Praise for *Mo*

"All the business information a mom needs to balance the needs of her family, her business and herself."

> —Suzanne Israel, president and CEO,
> American Women's Economic Development Corporation
> and former work-at-home mom

"*Mompreneurs*® is full of examples of mothers who have carved out successful home-based businesses and this helpful book provides easy-to-follow instructions for joining the ranks."

> —Alice Bredin, syndicated "Working at Home" columnist
> and author of *The Virtual Office Survival Handbook*

"What a terrific book for all those moms out there who want to stay at home and start their own Web businesses. All you need is a computer, an idea, and this book to guide you every step of the way. Here is literally everything you need to know to start an Internet business or find a way to telecommute from home. Learn how other moms did it, get inspired, and get going!"

> —Judith Nolte, editor-in-chief *American Baby* magazine

"*Mompreneurs*® *Online* is a fresh look at the essential entrepreneur's handbook. A must-read for the mom who wants to have the best of both worlds: quality time with her kids and productive time with her home-based business."

> —Aliza P. Sherman, founder of Cybergrrl and Webgrrls, and
> author of *Powertools for Women in Business: 10 Ways to Succeed in Life and Work*

"As a mom-to-be and advocate of home-based businesses, this book gave me great comfort and understanding about the realities of combining parenthood and career. I'd like to thank the Mompreneurs® for scouring the country to report on how dozens of real-life women learned that the Internet is the key to balancing home and business."

—Marilyn Zelinsky Syarto, former senior editor of Home Office Computing Magazine and author of *Practical Home Office Solutions* and *New Workplaces for New Workstyles*

"Patricia and Ellen have collected a wealth of resources for women looking to create a home-based Internet business. The book also has detailed how-to sections, checklists, and pros and cons that need to be considered. Perhaps most importantly, Patricia and Ellen have made the book personal. Stories of women—their frustrations and successes—are included and provide a solid and realistic foundation for their work. This book will be your go-to reference that is always within reach."

—Lindsey Johnson Suddarth, CEO and co-founder of Women Incorporated

MOMPRENEURS®
online
Using the Internet to Build Work@Home Success

PATRICIA COBE and
ELLEN H. PARLAPIANO

A Perigee Book

A Perigee Book
Published by The Berkley Publishing Group
A division of Penguin Putnam Inc.
375 Hudson Street
New York, New York 10014

Copyright © 2001 by Patricia Cobe and Ellen H. Parlapiano
Book design by Tiffany Kukec
Cover design by Jill Boltin
Authors' photo by Images by David

First edition: September 2001

Published simultaneously in Canada.

Visit our website at
www.penguinputnam.com

Library of Congress Cataloging-in-Publication Data

Cobe, Patricia, 1949–
    Mompreneurs online : using the Internet to build work at home success / Patricia
Cobe and Ellen H. Parlapiano, authors.
        p.   cm.
    Includes index.
    ISBN 0-399-52708-7
    1. Home-based businesses—Management.   2. New business enterprises—
Management.   3. Electronic commerce—Management.   4. Telecommuting.
5. Working mothers.   6. Work and family.   7. Internet.   I. Parlapiano, Ellen H.
II. Title.

HD62.38 .C628   2001
658'.041—dc21
                                                                                00-068447

Printed in the United States of America

10   9   8   7   6   5   4   3

DEDICATION

To Elliott, Josh, and Matt: Thank you so much for cheering me on until the final sentence. And to the memory of my parents, Myrna and Mac Cobe, who taught me to set the bar high.

PC

To my mom, Helen Hausler, and in memory of my dad, Chuck Hausler: Thank you both for teaching me that, with passion and persistence, all things are possible. And to Bob, Matt, and Amy for your unwavering love and encouragement.

EP

ACKNOWLEDGMENTS

We discovered "tech support" at its very best while writing this book. Hundreds of mompreneurs around the world—most of whom we have never even met in person—took the time to answer our online surveys, participate in our e-mail and phone interviews, and "virtually" share their challenges and successes. Why? Because mompreneurs believe in team spirit, and are more than eager to help each other attain the work/family flexibility we all cherish. Without these inspirational mothers, this book would not have been possible. We also extend our gratitude to the many websites devoted to entrepreneurship and home business, for allowing us to post our survey and get in touch with so many terrific, enterprising women.

We owe special thanks to two very important people who helped bring our venture to the page: Our agent, Carla Glasser, for her confidence in us and our concept; and our editor, Sheila Curry Oakes, whose patient guidance and sound suggestions helped mold Mompreneurs® Online into a comprehensive but easy-to-navigate book. Thanks, too, to Terri Hennessy, for overseeing the details that make it possible for a book to go seamlessly from manuscript to printed page.

Lastly, we thank our families, who provided both emotional and technical support during the intensive writing process. Pat's husband, Elliott, brought her home office into the twenty-first century with a new laptop computer, and helped her master all the bells and whistles with considerable patience. And her sons, Josh and Matt, rescued Mom too many times to mention with their technological savvy and Internet smarts. In Ellen's household, everyone had a hand in the book. Her daughter, Amy, took charge of alphabetizing all the surveys, while her teenage son, Matthew, did much of the behind-the-scenes Web research. And her husband, Bob, tabulated and interpreted all the statistical data from the surveys (and was equally good at cooking dinner during deadline times!).

Thank you all! And please continue to visit us and tell us your home business stories at our website, www.mompreneursonline.com.

Why the Web?

 Sound Byte

"Without the Internet, there's no way I could make a living working from home in my small town."

Terri Vincent, mother of one; Cody, Wyoming
Owner of TypaGraphics *(www.typagraphics.com)* and Partner in
eStore 2000 *(www.estore2000.com)*

Why a book about the Internet now, when so many big-name dot.coms are shutting their doors? Because smaller, mom-owned home businesses are alive and clicking on the Web! In the last few years, many large e-companies burst onto the scene fast and furiously, then fizzled out after overextending their financial resources. But mompreneurs grow their businesses slowly and steadily, in an effort to maintain control and balance in their work/family lives. Mompreneurs plot realistic, practical, and achievable business plans and goals. Mompreneurs start businesses because they want to call their own shots and have more family flexibility. They're much less likely than the average entrepreneur to seek funding at the start-up stages and risk relinquishing control of their enterprises. That means they don't have to worry about venture capitalists pulling the plug on their businesses. Most important, mompreneurs have discovered that a dot.com name alone is not enough to power business success.

But the Internet can be a very important tool when used in conjunction with other traditional business strategies. In this book we will introduce you to hundreds of mothers who have harnessed the power of the Web to discover their work-from-home potential and achieve success.

Since we published our first Mompreneurs® book in 1996, we've watched the Internet revolutionize the way we and other home-based moms work. While we still write articles and books (like this one) in the traditional print medium, more and more of our work is being done for the Web. Our online Mompreneurs® columns, chats, and message boards keep us wired to the pulse of the mompreneur movement. We have been inspired by the amazing number of mothers we met (online and off) who have embraced the Web to create flexible, profitable businesses in cyberspace with the express purpose of staying home with their children. And we know that there are lots more of you out there hoping to discover how you can do it too. The most common question we are asked by moms (and even by a number of women who aren't pregnant yet!) is this: "How can I make money with my computer so that I can stay home with my kids?"

Now more than ever, moms want better work/family balance in their lives—whether it's through launching a home-based business or linking up with companies offering flexible employment opportunities. A recent national survey, sponsored by the policy group Public Agenda, revealed that 80 percent of young mothers between the ages of 18 and 29 would rather be at home with their children than work full-time. The Internet is helping to make that dream a reality.

According to a recent study by Forrester Research, a firm that follows Internet trends, 54 percent of home business households are online. Home workers are present in 62 percent of all online North American homes. Forrester calls these homes "Digital Dens." We like to think of them as "Family Work Stations."

Where else can you nurse your baby while dashing off an important client proposal or processing a rush order? "Without the Internet I'd have to manually call eighty percent of my customers, and with a screaming toddler in the background that would not go over very well!" says Mary McCarthy, mother of one from Elk River, Minnesota, and owner of Comfy Bummy Diapers (www.comfybummy.com). Plus "it is so fast to work on the Internet," she adds. "I can e-mail a catalog and work when I want."

The Web is a natural fit for smart, cyber-savvy moms like you. "I read the morning paper on the Internet; I buy my children's clothes on the Internet; I even met my husband on the Internet!" says Rhonda Dykes, a mother of three from St. Joseph, Missouri. "When I decided to start my own business, it was only natural that it, too, would be Internet-related," states the owner of Admin Solutions (www.admin-solutions.com), which provides virtual office support to small businesses.

KEYWORD: FREEDOM

An e-Business puts you at the control panel of your work-family life. With the click of a mouse, you determine your hours and your availability to customers or clients. Most of your researching, marketing, and networking can be done online, giving you the luxury of turning from the screen whenever you want to hug or kiss your child. "I am living my dream," says Kristie Tamsevicius of Gurnee, Illinois, founder of Kristie's Custom Design (www.kcustom.com), which offers Web development, hosting, and promotion services. "Running an Internet business allows me the freedom to grow professionally. And I love being able to be with my babies every day. Life is all about moments. I don't want to miss any."

CLICK-ON CONVENIENCE

The Web offers unlimited work-at-home possibilities while requiring very little in start-up capital. "Doing business on the Internet is a cost-effective way to operate," says Mia Cronan of Greensburg, Pennsylvania, who runs Main Street Mom (www.mainstreetmom.com), a website dedicated to stay-at-home mothers. "All it costs me is my Internet connection, the extra phone line, and my domain hosting, for the most part. Even advertising and marketing can be done on a shoestring if you get a little savvy with what's available," she says.

The Internet "is the easiest link to the outside world without going anywhere!" adds Anne Fognano, who started Clevermoms.com, an online coupon and resale shop. It's much cheaper to run an e-commerce site than a brick-and-mortar store. There are no facilities or inventory to maintain.

Service businesses are thriving in cyberspace, too. "Every day I seem to find more ways that the Internet makes my job easier," notes Lisa Hornick, a mother of three from Dayton, Ohio, who runs Coulter & Gundy Development and Research Services. Her company helps nonprofit organizations raise money by identifying new funding sources. "With an Internet business, I can essentially do my job anywhere," she says. "Even if we move, I know I don't have to move my business."

CAST A WIDER NET

The Internet is your portal to a global village. You can run a world-class business right from home, even if that home is in Papua, New Guinea. That's among one of the many places American-born Melanie Wilson has lived while running the online *Vegetarian Baby and Child Magazine* (www.vegetarianbaby.com). Her husband is in the Peace Corps, and the family moves often. One summer was spent in Mongolia, and thanks to the Web, Wilson's business didn't miss a beat.

For virtual assistant Terri Vincent, the Internet has allowed her to expand her secretarial business beyond Cody, Wyoming—population 8,000. Pitching her services to a broader audience was a matter of survival. "I live in a small town whose main income is tourism during the summer," she explains. "Many businesses here are 'mom-and-pop,' and since PCs are so affordable, the pop runs the business while the mom does the computer work to save money. So they don't need me as much anymore." Besides recruiting more virtual services clients, Vincent has gone global in another big way. She recently partnered up with other cyberpreneurs from Australia, Peru, Canada, and Hawaii to launch an e-commerce site called estore2000.com.

With the Web, women are able to overcome adversity and build businesses where it wouldn't be possible otherwise. "I live in an economically depressed rural area, and if it were not for the Internet, I would never have been able to pursue my lifelong dream of owning a gift shop," says Renee Hogan of Marion, North Carolina, owner of Renee Barry & Co. (www.reneebarry.com), which sells collectibles and home décor items. "We have had several gift shops open and close in our town. People are still amazed when I tell them the product lines I carry. I have spoken with people at the hospital where I worked and they have compared me to Hallmark," this proud mompreneur says.

SCREEN NAME: SUCCESS

But no matter where you hang your shingle, the Web gives you a big-business image. "No one has to see that I operate out of my kitchen and dining room, and that I dry my soaps from a rack hanging from the ceiling because I have nowhere else to stack things," says Paula Polman of Mossberry Hollow Natural Care Products (www.mossberry.com). Believe it or not, she manufactures and sells her homemade soaps and natural bath and body products from a trailer in the Yukon! "I can look more official and bigger than my operations would suggest if you saw our small living space," this mom of one says.

With the right product or service, the size or scope of your enterprise really doesn't matter. "The Internet levels the playing field between the large conglomerates and the small business owner running her operation from the kitchen table," says Barbara Spangler, a mother of two who invented Reflections Safety Mirrors (www.reflectionssafetymirrors.com), a product that helps parents see their children in the backseat of the car without taking their eyes off the road. The overcapitalized "big boys" are now having a hard time getting the additional funds needed to achieve dot.com success. But prospects are good for small Web businesses that grow slowly and don't overextend themselves financially, predicts Julian Lange, professor of entrepreneurship at Babson College in Massachusetts.

BREAK DOWN THE BARRIERS

The Internet helps put moms with chronic health conditions or disabilities on even entrepreneurial footing, creating opportunities that would be difficult to handle in the traditional work world. "I have handicaps that make conventional 'jobs' hard on me," says Laura Strathman Hulka of McEwen, Tennessee, who was born with a hearing impairment and is now facing potential blindness from glaucoma. So this mompreneur opened a virtual branch of her used book store, Twice Told Tales (www.abebooks.com/

home/TWICETOLDBOOKS), and now focuses on all the Internet sales and contacts while her husband concentrates on the brick-and-mortar business.

Sandra Hamill of Toronto, Canada, was diagnosed with a crippling form of arthritis in 1998. To be able to continue supporting her three little girls with income from her home-based business, Cosmetics-on-the-Go, she developed a distance learning e-Biz (www.productionexperts.com). Hamill converted the workbooks and hands-on approach she had used to train makeup artists into an online correspondence course. "I rearranged the way I did my profession and actually created a new way to learn," she says with pride.

REAL-TIME FLEXIBILITY

Cyberspace also opens new doors for single parents and those with children who have illnesses, disabilities, or other special needs. These moms need to be home, and the Internet offers them a lifeline to provide for their families.

Jean Lentz of Reedsburg, Wisconsin, had been working as an on-site freelance programmer, but started her company so she could be more available to her older son, who has cerebral palsy. White Forest Software (www.whiteforest.com) offers website design and development, database applications, and customized software and computer consulting. "Creating websites is ideal for moms who want to work from home," she says. "When I have something ready for a client to see, I can publish it on the Web for review. Graphics and content can be sent back and forth via e-mail."

Working from home gives Wendy Harris the chance to spend more time with her oldest son, who has a mental health disability, without worrying about hassles from "a nonunderstanding boss." This mom of two from Valley Falls, New York, runs the National Association of Medical Billers (www.billersnetwork.com), a training information and support service for medical billers. "When my son was younger, we struggled a lot," she says, so when he turned 10, she decided to work from home. "It's been great," she says, and her son's condition has improved enormously as well.

In 1995, when we were writing our first Mompreneurs® book, the single moms we met who worked at home told us they sometimes found it difficult to earn enough money to keep the family afloat. With the Internet, it's possible to make ends meet . . . and more. "The best thing about being a dot.com mompreneur for me is that I am always here for my children," says Laura Brown of Ashland, Ohio, mom of two. "They were both very young when it became just me and them." She launched Aah, It's Done! Virtual Office and Travel Services, in 1999, and says, "The fact that I can be with them 24/7 and still keep a roof over their heads is the best feeling in the world. They are the reasons I work, and thanks to the Internet, I can always be there for them!"

THE SKY'S THE LIMIT!

We were absolutely bowled over by the creativity and diversity of all the mompreneurs we "met"—either virtually or face-to-face—while researching this book. In 1995, nearly 75 percent of the moms we interviewed said that their business was related to previous work done outside the home. With cyber-businesses, that number drops to 40 percent! The other 60 percent of the moms we rounded up for this book are tapping into their hobbies and talents to create businesses and fulfill lifelong dreams.

Many mompreneurs have also tapped into their parenting experiences, launching websites that showcase a clever invention, essential baby gear, child safety products, support services, or child-rearing advice. It makes sense—women are turning to the Internet in increasing numbers to seek information, shop, and connect with others. In an August 2000 study conducted by Media Metrix and Jupiter Communications, females made up 50.4 percent of the total U.S. Web audience—the first time in cyber-history that they've outnumbered males! While the total number of Web users increased by 22.4 percent, the number of women online increased by almost 35 percent, indicating their growing comfort level and acceptance of the Internet. By 2003, the study predicts, 78.9 million women will log on.

The Net is the gateway to brand-new career fields we hadn't even heard of several years ago—professions such as virtual assistants, personal coaches, online tutors, and e-zine publishers. Technology and vivid imaginations have combined to create a whole new workforce of moms out there—mompreneurs like Dawn Vaughan of Picayune, Mississippi. "The Internet has opened up an entire new world," says this mother of three who designs custom homes online (www.vhdesign.com). She communicates with clients almost entirely by e-mail, fax, and a password-protected Web page she personally constructs for each one. "I just love the fact that I can actually design a client's entire home without ever meeting them or visiting their building site," she says. Vaughan has attracted clients throughout North America, as well as in the Cayman Islands. "I've even been communicating with a possible client in West Africa!" she says. "There are no limits to my business now because of the Internet."

Like Vaughan, attorneys, nurses, bankers, teachers, and other professionals who would have been hard-pressed to find work-at-home jobs in their fields just a few years ago are carving out all kinds of interesting career niches without having to switch professions. We've met lawyers who are operating advocacy websites . . . special ed teachers offering information and merchandise for children with learning disabilities . . . nurses with online lactation catalogs . . . and public policy consultants running thriving e-businesses. There are no boundaries in cyberspace!

That's not to say that some professionals aren't finding new fulfillment by tapping into their hobbies. For example, Penny Tallent from Massachusetts was a registered nurse who no longer wanted to work the night shift. Now she can see her children in the daytime—she sets her own hours, selling her handmade soaps and bath items (www.fromtheheartsoap.com). Anne Englebach, another soapmaker (owner of Cove Creek Soaps), is actually an occupational therapist by training. And recreational baker Cecilia Ekberg left a corporate marketing job to start an online cookie business using her grandmother's Swedish recipe.

Even as recently as the late 1990s, there were few telecommuting opportunities or other reputable home-based options available for women who didn't want to run a business. Now the Internet makes it easier to uncover viable work-at-home jobs, as long as you know how to search carefully. (These home-based options are covered in Chapter 3.)

THE NEW MOM NETWORK

We found that community spirit is a large part of Web success. Many cyber-moms, driven by their own accomplishments, dedicate themselves to helping other moms prosper online. "Even if I never earned a dime, I would still continue to do this as a service to other moms. It gives me great satisfaction to get an e-mail from a mother thanking me for helping her find a work-at-home career," says Misty Weaver-Ostinato of Dumfries, Virginia, mom of two and founder of www.momshelpmoms.com.

"As a single mother of six, I've been experimenting with business ownership since 1991, first with a baby-sitting referral agency, started with absolutely no knowledge of business. As I was closing that business I received an insert in my welfare check about a course being held at the local small business development center. It came at a time in my life when I truly felt I needed to be home for my kids, all of them young and needing the love and affection only I could give them," says Donna Snow of San Jose, California. This enterprising mom enlisted a family member to stay with the children and fashioned a business plan to help provide the most qualified subs in the county to child care centers. Eighteen months later, she had a full-fledged business, with employees and clients. "I eventually had to close that business because it became too costly to run," she notes. "But as I sit here now, reflecting on my journey, I realize I went from an idea to a business plan to a business. It amazed me then, and still does today." Now Snow runs an e-Biz called Anything Business (www.anything-business.com), a virtual support system for others hoping to start a home-based business. She does everything from helping would-be mompreneurs evaluate skills to writing a business plan and growing a successful enterprise. She even offers a free weekly e-zine and business clinic for new owners who need cost-free advice. "This is why Anything Business was born," Snow says. "To give those who have the entrepreneurial dream a fighting chance!"

DATA BANK: *Why Did You Choose an Internet Business?*

Can do it from home. 33%
To reach people more quickly and less expensively. 31%
It's the future. 14%

WHAT DIGITAL MOMPRENEURS WANT

We'll tell you everything you need to know about starting, running, and promoting a business on the Net. And throughout this book, we'll include tips, advice, and inspiration from moms who have cleared a path to success in cyberspace. We went right to the source to find up-to-date answers to the most important work-at-home questions. We posted our extensive Internet survey on targeted moms' business websites and e-mailed it to our network of contacts. The result? We got instant feedback from all over the world! With the help of these inspirational mompreneurs, we will give you the tools to profit and prosper.

More Than Just Businesses!

For those of you ready to launch your own venture, we'll recommend the hottest, most family-friendly Web businesses, including virtual assistants, personal services, online teaching, e-tailing, and e-zines. We'll also provide ideas for expanding your existing brick-and-mortar business into "click and mortar" by establishing an online presence. We'll even show you how traditional home-based businesses like direct sales (Avon and Tupperware ladies) are going digital. Donna Valdes of Largo, Florida, signed on with Rexall Showcase to sell its line of preventive health care, sports nutrition, and weight loss products through the Internet. She's an independent rep who uses her website (www.donnavaldes.com) to distribute the products "with lightning speed," says Valdes. "Where else could I have started my own online business backed by a recognizable name for less than a hundred dollars?"

Many of you have told us that you simply want to find a reputable company that will hire you to work from home. We'll help you discover the Internet business or opportunity that best suits your talents, passions, and skills, plus help you avoid the countless cyber-scams that land in your e-mail box every day.

The Promise of Profits

A 2000 study by the Radcliffe Public Policy Center reported that 83 percent of women say that having enough time for family is more important than a high salary or job prestige. But you don't have to sacrifice financial rewards to find flexibility. We'll help you realistically plot and maximize your moneymaking potential, through nuts-and-bolts advice and inspirational stories from successful businesswomen—including our very own Web Celebs, mompreneurs who have gained fame on the Net.

It's great to love what you do, but it's even better to validate all your hard work by contributing to the family income. We'll tell you how to take your enterprise to the next level—how to turn your hobby, passion, or skills into a bona fide profit-making machine. You may not bring in the big bucks right away, but our tips and information should put your business on the fast track to being in the black. And eventually, you may wind up earning more than you did in the outside world. Indeed, many of the cyber-moms we meet tell us they're bringing in as much as they did before, if not more.

A Sense of Support

Although you may feel very isolated sitting at your computer most of the day, e-mailing invisible people or conversing in baby talk, YOU'RE NOT IN THIS ALONE! The Internet provides countless ways for you to reach out to others in the same boat . . . to network and find personal and professional support systems. Moms do such a good job "clicking" with other moms online, there are now hundreds of vibrant, virtual communities to welcome you. We'll introduce you to some favorites.

The "Gal Pals" you meet online can easily become some of your best e-buddies. That's what happened with Michelle Donahue-Arpas and Dawn Lloyd—two mompreneurs who linked up in cyberspace. Soon their friendship solidified into a business alliance, and the two started cross-promoting their sites—www.GeniusBabies.com and www.BabyUniversity.com. The pair agree that their relationship did more to increase their exposure and bottom lines than any other strategies, and now they've created an online mall filled with mom-owned baby shops.

Smart e-Networking makes it possible for mompreneurs to help each other maximize their work-at-home potential. We've discovered many moms whose websites revolve around helping other moms find home-based opportunities.

e-Marketing Strategies

"How do I stand out from the crowd and find my target market?" asks Ginger Jungling, a mom of one who runs a gift basket business from her Minnesota home (www.blissbaskets.com). We'll not only show you how to build a dynamic website, we'll share the secrets of making your site "sticky" so visitors return again and again. Our step-by-step marketing plan will help you build traffic and transform browsers into buyers. You'll learn how to use the Internet effectively as a marketing tool—to forge alliances with clients, customers, institutions, and other work-from-home mothers—and generate buzz about your business.

To Have It All With Minimal Child Care

Today's mompreneur is often working from her home computer with a baby sitting on her lap. And many are placing that computer in the hub of the household—the family room or kitchen—so they can tend to kids and business at the same time. "I'm the primary caregiver to my children and REFUSE to give this title up," states Melisa Cowden, mother of four and owner of Little Love Letters (www.littleloveletters.com), an e-Biz that markets motivational napkins to help build self-esteem in kids.

Like Cowden, you may be reluctant to call in child care and sacrifice time with your family. And this is a feeling that's shared by the majority of parents in America. According to the Public Agenda study, 56 percent of the respondents believe that no one can do as good a job of raising children as their own parents, and 71 percent percent of parents in the survey agreed that day care should be an option of last resort.

While the Internet does indeed make it easier to run a home business with minimal child care, you need to be open to the possibility of using some backup plans if you want to grow your business successfully. The great news is that cyber-moms have a variety of creative (and cheap!) solutions at their fingertips for those times when child care is absolutely necessary. You'll be hearing all about them in Chapter 4.

Click-On Resources

To keep a business running smoothly, every mompreneur needs help untangling the vast web of online resources. Within each chapter, and in an extensive resource guide at the end of the book, we'll lead you to the most reliable, easy-access sites on the Internet. With the click of a mouse, you'll find everything you need to start your business and make it prosper.

To Set an Entrepreneurial Example

Growing up alongside a home business can be a terrific learning experience for kids. Pat's two sons are now at the stage where they can use their entrepreneurial lessons to help evaluate future career options. And the boys have turned into patient teachers, too—providing Mom with much-appreciated tech support when a computer crisis hits!

Ellen's family is also filled with entrepreneurial spirit. She asked her daughter, Amy, to bring a friend to tour her home office on "Take Your Children To Work Day." Together, the girls posted and answered messages on the Mompreneurs® message board. When Amy asked her friend Tomomi what she thought of her mom's job, Tomomi answered: "I think I'd like to be a mompreneur someday!"

The Internet can empower you—not only to choose mompreneurship for yourself, but to set an incredible mompreneurial example for your children that will endure for years to come. We'll be your online guides to achieving cyber-success. So turn the page and log on to the future.

Use this handy checklist to navigate this book and chart your course to work-from-home success.

STEP 1: Tap Your Talents, Skills, and Passions (See Chapter 1).

STEP 2: Explore Your Work-From-Home Options and Decide on a Direction (See Chapters 1, 2, and 3).

STEP 3: Research the Market and Gather Information About Your Idea (See Chapter 1).

STEP 4: Build a Network of Support Through Entrepreneurial and Women's Business Groups, Professional and Trade Associations, and Online Communities and Chats (See Chapter 7).

STEP 5: Check Legalities—Decide on a Business Structure, Research Name Availability, and Apply for Any Necessary Permits, Licenses, Trademarks, Patents, etc. (See Chapter 6).

STEP 6: Register Your Domain Name (See Chapters 5 and 6).

STEP 7: Write a Business Plan (See Chapter 1).

STEP 8: Secure Any Necessary Financing (See Chapter 4).

STEP 9: Start Setting Up Your Website (See Chapter 5).

STEP 10: Get Your Business Cards, Letterhead, and other Marketing Materials Ready (See Chapter 7).

STEP 11: Set a Work Schedule (See Chapter 4).

STEP 12: Evaluate Your Child Care Needs (See Chapters 1 and 4).

STEP 13: Establish a Record-Keeping System (See Chapters 4 and 6).

STEP 14: Spread the Word About Your Business to Everyone You Know! (See Chapter 7).

STEP 15: Ready to Go! Welcome to the Work-From-Home World!

A Note from the Mompreneurs®

We've made every effort to insure that the Web addresses, prices, and other specifics listed in this book are current and up-to-date. But things change at light speed in cyberspace, so please understand if some information became obsolete after this book went to press.

We'd also like to extend our welcome to any dads reading this book. We know that many more of you are choosing the work-from-home life these days, and we hope that you, too, will benefit from the words of wisdom within these pages.

Good luck with all your work-from-home endeavors!

Pat and Ellen

CHAPTER ONE

Click Here: Discover Your Work-From-Home Potential

 Sound Byte

"The Internet can take you places you never dreamed of! All the resources you need for starting a home business are there at your fingertips."

Darcy Miller, mother of one; Austin, Texas
Owner of Little Did I Know *(www.littledidiknow.com)*

Do you fantasize about staying home with your kids while still contributing to the family income? Are you yearning to find a scam-free way to make money with your computer? Can you picture yourself building a successful business while bouncing your baby on your lap? (Or perhaps you already have an established home business that needs a Web presence.) Have you ever searched the Web fruitlessly for a certain service or product, then contemplated creating that hard-to-find service or product yourself?

The Internet can link you to your work-from-home dream. It has certainly helped us attain a work/family flexibility unlike any we've had before. Even though we've both been working at home for many years, we find that the Internet makes it easier than ever to balance our family and business needs under one roof. Because we do more of our conversing with clients by e-mail now, we no longer worry much that an editor might hear our kids bickering or screaming, "Ma! Where is my underwear!" Working on the Web keeps us connected to clients and customers all over the world, without our having to pick up the phone. We love the freedom of being able to turn away from our computer screens when our kids need a hug, homework help, or motherly advice. It allows us to work when *we* want to—even in the middle of the night!

That's not to say we haven't faced some new challenges. Ellen's daughter, Amy, recently complained she couldn't sleep because of a "clicking noise." And that "clicking noise" wasn't coming from any imaginary monsters under the bed! It turned out to be Ellen's fingers tapping on her computer keyboard as she raced through countless e-mails after tucking the kids in.

Because the Internet is open 24/7, it's easy to fall into the trap of working 24/7. But though you might be working at odd hours, the Web makes it possible for you to have a fulfilling and profitable career and still be home to hear your baby's first words (So what if those first words are "You've got mail!"). We'll show you not only how to discover your work-from-home potential, but how to manage and control your time so that your business does not wind up taking over your life. While writing this book, we talked to hundreds of moms who have harnessed the power of the Web to create kid-friendly businesses, discover flexible job options, and strike the perfect work/family balance. With a plan and some smart start-up strategies, you can, too.

WHERE'S *YOUR* WEB OPPORTUNITY?

Every day we hear from moms desperate to work from home, who say: "Help! I want to use the Internet to find a home-based job so I can make money without leaving my kids. But I have no idea what I can do. Please give me some advice—fast!"

Such desperation makes at-home moms particularly vulnerable to Internet scams. (We'll tell you more about these and how to avoid them in Chapters 2, 3, and 6.) We urge you to be wary of any job or business opportunity promising hefty profits and overnight success. Trust your gut. If it sounds too good to be true, it probably is. There is no quick-fix

From Idea to e-Biz

Take a look at how these mothers found inspiration in everyday experience.

Moment of Conception: Before heading on vacation with her children, Holly Jo West of San Marcos, Texas, makes laminated photo ID cards for each kid to use when checking in at the airport. After vacation, she tucks the cards in her pocketbook as a souvenir. Then one day, her two-year-old son Louis gets lost in a shopping mall. West whips out the ID card, which helps the security guard locate Louis in minutes.

A Business Is Born: West realizes that all parents and caregivers can benefit from having a child's photo and vital statistics at their fingertips when away from home. In 1997, she begins selling Kiddie IDs *(www.kiddieid.com)*, portable wallet cards that include the child's name, photo, and health information.

Moment of Conception: Andrea Milrad of Deerfield Beach, Florida, can't find a hockey-themed invitation for her son's first birthday party. Then she notices her husband's Florida Panthers tickets sitting on the kitchen counter, and her creative juices start flowing. She designs an invitation shaped like an event ticket, featuring hockey motifs and a picture of her son.

A Business Is Born: Friends and family rave about them. Those first fans become her first customers when Milrad launches Little BIG Man *(www.littlebigman.org)*, which sells custom birth annoucements and invitations in a variety of event ticket themes—from sports to ballet to concerts.

Moment of Conception: While living overseas in New Guinea and raising her baby as a vegetarian, Melanie Wilson longs to connect with other parents of vegetarian kids. She surfs the Web for support and resources, and realizes she is part of a huge untapped market.

A Business Is Born: In 1999, *Vegetarian Baby and Child Magazine (www.vegetarian-baby.com)* goes live. The online publication is targeted to parents of vegetarian and vegan children under three and offers a free Vegetarian Parents Database, as well as recipes and resources.

Moment of Conception: Linda McWilliams of Portageville, New York, has a hard time finding personalized baby keepsakes for her daughter, Khala. She figures other parents who have kids with unusual names must be having the same problem.

A Business Is Born: McWilliams launches Once Upon a Name *(www.onceuponaname.com)*, which creates lithograph artwork featuring the baby's name and the name's meaning.

Moment of Conception: Shelley Taylor's husband walks out on her one month after her second child is born. She searches the Web for practical single-parent advice, such as where to go for help paying the electric bill, and realizes that such information should be presented in one central location.

A Business Is Born: In June 1999, she launches Single Parent Central *(www.singleparentcentral.com)*, an online clearinghouse of information, resources, and legislative and lifestyle news for solo parents.

Moment of Conception: For years, Melisa Cowden of Austin, Texas, has slipped inspirational notes in her children's lunch boxes. After teachers and parents compliment her creativity, she wonders if the notes could somehow spawn a work-from-home business.

A Business Is Born: After a year of comprehensive research and development, Cowden unveils Little Love Letters, *(www.littleloveletters.com)*, motivational napkins decorated with upbeat messages designed to build children's self-esteem and generate communication between parents and kids.

solution when it comes to working from home. An e-Biz, like any other, takes time to develop and grow.

Besides, the very best business ideas come from within you—not from a kit or an e-mail solicitation. Instead of searching for ready-made opportunities, focus on your own talents, skills, passions, and experiences. These are the springboard for success. In Chapters 2 and 3 you'll find a comprehensive list of businesses and work-from-home options to match your needs and preferences.

TAP YOUR TALENTS AND PASSIONS

The more fervent you are about your work, the more likely you will be to succeed at it. So, it pays to build your business around something you love. "Don't do it just to make money," says Kathleen Driggers of HerWebHost.com, a webhosting service for women in business. "If you don't like what you're doing, you won't be happy no matter how much you make," says the Bremerton, Washington, mom.

Ann Allen's clothing design company is fueled by two of her passions: textile art and women's relationships. The Rochester, Minnesota, mother of three girls runs a company called Wearable Mamas (www.wearable-mamas.com), for which she creates and sells T-shirts, note cards, and other decorative items celebrating the special sisterhood shared by women everywhere. Allen's inspirational and unique designs feature women of all colors, arm-in-arm, facing the world together or reaching for the stars. "My business happened completely by accident," she says. "I created a T-shirt design for an online community of women called Feminist Mothers at Home. They loved the design so much, I decided to order a few extra shirts to sell at a local art event." The shirts sold briskly, and Allen began selling online almost immediately, to great success. In the year 2000, a friend of Allen's wore one of her shirts to the Million Mom March in Washington, D.C., and met another mom wearing a "Wearable Mama" tee. "I knew I had finally made it," Allen says.

As a mom of four, Jill Shortreed of Point Pleasant, New Jersey, had hosted her share of kiddie parties and had always been told she had a flair for entertaining. After her fifth child was born, Shortreed decided she didn't want to return to her full-time job as a banker, and began researching the party planning field. "We had several event-planning companies in the area, but none devoted solely to kids' parties," she explains. So she launched a children's party-planning business called Celebrated Times and increased her business greatly with a website (www.celebratedtimes.com). Her goal is to eventually hire others to do the actual entertaining so that she can concentrate on business affairs.

Perhaps your business will grow from a hobby, as it did for Anne Englebach of Marion, North Carolina. She's an occupational therapist by training, but loves making soap. "I started making all-natural, vegetable-based soaps for family and friends, and everyone liked them so much I decided to sell some to consignment shops," says this mother of five. Englebach launched her website in September 1999, and Cove Creek

Sideline Business: Sprinkling Pixie Dust

Nanci Rossetti of Forest City, Pennsylvania, works part-time three days a week as a lab technician at a local hospital. But the rest of the time she's busy planning trips to her favorite place on earth: Walt Disney World. Her home-based travel agency, Magical Journeys *(www.yourmagicaljourneys.com)*, specializes in affordable vacations to Disney theme parks all over the world.

Once Upon a Time: Rossetti fell in love with Disney World on her honeymoon in 1984. "As I walked down Main Street and first saw Cinderella's castle, I had tears in my eyes," she says. "It brought back warm childhood memories of sitting on my grandpa's lap watching *The Wonderful World of Disney* on TV." Rossetti and her husband vowed to make a return trip as soon as possible. Ten years and two kids later, they were finally ready, but when Rossetti started making plans she was shocked at the high prices.

From Passion to Profit: Determined to both find an affordable Disney vacation for her family and learn insider strategies, Rossetti took travel agent courses at a local junior college. Then she contacted her neighborhood travel agency and convinced them to hire her as an outside agent who worked on commission. Her intention was to just book trips for her own family. But in 1994, the Rossettis and their two young sons headed for Orlando— along with 73 friends and colleagues! "I just happened to mention the trip to coworkers at the hospital, and before I knew it I was checking on group rates!" Rossetti says with a laugh.

Word-of-Mouth Marketing: Soon she was booking money-saving trips for friends, colleagues, neighbors, and civic groups, while still working the evening shift at the hospital. "I have never had to advertise," she says. Most of her clients are referred by other satisfied customers. "Niche marketing is essential," she adds. "I decided to specialize in affordable Disney trips because that is what I know and love best." She later expanded to include other themed-attraction destinations, like Las Vegas.

Online Networking: Rossetti became a regular visitor at Disney-related travel websites, where she posted messages under the alias of Tink (short for Tinker Bell). She forged online friendships and a reputation for being nice, knowledgeable, and helpful. "If I heard about a cheap rate on a hotel, I'd tell people," she says. But she never tried to solicit their business. In fact, her cyber-buddies didn't even know she was a travel agent. Most online communities have strict rules against solicitation, she cautions. "If you post messages with a hard sell, you'll get booted right out." It's important to read the rules before posting anything that mentions your business.

How Business Grew: Rossetti cultivated a professional relationship with the webmaster (a person who manages a website) of a site for Disney enthusiasts, who invited her to write an article called "A Travel Agent's Guide to Travel Agents." She shared her cost-cutting strategies and her e-mail address, and became busier than ever. In April of 2000, after eight years of working as an independent contractor for various agencies, Rossetti launched Magical Journeys. She hopes that her home-based travel agency will someday become lucrative enough that she can quit her lab technician job and work full-time helping others discover the "Disney Magic."

Soaps was "officially born." Homemade bath teas, fizzies, lotions, and gift baskets are now for sale on her site, along with the soaps, and Englebach's market includes inns and specialty shops, as well as individuals simply looking for some pampering.

PLUG INTO PARENTHOOD

Your experience as a mom may be the spark for a booming e-Business. Louise Larson Janke, a former teacher from Trempealeau, Wisconsin, became frustrated when shopping for educational software for her two kids. "There were too many titles to choose from, and the well-intentioned employees at stores and mail order catalogs weren't knowledgeable enough to recommend titles that parents *and* kids would like," she says. Then she thought: What if all the best children's software was put in one trustworthy place for parents to access? And what if that place helped parents save time and money? That vision formed the mission of Tutor House Children's Software (www.tutorhouse.com), which reviews and sells children's software programs—all pretested by kids *and* parents.

Some enterprises are born from trauma. Ohio mom and registered nurse Barbara Spangler got the idea for her car safety mirrors after being in a near-miss collision with her kids. "I heard a startling cry from the backseat and turned ever so quickly to check my son and daughter," Spangler remembers. When she returned her attention to the road, she discovered she was just inches from the truck in front of her. The experience left her shaken, but inspired her to invent Reflections Safety Mirrors (www.reflectionssafetymirrors.com), which help parents see their kids in the backseat without turning from the road.

After the Malibu fires broke out a few years ago and her children's school was evacuated, California mom Allysen Friedman wished her kids had had an emergency survival kit with them. "My children had nothing to help them through the confusion—not even a Band-Aid or an ID card," she says. Subsequently, she and her husband created the "Ouch Pouch," a waterproof package containing a blanket, whistle, light stick, drinking water, and other emergency gear. It's sold online through their company website (www.anyabaganya.com), as well as offline through distributors. "We began selling the products offline, but it expanded almost immediately into an Internet business," she says.

💡 Mother of Invention

Dana Lowey Luttway's first baby, Daniel, inspired her to leave her job as a New York TV producer and become a stay-at-home mom. And after "the king of spit-up" ruined the last of his mom's clean shirts, Luttway took on another new role: product inventor. She created the Parent Smock, a protective bib for moms and dads. Next came the Stroller Stand, a kickstand that prevents umbrella strollers from tipping when bags are loaded on the back. Today Luttway has two sons and a company called ParentWise (www.parentwise.com), where she not only showcases her own products, but helps other moms bring their ideas to market by securing them licensing deals and paying them a percentage of the profits.

Here are her start-up strategies for anyone contemplating inventing a parenting product.

■ **Make Sure the Product Doesn't Already Exist.** Go to as many baby and children's stores as you can and talk to the clerks, managers, and buyers about your idea. (Well-established mom-and-pop shops are a particularly rich source for feedback, because the owners have seen many products come and go over the years.) Ask if they've seen a product like yours, and if they think there's a need for it. Do they think your idea would work? If not, why? If the product isn't already out there, ask yourself and your sources why that might be. There could be a good reason. Also do a patent search with the United State Patent and Trademark Office (USPTO; www.uspto.gov) to make sure the idea hasn't already been patented. (See Chapter 6 for details on researching and obtaining patents.)

■ **File a Provisional Patent.** This protects your idea for a year, giving you time to develop and test-market your product before plunking down thousands of dollars to file a utility patent (the one considered official by the USPTO). Provisional patents cost you only $75 to file, but you need to also factor in attorney fees, which might run anywhere from around $500 to $1,000 or more, depending on the product. (For more patent information, see Chapter 6.)

■ **Develop Your Idea Thoroughly.** While you have your provisional patent, make a prototype—a model of your finished product. (If you can't make the prototype yourself, enlist the help of craftspeople experienced in various manufacturing techniques. For example, a seamstress can help you create prototypes for clothing and other sewn items; a carpenter may help with items made of wood or laminate. If it's a complicated mechanical device, you will need an engineer to help you design it.) Once you've created a prototype, you can figure out what your product will cost to make and how much you need to charge in order to turn a profit. When calculating your profit margin, don't forget to factor in packaging, shipping, warehousing, and other hidden costs like retailer charge-backs (usually 5 to 10 percent).

■ **Sell Your Idea.** While still protected under your provisional patent, show your prototype to buyers and retailers to see if they're interested in ordering it. The best place to showcase a parenting or baby product is the Juvenile Products Manufacturing Association (JPMA) Show, held in Dallas every fall (www.jpma.org). Exhibiting at JPMA helps you determine whether there's bona fide demand for your idea. (If you're not yet ready to exhibit at JPMA, ask about getting a pass to "walk the show," which allows you to get a feel for the event, see what products are out there, and network with buyers and other juvenile product manufacturers.) It's wise to have one big order lined up before you begin the costly manufacturing process.

■ **Understand Your Expenses.** A simple item made of cloth might cost around $20,000 to launch, while a complex item made of plastic or metal could require $50,000 or more. (To find manufacturers, check the Thomas Register of American Manufacturers; www.thomasregister.com). Keep in mind that U.S. manufacturers of plastic and metal can charge a great deal, so you will likely need to look overseas for companies that can mass-produce your item cost-effectively. Legal fees can also soar quickly, so ask your patent attorney to cap them; Luttway asked hers not to exceed $5,000. (You can find a list of patent attorneys on the U.S. Patent and Trademark Office site; www.uspto.gov). Consider additional expenses like liability insurance, which can cost several thousand dollars per year. Many children's products also need to be tested in an independent safety lab to make sure they comply with industry safety standards. (For more information on safety standards and testing laboratories, search under "Product Compliance Safety Testing" at the United Inventors Association; www.uiausa.org.) "Inventing a parenting product can be a long and costly process," Luttway admits, but if your idea is unique, it's well worth the investment.

TUNE INTO A SPECIAL NEED

We're seeing more and more e-Businesses that champion a cause and reach out to families with special needs and interests. Inspired by a brother with disabilities, Judi Cohen of Martinez, Georgia, manufactures 'Lastic Laces shoelaces, which don't have to be tied. She markets them on her site WeBehave.com which also offers a variety of parenting products, many of them designed for children with disabilities and learning differences. Lori Thompson's e-Biz, The Attachments Catalog (www.attachmentscatalog.com), targets moms who believe in "attachment parenting," a philosophy that advocates long-term nursing, the family bed, and other bonding rituals. The Bremerton, Washington, mom sells gifts with nursing and mother/baby themes, all produced by stay-at-home moms.

As the number of aspiring work-from-home mothers explodes, there's a new wave of Web women dedicated to helping other moms fulfill their work-from-home dreams, through online support groups, job centers, and stores specializing in mom-made merchandise. Darcy Miller of Austin, Texas, calls herself a "mom on a mission." Everything sold in her online boutique, Little Did I Know (www.littledidiknow.com), is either hand-made or distributed by a stay-at-home mother. And her more recently launched site, MOO (Mother Owned and Operated; www.m-oo.com), includes tools, resources, and networking opportunities for moms starting or growing home businesses. "I feel so fortunate that I've had the opportunity to work, yet be home with my son," says the former Motorola executive. "I want to help other mothers do the same."

BRING YOUR WORK SKILLS TO THE WEB

Could you convert previous job experience into a work-from-home career? Rhonda Dykes of St. Joseph, Missouri, had always wanted to own a business that would utilize her 20 years' worth of administrative experience, pay well, and allow her to do what she loved best: "play on the computer." So she took her secretarial skills virtual. In 1999 she launched Admin Solutions (www.admin-solutions.com), which provides virtual office support to small companies and home businesses. "I do it all on the Internet," she says, "from communicating with clients to delivering their finished products."

Kirsten Ross of Warren, Michigan, combined her educational experience (she has a master's in Labor and Industrial Relations) and her 11 years of working in human resources to establish a career site specializing in alternative work arrangements for mothers called Womans-Work.com. Her site not only helps other moms discover flexible options like telecommuting and job-sharing, but helps its founder achieve better work-family balance in her own life.

Before the Information Highway was built, it was difficult for parents in fields like health care or law to bring those job skills home. But thanks to the Internet, even psychologists, doctors, nurses, architects, and attorneys are finding a niche for their skills on the Web.

TEAM UP

You don't have to run your business solo. Why not partner up with a like-minded entrepreneur? Deborah Elias and her husband formed their Virginia-based consulting firm (www.eliasconsultants.com), which pairs his expertise as an aircraft inspector and auditor and her specialty in scientific writing and editing. Shannon Rubio of State Spring, Texas, teamed up with her mom, an attorney. Together they fill and ship "Smile Boxes"—a cross between a gift basket and a care package—sold from their site (www.thesmilebox.com). "My mom and I have a shared love of computers (essential for an e-Biz!), plus we always dreamed of working together as partners," Rubio says.

Co-ownership means more flexibility, less financial risk, and sometimes, fewer hours for each partner. And now it's possible for mothers from different cities, states, and even countries to draw on each other's strengths to create a successful business. A good example is YarnXpress (www.YarnXpress.com), an online source of novelty and designer yarns and an interactive educational site for knitters and crocheters. Launched in January 1999, the business began as "an experiment with online auctioning," says owner and passionate knitter Sue Neiditch Schwartz of West Milford, New Jersey. "The first Web page built by my son was basically a scrapbook for displaying interesting yarns I had located for a handful of customers." More and more customers soon came, and the experiment expanded into a full-fledged online shop hosted by freemerchant.com. It got to the point where Neiditch Schwartz, who still worked offline as a school administrator, had to hire her children to work part-time and eventually partnered up with another family member in faraway Wisconsin. "I moved the inventory to Milwaukee, where my sister, another mompreneur, is running the fulfillment center," she says. Each partner is capitalizing on her own expertise to drive sales, and the sisters are branching out into the business-to-business marketplace.

MOONLIGHT FIRST

If you're hesitant to give up your "day job," you could start a sideline business and see if it takes off. Renee Hogan of Marion, North Carolina, wanted to quit nursing and stay home with her two children. "I sat on the bed with my husband and we brainstormed. I had always wanted to own my own gift shop." So she started Renee Barry & Co. (www.reneebarry.com), which sells popular collectibles and home décor items, and managed the website for over a year before she quit her full-time job as a registered nurse at the local hospital. When single mom Cindy Bean of Bowie, Maryland, needed a second income to supplement her full-time job at a major health insurance company, she utilized her 25 years of computer experience to launch Maryland Secretarial Services (www.webmss.com). She tends to the home-based word processing and desktop publishing firm on nights and weekends.

One single mom from Carmel, Indiana, spent several months researching the gift basket business and her competition before starting her own custom gift basket business. Though she currently holds another job outside the home, she hopes to take her business full-time by the time her youngest child is in school. "I would love to do it now, but as a single parent, supporting two children and paying the mortgage, it is just not possible," she says. However, this forward-thinking mom has already written her resignation letter, which she keeps posted at home to remind her of her goal. "I have faith that I will reach my goals," she says. "Even the most successful mompreneur has to start somewhere!"

BRAINSTORMING FOR IDEAS

To uncover the Internet work options that best suit you and your family, start with a bit of honest soul-searching. Sit down with a pad and pencil and jot down the answers to the questions below. When you're done, you'll have a clearer vision of your skills, interests, personality, and capabilities, so that you can start narrowing down the types of businesses and opportunities to look into (as well as those you should stay away from).

Ask Yourself These Questions

- If you could spend your day doing anything, what would it be?

- Are there things you love doing so much that you lose all track of time?

- What are your hobbies? Are you good enough at them to market your talents to others?

- Is there a service or product you've created for your own use that you could provide to others?

- List your passions. Are there causes, products, or services you care deeply about? Could these become the foundation for a business?

- What do you hate to do most? Can you avoid these things in your business, or find a way to delegate them to someone else?

- Have you ever thought, Boy, someone ought to invent . . . fill-in-the-blank? Could you be the one to make it happen?

- What previous job skills have you mastered? Can you offer these independently to customers or clients? Would you be happy doing that?

- Have you always wanted to pursue a different career? Is it time to switch gears and go after it? What skills or training would you need?

- Has anyone ever complimented your talents and/or skills and commented, "You should go into business"?

- Do you want to start a business of your own? Or would you rather find a flexible work option offered by a well-established company?

- Are you disciplined, self-motivated, patient, and persistent? These are essential personality traits for working from home.

■ What times of day would you work? What will the kids do while you work?

■ If you're planning to work when the kids are sleeping, will you have enough energy to keep up this kind of schedule? When will you and your husband or significant other carve out time for each other?

■ Are you flexible and able to work around the interruptions of your kids? Will you have backup child care options available for those times when the work demands your full concentration or for when you need to make phone calls?

■ Do you have the space in your home to carve out for an office—even if it's just a corner in the kitchen or family room?

■ Is your family supportive of your work-from-home dream?

■ What are your best personality traits? Maybe you're a good listener. Or perhaps you pride yourself on your "people skills." Think about the types of businesses these personalities suit. For example, good listening and talking skills are both essential in sales. (Don't worry, we'll give you lots more job options to match your personality and skills in Chapters 2 and 3.)

DATA BANK: *What Do You Like Best About Your Internet Business?*

Family flexibility/Making my own hours 59%
Networking/Helping others through my site 24%
Speed and efficiency. 5%

Virtual Reality

Internet Upside: You can plan your work schedule around the kids' naps.
Internet Downside: When you finally get your baby down for a nap, the computer goes down too.

Internet Upside: Your website never closes—it's working even when you're sleeping.
Internet Downside: You're working 24/7—and sleeping less than ever.

Internet Upside: You can take a break from the computer screen anytime your kids need a hug.
Internet Downside: Your husband hasn't had a hug in weeks!

Internet Upside: You have immediate access to clients and business information.
Internet Downside: Clients expect your immediate attention.

Internet Upside: You cultivate a supportive network of friends and colleagues through online newsgroups and message boards.
Internet Downside: You spend hours of precious work time conversing with strangers with online aliases like "Poopsy" or "Mumstheword."

Internet Upside: Speedy technology increases your productivity.
Internet Downside: Just when you finally master that speedy technology, it becomes obsolete.

Internet Upside: Instant Messages.
Internet Downside: Instant Messages.

Internet Upside: Kids can play quietly by your side while you tinker on your website.
Internet Downside: While you tinker on your website, your child quietly scribbles on your brand-new letterhead.

Internet Upside: You're linked to people and resources all over the world, without leaving home.
Internet Downside: You haven't left home in so long, you're forgetting what the outside world looks like.

WHAT YOU NEED TO SUCCEED

A Niche

The Internet is jammed with products and services, and getting more crowded by the minute. To survive, your e-Business must be unique, with a well-defined focus and a specific audience.

Bargain-hunter and stay-at-home mom Anne Fognano of Leesburg, Virginia, thought it would be great to have a place where parents could not only find great deals on kids' clothes, toys, and gear, but collect cost-cutting coupons to use when shopping at stores both online and off. She named her site Clevermoms Coupons and Online Resale Shop (www.clever moms.com) and sets it apart from the competition by abolishing consignment fees and commission charges and offering low-cost ads. The coupon portion of the site attracts over 4,000 thrifty shoppers a day!

Market Research

Once you have your business idea, you must do plenty of homework to make sure it's feasible. The Web offers a wealth of speedy resources for doing market research—from checking the competition to investigating patents to surveying potential customers and clients. (The sites listed in Click and Save, page 36, and in the Dot.Com Directory at the end of this book, page 271, will help get you started.)

Make sure there's enough demand for your idea. Using various search engines, scour the Internet to see what types of similar products or services are already out there and how you can make yours special. Call or e-mail similar businesses, posing as a prospective customer, and ask what they're charging. Network with potential clients and customers through online message boards, chat groups, and e-mail surveys. Find out if they'd use your product or service, what they like and don't like about it, what they'd change, and how much they'd realistically pay for it. And don't discount face-to-face contact. You can gather some great feedback on your business idea at the playground, the neighborhood mommy group, the PTA meeting—even from the bleachers at your daughter's softball game.

Work-from-home mom organizations and women's business groups (both online and off) are another essential source of information and inspiration. (You'll find them in Chapter 7 and in our Dot.Com Directory of resources.) There, you can mingle with other entrepreneurs and learn about their challenges and obstacles and how they overcame them. You may even meet a mentor willing to give you one-on-one guidance and support.

A Business Plan

Like a road map, a business plan helps you chart a successful course. It doesn't have to be complicated, unless you plan to apply for loans, in which case you'll need detailed financial projections. Every business plan should include a mission statement, business goals, a marketing plan, and estimates of start-up and operating costs and earning expectations. For help, use one of the free online business plan tutorials, such as those offered by the SBA (www.sbaonline.sba.gov) or the Edward Lowe Foundation Entrepreneurial Edge (www.lowe.org). Shareware programs also offer assistance. Check out: www.planware.org.

A Work/Family Schedule

You don't have to be tied to a rigid schedule, but you should set some boundaries for business and family. Plan when you'll work, and more important, when you won't. Although she originally thought working from home would give her the freedom to work whenever she pleases, Anne Ramstetter Wenzel finds it important to work regular hours. "I must resist the temptation to schedule appointments or errands while my seven-year-old is in school," says Wenzel, who runs an economics research and business writing firm called Econosystems (www.econosystems.com) in Menlo Park, California. "I can do many clerical tasks in the afternoon with him around, or late at night when I'm tired, but my business cannot function over the long haul without several hours of uninterrupted time several days a week."

The Internet can be habit-forming, adds Barbara Spangler of Reflections Safety Mirrors. "It's so easy to get caught up clicking from one link to the next, looking for that one break you need to catapult your business to the top," she says. We'll show you how to plan and protect your time in Chapter 4.

A Child Care Strategy

Though the Internet gives you the freedom to work with less child care, you shouldn't rule it out completely. It's important to have backup options—whether it's working around the school schedule or utilizing the child care program in the local church—so that you can do your job without interruptions and know the kids are safely supervised. "When I started my business, I did not want to believe that I needed child care for my kid," says Lara Fabans of Lodestone Software, Inc. (www.lodestone-sw.com), who often calls upon her mom and best friend to baby-sit. "But you do need something, even if it's just a few hours a week," the California web programmer insists. "It allows you to focus on your work and return phone calls, without *Muppets From Space* blaring in the background." Massachusetts party consultant Laurie Moore of PartyInABoxOnline.com does her best to work during her daughter's nap time, but she has also begun using a mother's helper in the afternoons so that there is not as much of a need to work in the evenings.

You may feel as if child care defeats your whole purpose of working from home, but it can actually help you preserve the family balance you crave, by helping you compartmentalize your time. There's no sense working from home if you're going to be frustrated when your kids want to play and you need to finish a deadline or answer a client's e-mail. A little bit of well-planned child care allows you to work exclusively during designated hours so the kids can have you all to themselves during "off hours." There are so many creative and cost-efficient child care options available. We'll tell you about them in Chapter 4.

CLICK AND SAVE: *Must-See Start-Up Sites*

>> *www.bcentral.com*   >> *www.lowe.org*

>> *www.bizstarters.com*   >> *www.onlinewbc.org*

>> *www.digitaldivas.com*   >> *www.onvia.com*

>> *www.digital-women.com*   >> *www.sba.gov*

>> *www.digitalwork.com*   >> *www.smalloffice.com*

>> *www.ideacafe.com*   >> *www.womensforum.com*

>> *www.inc.com*

CYBER–SUCCESS SECRETS

1. **Get Tech-Savvy.** Learn all you can about the Internet through courses in programming, e-commerce, and Web design and development. Many community colleges and tech schools offer these courses online, so you don't even have to leave home. Turnkey sites such as www.bigstep.com allow hands-on learning as you set up your site.

2. **Network.** Join Internet newsgroups devoted to work-from-home moms and digital women, as well as online forums related specifically to your field. You'll find that fellow dot.com moms are a very sharing and supportive bunch. (See Chapter 7 for inspirational ideas.)

3. **Recruit Help.** Consult with your lawyer and accountant before pursuing your idea to make sure you're clear on the legal implications. Also consider delegating start-up tasks that are beyond your range of expertise. Perhaps there's a friend or family member willing to do your graphics or Web design or to offer tech support as a favor or for a discounted fee.

4. **Have Realistic Expectations.** Consider how much time and money you can devote to the business. It's wise to start your ven-

Sizing Up a Business Idea

After having her second child, stay-at-home mom Susan Barone joined Rosie O'Donnell's TV Chub Club in an effort to shed her postpregnancy weight. "As I watched Rosie and the Chub Club coach inspire women with the 'Eat Less and Move More' motto, I thought, We should take this to the next level: 'Eat Less, Move More, and Look Great,' " Barone says. As a plus-sized woman herself, with years of experience working in the fashion industry, this Smithtown, New York, mom knew that larger women have limited fashions to choose from and want more of a say in what is being designed. "We need clothes that fit, make us feel good, and don't cost a fortune," she says.

Her Idea: Create a website for the plus-sized customer called Uniquely Me *(www. uniquelyme.com)*. There, women can express their fashion needs through online surveys, so fashion manufacturers and retailers can better understand what kinds of clothes are wanted for different seasons. For example, when manufacturers are working on holiday clothes, Barone asks members questions like: "Do you want long dresses?" and "Would you wear sleeveless?" With her industry experience, Barone understands the schedules and the capabilities of fashion manufacturers. "I know they can put out the merchandise if they have the proper information in enough time to incorporate into their new lines," she says. Revenue is generated through retailer advertising on the site, affiliate programs, and the survey subscriptions Barone sells to the fashion manufacturers.

Doing Her Homework: Barone spent a year reading everything she could about developing and marketing a website. "I wrote down all the elements involved in developing a business—such as design, advertising, affiliates, and software—and did searches on the Web. For example, I'd type in the word 'marketing' and then go into the various marketing company sites to research what they charged and what kind of services they provided. It's time-consuming, but necessary for success," she says. Before launching, Barone also took classes called "The Internet Professional" at New Horizons *(www.newhorizons.com)*, a nationwide school that offers Web courses designed to suit a mother's busy schedule.

Cost-Cutting Tricks: Barone kept her site as simple as possible. "You can do a simple ten-page website for about twenty-five hundred to thirty-five hundred dollars, if you're willing to do a lot of it yourself," she says. She also produced her own marketing materials and media kits with a desktop publishing program to save on printing costs.

Sizing Up a Business Idea, continued

Best Advice: "In addition to researching and understanding your target customer, you must also understand the general needs of the Internet shopper," Barone cautions. Don't market to an Internet customer the same way you would to shoppers in a retail store. Make sure your site is easy to navigate, with text and graphics that suit your audience. "If you provide your audience with the information they want and need in an accessible way, they will keep coming back to your site."

ture simply and expand it slowly as your kids get older and more independent. Though an Internet business is often less costly to start than a brick-and-mortar enterprise, overhead costs like Internet Service Provider fees and online phone bills quickly add up. (See "How Much Will It Cost" box on page 109 to chart your expenses.) As speedy as the Internet is, you can't expect overnight success. It could take a year or more for your Web business to become profitable. Many of the mompreneurs we met in the start-up stages were making under $10,000 a year. To grow and prosper, you're likely to need additional capital and the ability to outsource the tasks that are too time-consuming or technical. But the good news is that if you have a winning idea and are able to stick it out during the start-up stages, your salary could eventually exceed what it was in the traditional workforce. (We'll show you how to maximize your time and earning power in Chapter 4.)

5. **Be Patient.** Marketing a website is extremely time-consuming. Prepare to spend countless hours registering your site with search engines, exchanging banner ads, linking with compatible sites, and joining affiliate programs. "Mastering Internet marketing has taken longer than I anticipated," says Kirsten Ross, who runs Womans-Work.com. "You just have to keep going and focus on the end goal," she advises. "Know that you have something great to offer and stay positive that things will fall into place."

6. **Believe You Will Achieve.** You can do it, so don't give up. "If it's what you really want to do . . . go for it," offers Lynne Korff of

Cabot, Pennsylvania, who sells her own handcrafted ceramic giftware at www.korfforiginals.com. "I look at my girls and I think I am setting a pretty good example for them. I had a dream, which I attained—without leaving home!"

Web Celeb

Jan Jewell
Co–Chief Executive Officer of Birthday Express.com *(www.birthdayexpress.com)*
Kirkland, Washington
Mom of 4

Less than a decade ago, Jan Jewell was six months pregnant with her third child and enjoying success as a designer of high-end jewelry for an exclusive clientele. But on May 2, 1992, "My life changed completely," she says. Her baby, Sebastian, was born prematurely at 27 weeks, weighing just 1 pound, 10 ounces. As her tiny son struggled on life support in the neonatal intensive care unit, Jewell reevaluated her life and career choices. Though she was obligated to complete a rare gemstone design for an important client, "My heart was just not in it," she recalls. "It was so hard to finish that piece of jewelry when I really wanted to be sitting at my baby's bedside." Her husband, Mike, also found it difficult to focus on work. Brokenhearted about Sebastian's condition, he quit his job so he could concentrate on the needs of his family, and the Jewells lived off their savings as they waited for their son to grow, not knowing for months if he would make it. Though there were serious setbacks along the way, and he needed six blood transfusions, Sebastian slowly grew bigger and stronger. After two and a half months in the hospital, he came home, weighing less than 4 pounds.

"Once we knew Sebastian was going to make it, we started to think about new ways to work," says Jan. Over the course of a career in high-tech industries, Mike had become intrigued by the speed and efficiency of transferring files via e-mail, which was just in its infancy in 1992. Originally the couple planned to start an "e-mail marketing company," which would help various businesses get on the Internet, but the idea was ahead of its time and companies were not interested. So they began brainstorming about other potential business ideas.

"One day, we were walking through a toy store and I started thinking about my children's birthdays and how time-consuming it was to put together a great children's party," remembers Jan. "It would take me at least four or five trips to different stores before I had all the supplies I needed. I remember looking at Mike and saying, 'If we could just find a way to make it easier for busy parents to celebrate the lives of their kids, I think we might be onto something.'" And so, the idea for Birthday Express was born. The Jewells would provide a one-stop shopping source where parents could get everything to celebrate children's birthdays—from themed invitations to balloons to plates to games to favor bags to thank-you notes—all without leaving home.

Jan and Mike did extensive market research by sending out a 26-page survey to 150 moms across the nation, asking about party challenges they had faced and what types of products and services they needed to make the process easier. "The answers to those questions still drive our business today," says Jan. For example, parents wanted celebration advice, as well as supplies, so Birthday Express offers party-planning guides with activities, recipes, and decorating ideas related to a specific theme—whether it's a pirate bash for birthday buccaneers or a Cinderella ball for pint-sized princesses. "I feel a great responsibility to how a family's party will unfold that day. The ultimate goal is to make it a fun day for everybody."

Because the Internet hadn't yet caught on in the early '90s, Birthday Express started as a mail order catalog in 1994, funded by the couple's savings and cashed-in stock options. In April of 1996, the company expanded to the Web with BirthdayExpress.com, and by 2000, about half of the sales came from online orders. The couple's enterprise has experienced healthy growth—they now ship about 1,500 orders a day worldwide and have added a sister site, CelebrateExpress.com, offering party ware for grown-ups. Company sales are projected to exceed $30 million in 2001.

Sebastian is thriving, too. He and his younger sister, Sapphire, often model for catalog photos, which are cherished by their grandparents. "I was at my mother-in-law's recently, and she had all these beautiful framed school photos and family portraits of my nieces and nephews, but the only photos she had of my kids were from our catalogs," Jan recalls, laughing. "I realized I must make some time to have better family photos taken!" she says. But time is a rare commodity when you run an Internet business, she points out.

Though customer service representatives keep the company running round-the-clock, the Jewells try to keep their work confined to the hours the kids are in school and at extracurricular activities. They have sacrificed their social lives so that they can devote all of their nonworking time to their four children, who range in age from 7 to 19. Most weekends are spent relaxing on the family boat, where no laptops are allowed. ("We tried it once, but got seasick," admits Jan.) But at 9 P.M., when the younger kids are in bed and the house is quiet, the laptops go back on, and the co-CEOs frequently have "executive meetings" at 11 P.M. at the dining room table. "When we started the company, we were completely ignorant of how much work it would really take," says Jan. "Running your own company requires a very different mind-set than working as an employee," she explains, because you are ultimately responsible for every company decision.

And the job gets harder as you become more successful. "As a woman, I have bruised my head on the glass ceiling of my own company more times than I'd like to admit," says Jan, because investors are still predominantly male and women's leadership capabilities are still questioned simply because of gender. "Once investors became involved in my company, I had to fight to keep my title and position," she says. "It's a tough road for women business owners, and I think it will be for a long time. But it's important to persevere. If I have paved the way for one more woman to succeed in business, then I feel I have accomplished something very important."

CHAPTER TWO

Menu of Options: Finding the Best Business for You!

 Sound Byte

"If a mother feels she can make a difference, has an interesting concept, or thinks she can fill a void in the business world, she owes it to herself to try. The Internet is full of opportunities."

Mia Cronan, mother of three; Greensburg, Pennsylvania
Owner of EMC Media *(www.mainstreetmom.com)*

We have an image of ourselves as pretty savvy cyber-chicks—even though our children consider us newbies! Pat's sons still laugh at her inability to instantly locate a downloaded file on the pc. But we've been working on the Net since the dinosaur days of 1995, watching its impact on our lives and our businesses skyrocket. As we logged countless hours surfing for information and trends, supplying articles and content to various sites, and moderating chats and message boards on different venues, we have interacted with moms (and potential mompreneurs) in every stage of business development. But we couldn't have been more surprised by the sheer number and variety of businesses happening out there in cyber-space!

It's clear that smart mompreneurs are capitalizing on this business frontier—the products and services they're selling are limited only by their imaginations. Some are taking traditional workplace skills and converting them into successful Web businesses. Others are inventing brand-new job categories that could never have existed a mere decade ago. As Maureen Anderson, host of the syndicated radio program *The Career Clinic* (www.thecareerclinic.com), says, "Our society and economy are very much dominated by the flow of information, and that's what the Internet is all about. It opens up so many exciting business possibilities and allows small start-ups to reach a worldwide market at minimum expense."

TOP TEN FIELDS FOR MOMPRENEURS ONLINE

The vast scope and constant evolution of the Internet makes it almost impossible to categorize Web businesses into a traditonal top ten list. New and exciting work options seem to pop up every week! And mompreneurs are among the first to explore the different career paths in cyberspace. But our research has revealed certain e-Business trends among moms that we've been able to group under general headings— each with its own subcategories. These are the most popular online fields:

Website Consultants (Web designer, graphic designer, site developer, Web host, webmaster)

Virtual Assistants (office support services, human resources assistance, legal and medical transcription/billing, translation)

E-tailing (online shops, catalogs, gift baskets, crafts, and other e-commerce ventures)

Direct Sales (online marketing of Avon, Tupperware, Shaklee, Rexall, and other "person-to-person" products and services)

Online Coaching/Teaching (career, relationship, health and fitness, and personal counseling; job training, tutoring, computer courses, adult ed)

Communications/Information (newsletters, e-zines, public relations, research)

Parenting Services/Products (pregnancy and breast-feeding support; babies' and children's gifts, software, clothing, toys, and other products; parenting advice; safety services)

Event Planning (birthday parties, weddings, corporate events, party supplies)

Personal Services (concierge, personal trainer, travel agent, professional organizer)

Work-at-Home Support (resources, job counseling, business opportunities, entrepreneurial advice and tools)

For all of you who don't conveniently fit into any of these categories—and we know there are plenty—we're not going to stop here! Throughout this chapter and the rest of the book, we will be highlighting many more moms who have found success by discovering an untapped market niche, fulfilling social or personal missions, creating new ways to use past business experience in cyberspace, or turning a talent or passion into a thriving enterprise.

DATA BANK: *What Inspired Your Business Idea?*

Past work experience/skills 40%
A hobby/passion/talent 39%
An unfilled niche in the marketplace. 18%
Parenting experience. 18%
A dream or mission. 13%

TAKE YOUR SKILLS ONLINE

Maximizing the work skills and experience you already possess is one of the least stressful routes to cyber-success. Secretaries and word processors are turning into virtual assistants; teachers are creating online courses;

writers are contributing content to e-zines and informational websites; social workers and career counselors are becoming cyber-coaches; crafters are marketing their wares electronically; and merchandising mavens are running online shops.

With a little ingenuity and the right technology, almost any traditional "desk job" can be partially or totally done on the Internet—or at the very least, made more profitable with a Web presence.

Website Developer Joy Rotondi-Cann
Owner of Foodies, Marblehead, Massachusetts
Mother of 1
Website: *www.foodies.com*

JOB DESCRIPTION: A custom website design company for food-related businesses and other types of companies. Foodies.com serves as an online brochure for the e-Biz.

TAPPING SKILLS AND TALENTS: A background in motion picture production and her management skills have really paid off in custom designing websites. "Although I have an understanding of website coding and graphics, I'm not the technical person—I outsource that part of the business to my network of coders, database wizards, and other experts."

START-UP STRATEGY: She first did business on the Internet as a sales rep for six small gourmet food companies, showcasing their products on her website. Food sales didn't take off, but requests soon came in to help design other food sites.

TECH TOOLS: Computer with high-speed Internet access, scanner, printer, custom website design software, charts of web-safe colors.

CYBER-CHALLENGE: "Building up a reputation that permits me to charge my clients enough so I can make a decent profit."

SUCCESS SECRETS: Don't listen to the naysayers—if you really feel you have a great business idea, go for it! "When I started in 1996, many of my family members, friends, and colleagues were not exactly encouraging," Rotondi-Cann recalls. But she stuck with it and has since gained their respect.

MUST-SURF SITE: www.searchenginewatch.com

E-tailer Sherri Ingram Breetzke
Owner of The Creativity Zone, Melbourne, Florida
Mother of 2
Website: *www.creativityzone.com*

JOB DESCRIPTION: An online store that offers handcrafted gift items, including jewelry, candle holders, baskets, and kitchen accessories.

TAPPING SKILLS AND TALENTS: Worked as a systems programmer/analyst for a mail order company and wrote computer programs for all the departments—sales, marketing, inventory, accounting, etc. She used this experience to start and market a business on the Web.

START-UP STRATEGY: Many artisans don't have the background or interest to market their wares and handle all the paperwork, so Breetzke decided to fill that need. "I select and sell top-quality crafts on my website and take care of all the adminstrative details. So many others are selling pop items and name brands on the Web—my products are unique enough to differentiate my site."

TECH TOOLS: Computer with high-speed Internet access and UPS (uninterrupted power supply), scanner, credit card software, zip drive for backup, laptop.

CYBER-CHALLENGE: Marketing with a limited budget. Breetzke maximizes the free tools out there, taking advantage of word-of-mouth advertising from satisfied customers and using the Internet's search engines. She also writes articles and tips for other websites.

SUCCESS SECRETS: Have realistic expectations. A new business owner must be willing to work hard and not quit after three months if she hasn't made her first $100,000 yet! Profitability doesn't come overnight.

MUST-SURF SITE: www.adventive.com

Virtual Assistant Janice Byer

Owner of Docu-Type Administrative Services, Caledon East, Ontario, Canada
Mother of 1
Website: *www.docutype.net*

JOB DESCRIPTION: "The small business owner's answer to a personal assistant!" Docu-Type provides word processing, desktop publishing, website development, and other office support services via the Internet.

TAPPING SKILLS AND TALENTS: Byer has over 15 years of adminstrative experience, both working in an office environment and running her father's lawn care company from home. Virtual assisting was a logical next step.

START-UP STRATEGY: "I did extensive marketing to develop clients and become recognized as a true benefit to small business owners." Writing articles and submitting them to publications online and off helped create a large client base of both Internet and local business owners.

TECH TOOLS: Computer, laser printer and inkjet printer, scanner, high-speed satellite Internet access, a variety of desktop publishing, graphics, and office-related software, PC-to-phone program for free phone calls.

CYBER-CHALLENGE: Balancing work and family time. Her "plan of attack" is to make a to-do list every night of tasks that need to be completed the next day. "I try to spend as much time as possible with my family, and the nature of my work permits me to fit small assignments in between those times."

SUCCESS SECRETS: "Passion about my business is what drives its success," she claims. "This passion also helps ease tension—a benefit for my family *and* my clients!"

MUST-SURF SITE: www.staffcentrix.com

TAP YOUR TALENTS, PURSUE YOUR PASSIONS

Do your children's birthday parties or holiday gift baskets win raves? Has your hobby of making jewelry or sewing doll clothes been widely admired? Maybe you've become so adept at the computer, you're ready to tutor newbies or design websites. Or perhaps parenthood has sparked the idea for a business that provides a unique product or service.

Professional Organizer Debbie Williams
Owner of Let's Get It Together, Houston, Texas
Mother of 2
Website: *www.organizedtimes.com*

JOB DESCRIPTION: A virtual business in which she teaches organizational skills to parents and their families through e-mail, teleclasses, and telephone consulting.

TAPPING SKILLS AND TALENTS: As a hobby, Williams had organized the homes and offices of family and friends offline. "Now my vision is to teach the organizationally challenged everywhere that there is hope—they're not alone in the quest for balance in their lives!"

START-UP STRATEGY: Conducted research on the Net with focus groups and through surveys and networking with other businesswomen before finding her niche as an online organizing expert. Soon after, she launched her own website.

TECH TOOLS: Computer, DSL line, Microsoft Outlook, CallNotes (a voice-mail service), Caller ID, telephone headset.

CYBER-CHALLENGE: "My website is a work-in-progress, much like an oil painting—it's never completely done. But I have to force myself to quit tweaking it," says Williams. To avoid temptation, she goes online only during the specified times she blocks off in her daily work schedule.

SUCCESS SECRETS: Be an Internet team player to build your business network and support network. "Those who are afraid to share content and tips, swap links and ads, or respond to e-mail inquiries are doomed to fail."

MUST-SURF SITE: www.suite101.com

FIND YOUR NICHE ON THE NET

Perhaps your business is the culmination of skill, talent, passion, and the proverbial lightbulb going off in your head. In the vast expanse of cyberspace, not even the sky is the limit! Many of the mompreneurs in our survey discovered or created very unique niches, and then filled them with innovative moneymaking businesses.

Baby Biz Proprietor Mary McCarthy
Owner of Comfy Bummy Diapers, Elk River, Minnesota
Mother of 1
Website: *www.comfybummy.com*

JOB DESCRIPTION: An online retail store offering natural baby products, including cloth diapering supplies and skin care products, along with a free newsletter.

TAPPING SKILLS AND TALENTS: Before her baby was born, McCarthy worked as an assistant in an office, but always dreamed of owning a business—especially since her dad had a home-based company. The birth of her son actually sparked the idea for this business, and her college marketing courses helped it grow. "I contracted with a website designer to code the site, but I drew pictures of the products, laid out the pages, wrote product descriptions, and heavily promoted the business."

START-UP STRATEGY: As a new mother, McCarthy enjoyed using different kinds of cloth diapers, but had trouble finding them in her area. So she decided to open a virtual storefront to sell the products she loved so much. "I analyzed hundreds of other websites before deciding on the look I wanted."

TECH TOOLS: Computer with high-speed Internet access, scanner, printer, accounting, publishing, and invoice-printing software.

CYBER-CHALLENGE: Figuring out how much stock to order the first time around. "I had never run a retail business, so I went ahead and ordered the minimums required for wholesale companies, and that worked out okay."

SUCCESS SECRETS: Join an e-mail list for work-at-home moms. "It's great to connect with other mothers who are going through the same things. The support and information I have found from these groups is unbelievable."

MUST-SURF SITE: www.onlinewbc.org

Online Instructor/Coach Linda Simpson

Owner of American Medical Transcription Education (AMTE), Sturbridge,
    Massachusetts
Mother of 2
Website: *www.grecoenterprises.com/amte*

JOB DESCRIPTION: Administering a nationally recognized online medical transription training program, using an interactive, step-by-step syllabus to take students through essential medical and scientific information and terminology. It includes transcription practice, report formats, and other teaching tools, plus coaching.

TAPPING SKILLS AND TALENTS: "I worked as a certified medical transcriptionist for many years and was able to translate my expertise into the new field of electronic education." Online support is a big part of Simpson's business, so she also has to be available (and patient enough) to constantly answer e-mails.

START-UP STRATEGY: Through her work experience, she realized how difficult it is for hospitals and transcription services to find adequately trained help. Creating a website seemed to be the best vehicle for attracting students and selling the course.

TECH TOOLS: Computer, high-speed Internet access, word processing program, sound card and foot pedal (for CD-ROM training), transcribing machine with headset and foot control (for training with tapes).

CYBER-CHALLENGE: "I really enjoy getting students' feedback and answering their questions, but it sometimes seems that I spend too much time responding to e-mails from people who never become customers."

SUCCESS SECRETS: Persistence—especially when it comes to monitoring your website. Make sure you or your webmaster keeps reregistering you on many search engines. (See Chapter 7.)

MUST-SURF SITE: www.HomeWorkingMom.com

E-zine Publisher Susie Cortright

Founder of *Momscape,* Breckenridge, Colorado
Mother of 1
Website: *www.momscape.com*

JOB DESCRIPTION: An online magazine devoted to nurturing the nurturers and building a support network of mothers. Cortright writes and edits essays, articles, daily "soul snacks," and other empowering pieces.

TAPPING SKILLS AND TALENTS: Her career has always revolved around freelance writing and editing, but she had trouble meeting newspaper deadlines with a new baby in the house. To complicate matters, Cortright lives in a log cabin in a resort town 11,000 feet above sea level in the Rocky Mountains, where job opportunities are rather limited! "*Momscape* combines my passion for the written word, a need for more flexible deadlines and earning opportunities, and a desire to connect with a community of like-minded moms."

START-UP STRATEGY: Seeking and getting advice on the Web helped her get off on the right foot. "There's a tremendous cooperative spirit on the Internet—even direct competitors are happy to exchange ideas and tips." To build on relationships and help generate content, she includes feedback forms with her e-zine.

TECH TOOLS: Computer with 56K modem Internet access, software for creating graphics and maintaining website.

CYBER-CHALLENGE: It's hard to say, "I'm done for the day." Her office is just a few steps from her bedroom door (and the Internet is always accessible), so she often finds herself working when everyone else in the house is asleep.

SUCCESS SECRETS: "I'm a better and more understanding mom if I can take some time each day—even fifteen minutes—to be alone with my thoughts, or go for a run, or read a chapter in a novel." Cortright extends that philosophy to the pages of *Momscape*—her e-zine validates the choice to nurture yourself once in a while by framing it not as a selfish act, but as an act of love toward yourself and your family.

MUST-SURF SITE: www.womensforum.com

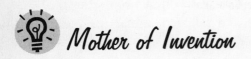

Mother of Invention

Amilya Antonetti was well aware of how important the Internet was going to be way before she became a mother. Having clocked countless hours working for telecommunications giants AT&T and MCI, she was "in the know" from the early days. What this San Leandro, California, mom never imagined was that her portal into this virtual world would be the solution to the health problems that plague her son and millions of other people. With the launch of SoapWorks, Inc., in 1995, Antonetti began a personal and professional journey that becomes more rewarding every day.

THE INSPIRATION: Antonetti's son, David, was born with severe asthma and MCS (Multiple Chemical Sensitivity). In an effort to figure out what was causing her baby's crippling attacks, she began to keep a journal. "After months and months of pain, agony, and frequent trips to the hospital, I realized that the culprit was the normal, everyday cleaning products I was using in my home," says Antonetti. "They were toxic!"

This frightening realization motivated Antonetti to gather more information and seek out parents with similar illnesses in their families. As her journey progressed, she learned more about the relationship between disease and common household products, and decided to share her discoveries via the Internet.

AN E-BIZ IS BORN: In short order, Antonetti reserved several domain names and launched www.soapworks.com as an information site. In the meantime, she started cleaning her house with ingredients her grandma recommended—baking soda, vinegar, soda ash, borax, and lemon and grapefruit juice. Husband Dennis, a third-generation soapmaker, threw some of his expertise into the pot, too. The resulting homemade cleaners not only helped David regain his health, they gained a loyal following of fans.

That was enough for this mom-on-a-mission to forge ahead! Dennis left his law practice, then they liquidated their assets and hired expert formulators to perfect the product line. With input from other parents, Antonetti fine-tuned the formulas and began manufacturing natural, rapidly biodegradable household and personal care products. All are made from vegetable-base soap and are designed for adults and children who suffer from allergies, asthma, skin sensitivities, and weakened immune systems due to disease or treatments like chemotherapy and radiation.

THE GROWTH: The products were trademarked and patented and began to be marketed in retail outlets on the West Coast. In order to reach customers everywhere, Antonetti soon developed a mail order catalog and added an e-commerce component to www.soapworks.com. She works tirelessly to make her website more valuable to visitors. In the fall of 2000, she kicked off a "Back to School" campaign to coordinate with the introduction of two new site features—mom-2-mom networking and easy-access reference guides. "We have become a trusted source for people who are trying to detox their homes, make better choices, or help a loved one deal with a challenge," says Antonetti, "by providing real information and knowledge on how we beat it and won!"

THE CHALLENGE: Cash flow was a problem at first, but Antonetti leaned on her nurturing skills to overcome it. "I learned to invest in and build relationships with my vendors, suppliers, and banks, always being upfront about the positive and negative things that were happening with Soap-Works," she says. By establishing trust and showing results, she was able to get extended terms and have new products and ideas funded by other people's money.

REALIZING THE DREAM: Antonetti combined her experiences as a parent and a businesswoman to transform her dream into a reality and fill a glaring gap in the grocery category. "I knew it had to be done by a mom, a woman, and someone like me." To help propel her dream forward, she has built a team of people with diverse talents and similar experiences and goals. Together, they've created a thriving business with a huge heart.

FAMILY FIRST: The SoapWorks team is very family-oriented, and the work space reflects that focus. "I walk around with a big smile on my face from seeing my coworkers' children running around the office, or learning Spanish or reading and writing skills in the conference room." Many kids come by after school, and the parents on staff pitch in to lead various activities. "We have an arts and crafts mom, a garden mom, a hockey mom, a soccer dad, a football dad, and so on," she points out. Antonetti's husband continues in his leadership role as vice president of the company (mom is president!), and their happy, healthy son, David, is an integral part of the after-school scene.

SECRET TO SUCCESS: Stay balanced. After SoapWorks was featured on TV and several magazines picked up on the story, the company was on the map. But Antonetti doesn't let all the hype get to her. She is just as committed to being at her son's hockey game as she is to attending a company meeting. She strives every day to be an involved and present mom, without losing sight of her important mission.

E-Bizzes to Buzz About

Some business ideas germinate from a highly personal, social, or political mission, and mompreneurs are finding the Internet to be a very effective platform for helping others.

* *www.sidelines.org:* Candace Hurley of Laguna Beach, California, endured fertility treatments and a miscarriage, then went into premature labor during a pregnancy that ultimately produced a healthy baby. Her experience prompted this mompreneur to start a nonprofit network of support groups for women with high-risk or complicated pregnancies. Hurley, now the mother of two boys, has connected thousands of women around the world through her website.

* *www.hearinghealth.net:* Angie King's role as president of the National Campaign for Hearing Health's advocacy program, Hear Us, resulted from a personal battle involving her two deaf daughters. The Salina, Ohio, mom now brings her fight for newborn hearing screening and cochlear implants (an inner-ear operation) to the website to raise national awareness among parents and the health insurance industry.

* *www.fieryencounters.com:* Joelle Burnette worked as a newspaper reporter on the police and fire beat in a small California town before she became a mother. That was enough to motivate her to actively raise funds for severe-injury burn survivor charities. Working from home after her son was born, she launched a website—featuring a family-oriented firefighter album, a quiz, a contest, collectibles, and fire safety and emergency preparedness tips—which has prompted donations from around the world.

* *www.k2z-ebooks.com:* Kathy Alexander started a self-publishing e-Biz in her Roswell, Georgia, home in order to care for her ailing mother. Hot off the press—an eBook about taking care of aging adults, written by Alexander and her mom. It's a firsthand collection of tips they've gathered from personal experience.

* *www.suzannesfoods.com:* Suzanne Locklear of Garden City, Idaho, was twice diagnosed with breast cancer while still in her thirties. Scared into eating a healthier diet, this mother of three created a vinaigrette salad dressing to perk up fruits and vegetables. It was so good, Locklear was persuaded to market it, and now sells five varieties of Suzanne's Sensational Dressings from her website. A portion of the profits goes to breast cancer causes.

★ *www.traverse.net/childcare:* Brenda Forton, a former home-based day care provider, knew firsthand how difficult it could be for working parents to find quality child care in her Michigan community. When her own children started school, she licensed with Child Care Seekers, a national organization, to create a free directory and referral service for northwest Michigan that parents can easily access on the Internet. It has since become one of her area's top child care advocacy programs.

OPPORTUNITY KNOCKS ... ON YOUR COMPUTER SCREEN

Direct sales companies like Avon, Tupperware, Mary Kay, and Shaklee have always been a magnet for moms. The products are a natural fit, the hours are flexible, and the customers are built into a woman's traditional network. If you like the idea of direct sales/multilevel marketing but can't (or don't want to) leave home on a regular basis, you can now sell cosmetics, kitchenware, books, technology equipment, vitamins, and more without ringing a doorbell or hosting a party! All the major players have an Internet presence or are planning one in the near future.

Although Avon had been involved in e-commerce since 1997, in the fall of 2000 this pioneering company "entered the next evolution in the direct-selling challenge," says Laura Castellano, an Avon spokesperson. "We realized that our sales reps were pretty Web-savvy, and we wanted to make the Internet an enabler for them to boost business." Avon now provides each e-representative with her own professional-looking home page, 90 percent of which is designed to reflect Avon's image; individuals can personalize the remaining 10 percent with their own touches.

Customers simply go to the main website (www.avon.com) to locate and access a rep in their area 24/7. By getting in on the Internet action, the e-representatives, in turn, can receive online training as beauty advisors, attract new customers or reconnect with former ones, schedule appointments, place orders electronically, offer tips, recruit staff—and get their commissions.

Several other direct sales and multilevel marketing (MLM) players—both those that are household names and some of the newer kids on the block—are joining the e-revolution. These include Tupperware, Amway, and 1-800-Partyshop. Just log on to each company's website to find out how to become a salesperson. Consultants can choose to branch off from the parent website and/or establish a small site of their own. Georganne Fiumara, founder of HomeWorkingMom.com, feels that company-provided "replicated websites" are not always sufficient marketing tools. "It sometimes makes sense to start your own website in addition to any replicated sites you may get," she explains. "Then you can use your editorial content and unique style to promote your business and link it to your replicated site."

Direct Sales Goes Digital

Among the mompreneurs we surveyed, these were the most popular business opportunities pursued on the Net:

- Arbonne International (skin care)—*www.arbonne.com*

- Avon—*www.avon.com*

- Discovery Toys—*www.discoverytoysinc.com*

- Excel (telecommunications)—*www.excelir.com*

- Mary Kay (cosmetics)—*www.marykay.com*

- Nature's Very Best (personal care products and gifts)— *www.naturesverybest.com*

- 1-800-Partyshop—*www.1800partyshop.com*

- Pampered Chef (kitchenware)—*www.pamperedchef.com*

- Rexall Showcase (health care products)—*www.rexall.com*

- Shaklee (nutrition and personal/household care products)—
  www.shaklee.com

- Tupperware—*www.tupperware.com*

Information about pursuing opportunities with these companies can be found on their websites.

Party Girl Lisa Pelton
Easy Parties for YOU with 1800partyshop, Rosemount, Minnesota
Mother of 2
Website: *www.1800partyconsultant.com/1792*

JOB DESCRIPTION: Plans parties for customers, including the theme, activities, decorations, etc. She then provides the necessary party supplies by ordering them through the parent company's website or its print catalog.

TAPPING SKILLS AND TALENTS: She always loved hosting parties, and wanted to help others see the ease with which they could plan and pull off a terrific event. After being involved with a home business opportunity that required a sizable investment, Pelton jumped at the chance to join a company that demanded no inventory, no home parties, excellent tech support . . . and that was based on the Internet.

START-UP STRATEGY: Make party planning a family affair to ease the workload and have more fun. "My children paste labels on catalogs and are eager to assist with face painting and game activities at kids' parties," says Pelton, "and my husband is a great sport about packing and setting up for trade shows."

TECH TOOLS: Computer, printer, modem Internet access, desktop publishing software.

CYBER-CHALLENGE: It's great (and economical!) to have a site provided by 1800partyshop, but eventually Pelton would like to personalize her website and shorten the name so it's easier to remember and access. "I strongly believe in starting out small and not investing in office needs until a business is bringing in enough money to pay for them."

SUCCESS SECRETS: "Set your business schedule and your goals, then share them with your family." She periodically takes the time to sit down with her children and explain how *everyone* benefits when she is allowed to focus on her work during business hours and is supported in reaching her goals.

MUST-SURF SITE: www.1800partyshop.com

Tupperware Lady Phyllis Jozwik
Direct Sales Consultant, Edison, New Jersey
Mother of 1
Website: *www.momsnetwork.com/suites/shop/tupperlady*

JOB DESCRIPTION: Independent Tupperware consultant using the Web to sell kitchen tools and cookware. Also offers services for reorganizing the kitchen.

TAPPING SKILLS AND TALENTS: She has always enjoyed using Tupperware products, and after attending a party decided that this would be a good opportunity for a home-based business.

START-UP STRATEGY: With an active three-year-old daughter, this mom had very little energy left at night to host parties and demos with customers. She figured an online business would provide greater flexibility in her schedule ("I could work in my pajamas from my laptop!") and a much broader customer base (beginning with out-of-state friends and relatives).

TECH TOOLS: Laptop computer, high-speed Internet access, printer, fax.

CYBER-CHALLENGE: Driving traffic to her site. "My website has been up and running for just a short time, and I have to find ways (and time) to promote it more effectively."

SUCCESS SECRETS: "I work at odd hours—six in the morning or ten at night—squeezing in phone calls and offline business around my daughter's day." She works online while her daughter is sleeping, hanging out with her daddy, or playing with friends. With the flexibility this schedule allows, Jozwik rarely feels crunched for time or stressed out.

MUST-SURF SITE: www.momsnetwork.com

CLICK AND SAVE: *Scam Check*

>> *www.scambusters.org*

>> *www.scamwatch.com*

>> *www.usps.gov/websites/depart/inspect/emplmenu.htm*

>> Take a look at the posts and message boards on *momshelpmoms. com, homeworkingmom.com, hbwm.com,* and other work-at-home sites for mothers—women love to share their stories, both good and bad!

HELP WANTED: MOMS PLEASE APPLY

Some enterprising mothers are using the World Wide Web to open a wide world of opportunities for other mothers. Most of these mom-to-mom businesses are small-scale ventures where the buy-in is nonexistent or minimal, and the rewards can be sizable. Here are a few of the legitimate opportunities offered by and for work-from-home moms:

MOMPRENEUR: Mary Tobin, Wilmington, North Carolina
E-BIZ: The Stork Flock (www.storklady.com)
DOT.COM OPP: Tobin's business began when she was trying to find a cute sign to welcome her employer's newborn twins. She created a stork-shaped sign, stuck it on their front lawn, and was soon fielding requests for more. Her idea eventually grew into a sign rental businesss, and her very first customer was a neighbor of former president George Bush and his wife, Barbara. "I even got to meet them when I picked up the stork!" Tobin remembers. She now sells business packages from her website.

Fraud Finder

For all the legitimate opportunities to do business on the Net, there seem to be as many bogus multilevel marketing schemes and shady direct-selling deals. Unfortunately, cyberspace opportunities can be harder to evaluate than those in the real world, says Georganne Fiumara of *HomeWorkingMom.com* So how can you tell the good from the bad? Here's what she suggests:

★ Make sure there's a product or service behind the opportunity. A sales or multilevel marketing site should be offering tangible products or services to sell, not just the opportunity to sell the idea or recruit other suckers. That's the same principle of "misleading opportunities" that envelope-stuffing scams have used for years. The most common misleading opportunity in cyberspace? Selling copycat websites.

★ Beware of million-dollar promises. Find out how much you can realistically expect to earn. A common pitch being used online is "guaranteed earnings in a protected market area." Another ploy—a listing of quotes from people who have been successful and how much money they've made. If something sounds too good to be true, it probably is.

★ Never send cash, a check, or a money order. If you do decide to invest in an opportunity, use a credit card so you have proof of purchase. Online payment systems like *PayPal.com* and *Ecount.com* also provide protection in the event of fraud, deception, or nondelivery of goods.

Misty Weaver-Ostinato, founder of *momshelpmoms.com*, a site that provides resources for moms and evaluates home-based business opportunities, has this to add:

★ Treat a business opportunity as you would a job. Ask what your duties will be, how you are expected to represent the company, and if you can contact other reps before you put up any money. If your questions go unanswered or the site refuses to send you information before you make a decision, watch out!

★ Don't empty out your piggy bank. Initial investments in legitimate, small-scale Internet business opportunities usually range from between $29 to $500, with kits averaging around $100. If you're asked for more of an investment, proceed with extra caution.

★ Check with the Better Business Bureau. Even if you know an Internet opportunity is legitimate, you can find out if any representatives or consultants filed complaints about the company by contacting the Better Business Bureau *(www.bbonline.org.)*

MOMPRENEUR: Jennifer Dugan, Los Alamos, New Mexico

E-BIZ: Dugan's Travels (www.onlineagency.com/duganstravels)

DOT.COM OPP: After her first son was born, Dugan was working from home as an outside sales rep for a travel agency, booking trips through the Internet and surfing the Web, when she got her brainstorm: She would recruit travel agents through her website to work with her on commission. She has since brought in a "family" of moms from all over the country. Paying for personal liability insurance is the only cash outlay each agent must make.

MOMPRENEUR: Marybeth Henry, Herndon, Virginia

E-BIZ: WAHMfest (www.wahmfest.org)

DOT.COM OPP: Henry was asked by a local hospital to give a talk to new moms on starting a home-based business—and conceived her own business idea. She had developed a resource list for the talk, but then figured it would be better for interested mothers and those who could help them to come together face-to-face. WAHMfest—an expo that connects parents with legit business opportunities *and* helpful resources (like the Chamber of Commerce and professional organizations)—was born. Most of Henry's "face-to-face" networking is now done on her website, where she also offers parents inexpensive kits for organizing live expos around the country.

MOMPRENEUR: Tammy Harrison, Logan, Utah

E-BIZ: Marketing and Creativity for Small Businesses (www.jdharrison.com/queenofpizzazz.htm)

DOT.COM OPP: Online businesses contact Harrison, a marketing specialist, for help in finding independent advertising reps for their sites. The reps are responsible for selling ad space to other websites and electronic publications, and earn commissions based on sales. Harrison provides training through a booklet she developed, e-mail correspondence, and Instant Messaging. No investment is required; each rep works as an independent contractor.

MOMPRENEUR: Heather Quarnstrom, Wauconda, Illinois

E-BIZ: 3JC Enterprises (www.3JCEnterprises.bigstep.com)

DOT.COM OPP: Quarnstrom's Internet gift shop began as a catalog mail order business. She soon saw the benefits of moving online, and built a website to peddle her selection of glass collectibles, jewelry, plates, toys, and tools to both retail and wholesale customers. The website also offers low-cost business opportunties to moms who want to sell 3JC Enterprises' wares from their own sites.

MOMPRENEUR: Kim Martins DeYoung, Scarsdale, New York
E-BIZ: Metromom (www.metromom.com)
DOT.COM OPP: DeYoung started her business as Metromom Maternity—a line of high-quality maternity clothing that she designed, produced, and sold from home. She launched her website on Mother's Day, 1999, and is expanding her business to include coaching and other services that can help moms keep their lives in balance. To encourage working from home, DeYoung also offers opportunities to sell her clothing line.

MULTITASKING CYBER-MOMS

Do you have too many ideas to fit into just one business? We came across some mompreneurs who are so enthusiastic about the limitless possiblilities of cyberspace, they're running two or more Web businesses at a time! Of course, moms are skilled at keeping several balls in the air at once, so this minitrend, also known as "multiple income streams," didn't particularly surprise us. And when the fringe benefit is greater earning potential—without much more cash outlay—it's a win-win deal.

Virtual assistants typically wear many hats, but a few enterprising moms have taken the concept to new heights. Cheryl Infanzon offers a smorgasbord of services—database management, spreadsheets, word processing, graphic design, PowerPoint presentations, event planning, and travel itineraries—from www.virtualassist.homestead.com/va.html in Hatfield, Pennsylvania. Tina Jacks of Kirbyville, Texas, certainly lives up to her name—she's a jack-of-all-trades! Her business, At-HomeWorks.com, provides a combination of services, including free online resources for work-at-home moms, website development, Internet and computer tutoring, and a newspaper column.

Are Auctions the Answer?

Love to collect memorabilia or browse flea markets? You may be able to earn cool cash for your hot finds—without ever leaving the comfort of your computer chair. eBay started the online bidding craze back in 1995 and, by early 2000, there were over 200 Internet auction sites.

All make it relatively easy to sell your merchandise with just an e-mail address and a little perseverance. Beth Schumann, a mom from Virginia, was inspired by her daughter's Beanie Baby enthusiasm to start collecting the cuties herself. When that market began to fizzle, she branched out into Barbie dolls and other collectible toys. In less than six months, she completed hundreds of sales on eBay, and now hopes to market the items from her own website as well. (For more on earning money through online auctions, see "Click Cash" in Chapter 3.)

A few words of warning: "Fake customers" do frequent these sites—lurkers who think it's fun to come in with a high bid and then disappear. With a little practice, you can learn how to zero in on the sincere bidders so you don't waste time on deadbeats and lose out on sales. Far more serious and more difficult to control are dishonest buyers who use stolen credit cards, bogus money orders, and bad checks to pay for merchandise.

Mompreneurs like Jacks are not that unusual—others have pieced together several distinct services to create a crazy quilt of income opportunities. Rosalie Kubik Ferris, a mompreneur from Ware, Massachusetts, is involved in three ventures, all of which are somehow related to her family lineage. DUQwear is an Internet catalog business providing unique clothing to Duquette descendents (www.duqwear.hypermart.net), DUQUET(TE) Family Forest is her online genealogy service, and Ferris Clan Web Design is self-explanatory. "All of these businesses sprang from hobbies and passions," says Ferris. And former teacher Liane Serna of Boca Raton, Florida, is a distributor of aromatherapy products, an online tutor, and a mystery shopper on the Internet.

Mompreneurs who have energy to spare no longer have to be tied down to—or bored by—just one job. The Internet allows you to pool your various talents, skills, and passions and juggle several businesses at once.

Web Celeb

Laura Berman Fortgang
Founder and President of InterCoach, Inc. *(www.intercoach.com)*
Montclair, New Jersey
Mom of 3

"It takes courage to have a balanced life, says Laura Berman Fortgang. "You have to learn how to say no." She should certainly know. As a popular career and life coach, author, and public speaker, and a mother of three children under the age of four, Fortgang not only helps people all over the world achieve work/family balance, she tries to live it herself every day!

Fortgang started her coaching business in 1994, several years before she was a mother *and* before the word "coach" expanded to mean more than sports and a whistle! At the time, she had reached a turning point in her life, having driven herself into a tizzy trying to pursue an acting career while waitressing, teaching aerobics, and working as a shoe model to make ends meet. "I had worked with a coach to help me build the tenacity I needed to succeed in my theater career, and realized how coaching could benefit everyone, from actors to top-level executives," she recalls. "I also knew that I wanted to design something that would allow me to work from home with the kids I hoped to have someday." So with $10,000 in waitressing savings, Fortgang founded InterCoach, a name her husband thought up to reflect the interpersonal nature of coaching. The name became even more meaningful when the company went on the Internet in 1998.

An acknowledged "chicken" when it comes to financial risk-taking, Fortgang made a conscious decision to allow InterCoach to grow from within, refusing to seek out loans, venture capital, or investors. Paring down her lifestyle and going after corporate clients, she was able to double her income every year. By the time her first son was born in 1997, Fortgang had grown from a self-employed personal coach on the cusp of an emerging profession to a full-fledged certified coaching company recognized as a leading force in this trendsetting field. She has since written two books—*Take Yourself to the Top: The Secrets of America's #1 Career Coach*

(Warner Books, 1998) and *Living Your Best Life* (Tarcher/Penguin Putnam, 2001)—made appearances on *Oprah* and *The Today Show,* and lectured internationally.

Fortgang now supervises a staff of independent coaches to help lighten her load, but still works from home, coaching clients by phone and e-mail "from the biggest room in the house." From there, she organizes her seminars and presentations, educates people about the coaching profession from her busy website, and performs work/life makeovers. If a client wants a face-to-face meeting, she rents an outside conference room for the day.

Exactly how does Fortgang manage to balance her hectic life? She sets her office hours around her child care schedule and when her workday ends devotes at least six hours to full-time mothering. "If I see that balance slipping, I consider reorganizing my priorities or hiring help for my business," she says. Eager to share her professional tips with mompreneurs, credentialed coach Laura Berman Fortgang generously put together the following minicoaching session:

- Make time to build a community around your business. Isolation is a big factor when you work from home, and you must make an effort to maintain relationships and "people contact"—even if it's over the phone.

- Market your business creatively without spending a fortune. When she started out, Fortgang gave free lunchtime workshops at corporations to build up her client base.

- Think of yourself as a "company," not a "sole proprietor." That vision and attitude influences the way you present yourself to clients and customers.

- Be willing to push the envelope. We live in a time when women-owned businesses are starting and succeeding at an incredible rate.

- Be very clear about what you want out of your business. List the "ideal" goals you wish to accomplish and "ideal" kinds of work you want to do so you have the power to say no.

CHAPTER THREE

The Flex Track: Telecommuting and Beyond

 *Sound Byte*

"Many moms want the flexibility to work from home, but don't want to invest the time and money starting a business. They'd rather be employed by established companies that will allow them to work off-site."

Heidi Piccoli, mother of two; Riverside, California
Founder of Moneymakin'Mommy *(www.moneymakingmommy.com)*

When we talk to moms across the nation about the joys of running our home businesses, so many of them say to us, "But I don't want a business." They tell us that they simply want to find a way to work from home and earn a steady paycheck (ideally with health care benefits). Some are hoping to continue professional careers on a more flexible track, through telecommuting or part-time work. Many are looking for home-based clerical positions, like data entry and telemarketing. Some have no idea what can be done from home, but are desperate for suggestions. All however, share one common goal: the desire to earn money without sacrificing time with the kids.

When we worked full-time in the corporate world, in the days before the Internet revolution, we had three options when our children were born. We could stick with our full-time jobs as magazine editors and juggle our career and family needs. We could quit working completely, and give up a needed salary to become stay-at-home moms. Or, we could leave our full-time jobs and start home-based businesses, in an effort to create more family balance while still contributing to the family's financial bottom line. Well, you know which route we chose. It was rare then to see many moms telecommuting, job-sharing, or working part-time. And the only other home-based options available were scams like envelope-stuffing. But things have changed considerably, thanks to the Web and trailblazing moms who have broken the barriers of 9 to 5, and paved the way for you to do the same.

THE WIRED (AND WIRELESS!) WORKPLACE

Today, 30 percent of the U.S. workforce engages in nontraditional employment, including project work, telecommuting, and part-time assignments, according to the Economic Policy Institute. Technology and the tight labor market of the late '90s and early 21st century have fueled the trend. "Even new college graduates are negotiating for flexible hours when applying for jobs," notes Kirsten Ross, mompreneur and founder of Womans-Work.com, a website dedicated to helping professional women find alternative work arrangements. "Employees are in the driver's seat," she says. The Internet and tech tools like e-mail, web phones, laptops, and personal digital assistants make it possible to work anywhere—whether it's from a corner table at Starbucks or a home office across the hall from your baby's nursery. "Technology has changed the face of the workforce," agrees Kathleen Shelby, who, with fellow mom Lisa Marks, runs Flex-Time Solutions, a Maplewood, New Jersey, interim staffing firm that places marketing, public relations, and communications professionals in project positions. Shelby and Marks run the company from each of their home offices, which are completely connected by networked computer, phone, and intercom systems.

Not only are your choices more flexible than ever, but you have better ways to find the job of your dreams. Employment agencies specializing in flexible work alternatives are cropping up across the nation to help moms in various professions achieve better career/family balance. And with the

advent of online job boards, you can post your resume and scan the classifieds for home-based opportunities at all skill levels—whether you're an
MBA or a secretarial school grad. The newest trend is moms-only job
resource centers, owned and run by mompreneurs who are dedicated to
helping you locate reputable employment with built-in adaptability.

Mom-2-Mom Job Network

Take a look at some of the job resources available—all started by work-from-home
mothers.

Company and Its Mission:
Dot Com Mommies
(www.dotcommommies.com)
This website targets moms who may not have extensive professional experience,
yet want a scam-free way to work from home. It lists nationwide work-at-home
jobs and other online income opportunities, plus offers moms the chance to earn
commissions by selling ads for the site.

Founding Mompreneur and Her Motivation:
Stacy Perez
(mother of 1 from Hanover Park, Illinois)
"After my son was born I tried all kinds of work-from-home jobs and learned lots
about what's reputable and what's not. I started Dot Com Mommies because I
wanted to take all my knowledge and resources and make them available to other
moms."

Company and Its Mission:
Flexible Resources, Inc.
(www.flexibleresources.com)
This employment agency places experienced professionals in flexible work arrangements, including part-time, job-share, telecommuting, and project assignments. Based
in Connecticut, the company also has offices in New York City, Boston, Los Angeles,
and Montclair, New Jersey, many of which are run by work-from-home moms.

Founding Mompreneurs and Their Motivation:

Nadine Mockler (mom of 3 from Pleasantville, New York) and

Laurie Young (mom of 3 from Norwalk, Connecticut)

Mockler and Young met while working as advertising agency accountant executives in the mid-'80s. After their kids were born, they yearned for better life balance, and knew other career women wanted it too. They formed Flexible Resources in 1989, with a single objective: "To pioneer flexibility in the workplace."

Company and Its Mission:

FlexTime Solutions

(www.flextimesolutions.com)

This interim staffing firm specializes in placing marketing, communications, and public relations professionals in project, part-time, and flex-time jobs in New Jersey companies, in fields like financial services, pharmaceuticals, health care, and consumer products.

Founding Mompreneurs and Their Motivation:

Kathleen Shelby (mom of 2) and

Lisa Marks (mom of 2), both from Maplewood, New Jersey

Shelby quit her job in corporate management in the mid-'90s so she could spend more time with her two-year-old, and realized, "I needed a company that would place me in an alternative work arrangement, so I could scale back without forfeiting my career." While she was brainstorming with friend Lisa Marks, a workplace recruiter, the idea for FlexTime Solutions was born.

Company and Its Mission:

GET A MOM

(www.getamom.com)

An employment e-source for professional mothers in the technology, legal, and accounting fields. It provides job placement, a support network of other work-at-home moms, and links to online resources.

Founding Mompreneur and Her Motivation:

Started by Andrea Mudd, a work-at-home mother, who also owns a successful at-home piano studio. She saw a need for a site that provides flexible placement with legitimate companies.

....

Company and Its Mission:

Jobs and Moms Resource Center

(www.jobsandmoms.com)

Offers resources, advice, and helpful links for moms in search of new career directions, flexible work options, and home-based information. Also links you to career counseling services through telephone coaching and online courses.

Founding Mompreneur and Her Motivation:

Nancy Collamer

(mom of 2 from Old Greenwich, Connecticut)

Before becoming a work-at-home mom, Collamer worked in corporate human resources and also owned her own employment agency. "I felt the Internet was a wonderful way to reach a wide audience of mothers who are in need of career counseling and job-search strategies so they can land the flexible jobs they desire."

....

Company and Its Mission:

MoneyMakin' Mommy

(www.moneymakingmommy.com)

This website offers an extensive list of telecommuting and other work-at-home jobs across the nation, culled from the major online job boards and placed in one central location. It also features home business advice and resources.

Founding Mompreneur and Her Motivation:

Heidi Piccoli

(mom of 2 from Riverside, California)

Needing to contribute to the family income yet wanting to stay home with her kids, Piccoli searched online for telecommuting jobs. "There are lots of opportunities out there, but they're tricky to find. I wanted to help simplify the search for moms who are desperate for a safe and reputable way to make money from home."

....

Company and Its Mission:

WAHMfest

(www.wahmfest.org)

WAHMfest (the "WAHM" stands for "Work-at-Home Moms") is an annual live job expo that connects parents with legitimate work-at-home opportunities and business resources. It began in northern Virginia, but has expanded to several other U.S. states, as well as Canada.

Founding Mompreneur and Her Motivation:

Marybeth Henry

(mom of 2 from Herndon, Virginia)

"As a mom, I knew how important it was to have the freedom and resources to work from home, and wanted to share my strategies with others. I did a talk on work-at-home options for a new moms' group at a local hospital, but realized that what was really needed was a central place where moms could come face-to-face with companies offering at-home jobs. Eventually I'd love to see WAHMfests in every state!"

Company and Its Mission:

Womans-Work

(www.womans-work.com)

This website helps professional women across the U.S. find alternative work arrangements like job-sharing, telecommuting, and part-time positions. It features a job posting board, a service that matches job-sharing partners, resume and interview tips, and community areas where parents can network and share job leads. It also offers resources for companies that want to be more family-friendly.

Founding Mompreneur and Her Motivation:

Kirsten Ross

(mom of 2 from Warren, Michigan)

When her first son was born, Ross cut back her full-time job in human resources to a part-time schedule. "I thought other women should have flexible options and that more companies should provide them,"said Ross, who was inspired to start a business. Initially she planned a website that paired job-share partners, but then a coworker's wife suggested she include job postings, too.

YOUR FLEXIBLE WORK OPTIONS

A recent report by Catalyst, the nonprofit organization devoted to advancing women in business, found that career advancement does not have to get sidelined when moms modify work schedules in an effort to achieve family balance. The study tracked the career outcomes of women who were first to try flexible work arrangements at corporations over a decade ago. All of the women now hold mid- and senior-level positions, and most credit the availability of part-time work during critical child-rearing years as the key to maintaining career momentum.

What constitutes an alternative work arrangement, or flex time, as it's often called? It can be anything that differs from the traditional 9-to-5, 40-hour workweek. It might be a full-time job with flexible hours, a permanent part-time position, a job-sharing or telecommuting arrangement, or a long- or short-term project. "Extended flexibility is the wave of the future," says Nadine Mockler, cofounder of Flexible Resources, Inc., a staffing and consulting firm that specializes in flexible work arrangements for professionals. The global economy creates a 24/7 workplace in which everyone is fully wired together, Mockler explains. "People must work varied hours, often with a job-share partner, in order to get the work done. Companies want employees who are willing to put in long hours. There's no way anyone can do that long-term and stay motivated unless they can make their own rules about when and where they work. More and more we are seeing 'flexible hours' extended beyond the traditional part-time arrangement, with the freedom for moms to telecommute and work when they are at their best." For example, a marketing professional with a young child might work from early morning until early afternoon, take off for a few hours to be at home with her child, then return to work in her home office, burning the midnight oil. "She might put in a ten-hour day," says Laurie Young, Mockler's partner and company cofounder, "but she has the balance she craves and can give her employer a more energized, focused mind-set."

Following are some of the choices you have in this high-tech work world.

TRY TELECOMMUTING

Telecommuting (often referred to as teleworking) is by far the most popular alternative work arrangement for mothers. According to a survey sponsored by AT&T and the International Telework Association and Council (ITAC), there are 16.5 million teleworkers in the U.S., and that number is projected to reach 30 million by the year 2004.

A typical arrangement has telecommuters working from home two or three days a week and the rest of the time on-site. But today there are a variety of other groundbreaking ways telecommuting can be set up, thanks to the Internet and its power to keep you connected to corporate headquarters—anytime, anyplace.

Many high-tech companies (and even a few conventional establishments, like banks and law firms) now allow employees to work *exclusively* from home. As webmaster and managing editor of publications for Oracle Applications Users Group, Atlanta mom Katie Lail gets to wear sweatpants (and go without makeup!) every single day. She found her full-time telecommuting job through a member newsletter from Homebased Working Moms (www.hbwm.com), a work-from-home parent organization. About once a month Lail commutes from the suburbs to attend meetings in Oracle's Atlanta office; she also travels to semiannual educational conferences and meetings in the San Francisco headquarters. (Even her boss telecommutes—from San Antonio, Texas!)

Susan Perrin of Olathe, Kansas, works from home 15 to 20 hours a week, doing loan setups for the mortgage department of Hillcrest Bank, right around the corner from her house. The part-time job (which she found by looking under "Mortgage" in the newspaper classifieds) is perfect for her background in mortgage underwriting. "The bank calls me when they have paperwork that needs processing; I pick it up and turn it around in twenty-four hours," she says. "I love having the freedom to work on loans at night and take my two boys blueberry-picking in the middle of the afternoon," Perrin says.

Some teleworkers may live thousands of miles away from company headquarters. For four years, Kathy Snead, a mom of two from Jacksonville, Florida, telecommuted full-time for iVillage, the Internet women's network that's based in New York City. After leaving that job, she took a similar position for WebMD in Atlanta, where she also works exclusively from home, helping the company build an online community. "As a divorced mom and parent of a special-needs child, it's particularly important for me to be able to work from home," says Snead. "I've always had two goals in my life: to have a career and to have a family," she says. "It means the world to me that I can be at home writing a proposal that's valuable to my company, yet still be on call for hugs and kisses from my kids. Of course, the trade-off is that I have to ignore my dirty dishes during work time!" she says with a laugh.

Telecommuting Tips From the Trenches

Teleworking moms agree that self-discipline, a regular work schedule, and constant communication with your employer are key to making the arrangement work successfully.

■ **Go Over Ground Rules.** Establish with your boss and coworkers the hours you are expected to be available, and how you will stay in touch. For example, Snead works from 8:30 A.M. till about 5 or 6 P.M., and communicates with her colleagues through e-mail, Instant Messages, and phone conferences. She's made it clear that she's unreachable during dinnertime, but faithfully logs back on the computer after the kids are in bed to make sure there are no urgent e-mails.

■ **Be Reliable.** Return calls and e-mails promptly, and let colleagues know when you may be away from your desk for extended periods. If she has to go to a doctor's appointment or school meeting during the day, Snead always alerts coworkers in advance, so they can get her any important information or projects before she leaves. She also sets up an automated e-mail message which says when she'll be back. Voice mail is another way to stay in the loop. Susan Rietano-Davey, a mother of four who runs a Flexible Resources satellite office from her Connecticut home, updates her voice-mail message every day to let callers know the date, whether she's in or out of the office, and when she will return the call. "I always make an effort to return calls by the end of the business day," she says.

■ **Plan on Child Care.** Employers will expect it and you will need it to get your job done. "One of the biggest fallacies about teleworking is that you can do it without child care," says Kathleen Shelby of Flex-Time Solutions. Luckily, working from home allows you more flexible choices. If your kids are over five, school may provide the child care coverage you need. Snead tackles her high-concentration tasks from 8:30 A.M. to 3 P.M., while her kids are out of the house. If you've got babies or preschoolers, you might opt for an in-home sitter or a family day care arrangement.

■ **Document Your Accomplishments.** Make management and coworkers aware of the work you're producing, so no one questions what you're doing all day. Send frequent updates and memos (several times a week) to apprise your boss and coworkers of projects under way, as well as any you've completed. When you send e-mails to clients or coworkers, make sure your boss and other key supervisors receive copies, too, so they have tangible evidence of your efforts. "Make sure they feel your presence, even though you're not there in person," stresses Snead.

■ **Put In Face Time.** Even if you're lucky enough to work from home every day, plan to show up at the corporate office periodically for meetings and other functions. Snead flies to corporate headquarters in Atlanta about once a month to meet face-to-face with her WebMD team. Not only does it offer a visual reminder of your value to the company, but it helps you reinforce the relationships you've forged through less personal methods like e-mail and phone conferences.

■ **Protect Your Equipment.** The company might provide you with the tools you need to work from home, but it's your responsibility to make sure the system always works efficiently. "Here in Florida, a flash thunderstorm could crash my computer in seconds," says Snead. She makes sure she prevents such mishaps by using a heavy-duty surge protector and backing up her work constantly.

■ **Get Frequent Feedback.** Schedule face-to-face meetings with your manager at least once a month, recommends Rietano-Davey, to review how you're doing, discuss the progress of the telecommuting arrangement, and iron out any kinks.

CLICK AND SAVE: *Telecommuting Resources*

>> *www.telecommute.org*

>> *www.telecommuting.about.com*

>> *www.gilgordon.com*

>> *www.telework-connection.com*

GO PART-TIME

Corporations are warming up to the idea that professionals don't necessarily have to put in a 40-hour workweek to be productive. "Many of the companies that list with our site say they are willing to consider part-time employment," says Kirsten Ross of Womans-Work.com, which links moms with flexible job options. "Even if a company doesn't have a formal policy on part-time or flex time, they're often willing to try it on a case-by-case basis."

Ross was a part-time professional herself before she started her e-Biz. She was working full-time in human resources for a major health care corporation when she became pregnant with her first child. She approached her boss about the possibility of working part-time after the baby arrived. Fortunately, her manager was supportive, promising, "We'll make this work." By cutting back on the number of departments Ross supervised, management rearranged her schedule so that she only came in to the office two days a week. On a third day Ross agreed to be available from home by pager, e-mail, and voice mail.

More common part-time arrangements involve shortening the hours in the workday (maybe working 9 to 1 every day instead of 9 to 5) or shortening the workweek to four days, says Pat Katepoo, flex coach and

Virtual Chief Operating Officer

In September 1995, when her second son was a year and a half, Connie Johnson-Hambley left her high-powered job in banking so she could devote more time to her children. She felt the formal corporate world was too rigid, and wanted to chart her own course—one that included the flexibility to work from home. She began her own business refinishing and repainting children's furniture, but never lost touch with her corporate colleagues. Along the way, she received many offers for jobs in banking, but always politely declined them, suggesting other well-qualified candidates.

Then in 1999, Johnson-Hambley got an irresistible proposition. Belinda Barton, Inc., a small mom-owned company which creates children's furnishings, asked her to come on board as its chief operating officer. The company needed her expertise and seasoned guidance, and was willing to be as flexible as possible to get it. The New York–based company allows Johnson-Hambley to work exclusively from her home office in Boston. "It is a high-level job without the stress of high-level absence from my home and life," Johnson-Hambley says. "It's exciting to know that being a stay-at-home mom can be so fulfilling and dynamic."

Here are her success secrets:

Keep Up Your Contacts: Although she'd been out of the corporate workforce for some time, Johnson-Hambley kept friends and colleagues posted on what she was doing through regular phone calls and e-mails. An acquaintance familiar with her background in law, finance, and children's marketing recommended Johnson-Hambley for Belinda Barton, Inc., which was expanding its staff.

Tap Technology: "Our working relationship could not exist if it were not for the Internet and the high-tech tools we have at our fingertips," Johnson-Hambley says. Her home office is outfitted with a computer and cable modem, video conferencing equipment, a scanner, a fax, and multiple phone lines.

Plan Work and Family Time: Daily work tasks (editing business plans, raising money through angel and venture capital networks, and creating marketing strategies) are planned around the kids' school and extracurricular commitments. Though she's often able to answer e-mail with her toddler on her lap, she's careful to make sure the kids are well-supervised before she makes conference calls.

Get Creative With Child Care: When she needs uninterrupted time to work, Johnson-Hambley barters sitting time with neighbors so her three children always have a friend or two to play with. If she has to attend outside meetings, she'll ask her former nanny to care

Virtual Chief Operating Officer, continued

for the kids in her home, or she'll drop them off with a trusted day care provider just up the street. In the summers she teams up with a small group of local moms who have kids the same age as hers and creates a neighborhood day camp. The moms take turns planning the activities and supervising the kids, so each mom gets a couple of days "free" to work each week.

Best Trick for Juggling Work and Family: Voice mail. "If you're snuggling with your two-year-old and the phone rings, let voice mail get it," Johnson-Hambley urges. "The caller can wait ten minutes to talk, but the snuggles are what you're home for, right?"

founder of WorkOptions.com (see "Mother of Invention," page 83). "A part-time work option can be just the ticket to a downshifted pace, while helping you remain active and visible in your career," she says.

But what if you've temporarily left the workforce to nurture your young children, and now want to find a way to work part-time? Don't underestimate the value of your mom skills. Carol Jula, a mom of two from Corinth, Texas, never dreamed that her stint as PTA president would lead to a paying job. She had spearheaded a school fund-raiser in conjunction with iThought.com, the Internet yellow pages powered by consumer opinion. Jula's mission was to convince parents to rate as many local businesses as possible for listing on the iThought site. In turn, iThought would donate a certain amount of money for each review recruited by the school. "Our school had the most reviews of any school in the whole state of Texas!" Jula says proudly. iThought execs presented the PTA with a $6,000 check, and were so impressed with Jula's motivational qualities they asked her to join the company. She now works 25 hours a week exclusively from home. As community coordinator, she is responsible for recruiting local businesses and nonprofits to list with iThought. Every Friday she has a lunch meeting with the iThought staff in Dallas, where they discuss strategies. She loves her home-based job so much, she's considering working full-time.

PARTNER UP THROUGH JOB-SHARING

If you're hoping for a few days off each week and don't mind working on-site, a job-share arrangement may be your best bet. You and a partner share a full-time job, but each work designated days in the office. Rose D'Orazio and Shari Hope share the position of advertising records assistant in the finance department of AOL Time Warner. It's the perfect arrangement for these New York moms, who get at least two days off each week. Hope works Mondays and Tuesdays, D'Orazio works Thursdays and Fridays, and they alternate coming in on Wednesdays. They receive half the salary and half the vacation time of a full-time position, but get complete health care benefits.

Job-sharing is easier to arrange when you're already established with a company and you have a specific partner in mind. D'Orazio and Hope had worked together for years as ad records assistants before they had their kids. However, even new applicants can pursue job-share positions at corporations, notes Kirsten Ross of Womans-Work.com, *if* they team up with a partner beforehand. "You can then send in resumes and go on interviews together," says Ross, noting that many of the companies listing jobs on her site welcome applications from job-share partners.

Communication is crucial for job-sharing to succeed. D'Orazio and Hope talk several times a day. "We're always available to each other when we're home," D'Orazio says. They also leave detailed notes for each other in the office so the transition is seamless. "I think we're actually more productive now than we were when we each worked full-time at this job," says D'Orazio. Having less time to get the work done challenges you to work more efficiently on the days you're in the office, she explains.

Job-sharing won't work for everyone, however. "You've got to be the kind of person who's willing to share recognition," notes Ross. Partners need to have complementary skills and a common vision. "Shari and I have very different work styles," says D'Orazio, "but we share the same motivation: our children. What better reason could there be for making this work?"

OPT FOR FREE AGENCY

"Free agent" is a fairly new term that's been coined to describe the free-lance professional who is hired to work on a project basis, either on- or off-site. Projects can last anywhere from a few weeks to a year or more, and vary in scope according to your expertise. Perhaps you'll be hired to type an employee manual. Or maybe you'll design the graphics for a brochure or a website. Jobs like these can be found via word-of-mouth networking, through employment agencies specializing in flexible work options or interim staffing, or at online job boards devoted to free agency (see "Surfing the Online Job Boards," page 87). Online job boards at professional trade associations are another great source.

Kathy Sherman, a technical writer and mom of two from Walden, New York, has found a variety of project jobs through online boards at www.monster.com, www.tristatejobs.com (serving New York, Connecticut, and New Jersey) and the Society for Technical Communication (www.stc.org), a professional organization devoted to her field of expertise. She's currently contracted to do a long-term project for Bell Atlantic (renewable every year), working four days a week on-site and one day at home. But she has had many tech-writing projects that were completely or mostly home-based, including contracts with the New York Stock Exchange and MECCA software.

As a free agent, you work as an independent contractor and get paid by the hour or the project. Since you're not considered an employee of the company, taxes won't be withheld from your checks, so you'll be responsible for filing the appropriate tax forms with the IRS and paying estimated taxes. You are also not likely to get health benefits, though many interim staffing firms are now offering insurance benefits to their clients.

Project work is sporadic, so as a free agent you'll need to continually market yourself and line up new gigs if you want to make a steady income. And keep in mind that some freelance projects might require months of on-site work, so child care will be a consideration. But you will have control over which jobs you take, and the luxury of having blocks of free time between jobs if you wish.

TAKE YOUR CURRENT JOB HOME

The easiest route to a flexible work schedule is to start with the job you already have. When you have a proven track record and are valuable to your company, management is likely to be more receptive to modifying your work hours and location. But you must present a well-thought-out, written plan that not only details how the arrangement will work but that stresses its benefits to the company. "The people who are most successful landing flexible arrangements are those who are confident that they can deliver results to the corporate world using a combination of their talents and technology," says Kathleen Shelby of FlexTime Solutions.

Before you approach your boss, follow these essential steps.

Decide on a Plan

Figure out the flexible work arrangement that best allows you to fulfill your job responsibilities. Consider what parts of your job can be done from home, and which might require you to be in the corporate office. "Be realistic," cautions career consultant Nancy Collamer of jobsand-moms.com. For example, telecommuting won't work if your job demands on-site coverage or extensive face-to-face contact, she explains. "Job-sharing might be a better solution in this situation."

Go on a Fact-Finding Mission

Research the company's policy on flex time. Even if there's no official policy, the company may offer it on a case-by-case basis, notes Ross. Have other moms at your company been successful at obtaining alternative work arrangements? Talk to them about the challenges of negotiating and implementing the plan. Have there been failed attempts at flex time? If so, try to determine why the arrangements didn't work so that you can show management how your situation will be different. Also investigate the family-friendly policies of other companies—particularly those in your field. When you write your proposal, you'll want to include examples of successful flex-time arrangements at your company and similar companies, as well as recent studies or statistics on the corporate benefits of flex time.

Put It in Writing

A carefully researched written proposal shows your dedication and commitment to making flex time work. Don't focus on how your family life will be easier; rather, stress the advantages of your plan to the company and back it up with hard facts and figures. For example, studies have shown that part-timers cost less in overhead, are more productive, and have lower absentee rates. Point out how the arrangement will conserve office space and ultimately save the company money. Talk up your value to the company and stress your past achievements. Mention any ways that you have helped increase corporate revenue—for example, by landing big clients or managing important high-profile projects.

Explain in detail exactly how the arrangement will work. How many days per week will you work from home? How will you handle your current workload? How often will you go into company headquarters? How and when will you be available to colleagues back at the office, and what equipment will you need to keep you connected? What arrangement have you made for child care? "You need to anticipate as many of the employer's concerns as possible, and show how you will provide seamless coverage of your job," says Ross.

 *Mother of Invention*

Pat Katepoo has always been good at strategic planning. Back in the late '80s, as a bride-to-be and director of nutrition services at a Honolulu medical group, she anticipated the stresses of juggling a 40-hour workweek with the needs of her new husband and young stepson. "I had watched what my full-time working friends went through when children were added to the mix," she says. "It looked very hectic and tiring—and more than I thought I could handle!" So Katepoo and her boss collaborated to create a new version of her job—one with a shorter, 30-hour workweek. And Katepoo found herself working flex time long before it was fashionable. The arrangement made a "sanity-saving difference in managing both work and home," she says.

Today, Katepoo helps other moms achieve better work family balance with an electronic workbook called *Flex Success: A Proposal Blueprint and Planning Guide for Getting a Family-Friendly Work Schedule,* sold exclusively through her website at www.workoptions.com. This thorough, 100-page manual helps employees negotiate for telecommuting, job-sharing, compressed workweeks, and part-time arrangements at their current jobs by taking them step by step through the process of preparing a written proposal. "You can't 'wing it' when you ask your boss for a flexible work arrangement," Katepoo emphasizes.

Katepoo's own business plan for *Flex Success* evolved with time and technology. Here's how her successful product progressed from idea to e-book.

THE INSPIRATION: While enjoying a relaxing weekday off, Katepoo wondered, Why can't all my friends do this? She started thinking about how she might help other families achieve similar work/life balance.

THE HOMEWORK: She researched every existing article and book that she could find on negotiating flexible work arrangements and contacted organizations devoted to the issue. "Everything I read stressed that a written proposal was the key component in getting a boss to consider a flexible work plan," she says. "Yet I saw from my research that there were no directions available for writing a flex-time proposal." She decided to create a workbook that would guide women through the steps of writing the proposal.

THE BRAINSTORMING: She jotted down the topics most important to consider when preparing a flex-time proposal, such as researching a company's policies and anticipating a boss's concerns, and arranged the material in an easy-to-read style, using checklists, charts, and bullet-pointed tips.

THE START-UP: After about six months of researching and writing, Katepoo self-published her guide in August of 1993 and began selling it locally in Hawaii through work/family seminars.

THE HURDLE: Katepoo had hoped to work directly with companies interested in offering flexible arrangements so that she could reach a larger audience of women. But Hawaii's economy was not strong at the time, and companies were not receptive to her idea. So she shelved her plans temporarily.

THE DIGITAL TRANSFORMATION: In January 1995 Katepoo went online for the very first time and taught herself how to navigate the Web. She began networking with other entrepreneurs through online work-from-home forums and e-mail newsgroups, and started thinking about the potential of selling *Flex Success* via the Internet. By 1996 she had converted her workbook to a disk and begun selling it by mail order.

AN E-BIZ IS BORN: In May of 1997, Katepoo launched her website, www.workoptions.com, and began selling the disk online, though it was still delivered by snail mail. Katepoo followed up every order with an e-mail note, asking moms whether the proposal helped them land flexible work arrangements. Thank-you letters from thrilled moms poured in and she incorporated the testimonials into her marketing materials. Word of *Flex Success* spread, and sales blossomed. After noticing an increased demand for *Flex Success* to be delivered immediately, Katepoo began selling it in electronic form so moms could download it right into their computers. Today, *Flex Success* is sold solely in electronic form through Katepoo's website. "It's hard to beat digital download," Katepoo says. "Thanks to the Web, I can run my business from an island in the middle of the Pacific Ocean and instantly deliver *Flex Success* to customers all over the world."

JOB HUNTING IN CYBERSPACE

We're not going to tell you it's easy to find the work-at-home job of your dreams, but using an online job bank (see "Surfing the Online Job Boards," page 87) will certainly simplify your search. We were surprised at the diversity of the home-based positions we saw listed as we cruised the various online boards. One Internet company needed a part-time online host to work from home. Another firm, based in New York, advertised for a freelance web designer, and stipulated: "Relocation not necessary; off-site work acceptable."

Tech firms and Internet companies are most likely to offer work-at-home options, so it pays to get the skills you need, says Heidi Piccoli of moneymakingmommy.com, which lists telecommuting jobs and other work-from-home options. Piccoli used books and tutorials to teach herself HTML (Hypertext Markup Language), Dreamweaver, and PhotoShop, and landed a project job at a tech company for $30 an hour. "These companies are desperate for good people and willing to train you," she says. Another hot area is translation. "As companies are building their websites, they need people who can help translate the material on their sites into different languages," Piccoli says.

Unfortunately, jobs like these are in high demand and may be filled in nanoseconds, before you even get the chance to apply. And "ninety percent of home-based jobs aren't advertised," says Piccoli, because companies don't want to be inundated with resumes from nonqualified candidates. Instead companies will often look at the resume banks at online job boards to identify hot prospects. So "you not only have to answer ads on online job boards, but you have to get your resume posted there too," Piccoli emphasizes. Here are her tips for using job boards successfully and safely.

Search Selectively

To get right to the home-based jobs, type in specific key words and phrases, and surround them in quotation marks or parentheses to focus the search. Try typing in: "work-from-home"; "work-at-home"; "telecommute"; "telecommuting"; "telework"; "teleworking"; "home-based"; "off-site"; "virtual assistant"; "virtual office"; and "part-time". Also search by field of expertise. Kathy Sherman looks at ads for technical writers, and then hones in on the ones that allow off-site work.

Showcase Your Independent Work Style

When you post your resume, stress your ability to work on your own. If you have previous telecommuting or other work-at-home experience, make sure you emphasize it.

State Your Goals and Related Work Skills

Aimee Stewart of Toledo, Ohio, posted her resume on guru.com in the hopes of finding a home-based career that would tap the writing skills she used in her former job as director of multicultural and international services at a local college. Her resume said she was looking for writing and consulting positions. She got an e-mail from a company planning a website that provides financial aid for college students, and now works 20 hours a week from home, creating content for her company's site and reviewing other financial aid websites to link with.

Avoid Pay-For-Work Sites. Access to job listings should be free. If you're asked to pay a subscription fee or upfront entry fee, beware! There are plenty of free sites available, so don't waste your money!

Surfing the Online Job Boards

FOR	CHECK OUT	WHAT THEY OFFER
Jobs in all fields	www.monster.com www.hotjobs.com www.careerbuilder.com www.headhunter.net	*Jobs nationwide, many with part-time, project, and work-from-home capability. You can also post your resume so employers can contact you.*
Temp positions	www.net-temps.com	*A good assortment of temporary jobs (some of which are home-based) in all fields, from administrative and clerical to sales and marketing.*
Telecommuters	www.workaholics4hire.com www.tjobs.com	*Telecommuting jobs in all fields—including administrative and clerical positions, data entry, desktop publishing, and web design.*
Free Agents	www.freeagent.com www.guru.com	*A listing of short- and long-term project jobs for freelancers and independent contractors in a variety of professions, both on- and off-site. You can also create and post a personal profile with your job skills and experience so that clients can find you.*

Surfing the Online Job Boards, continued

FOR	CHECK OUT	WHAT THEY OFFER
Showcasing your talent for others to bid on	talentmarket.com www.icplanet.com	*Job-matching services for highly skilled independent contractor/consultants in various fields of expertise. You post your resume, and interested employers can bid on your services.*
Bidding on jobs	www.ework.com www.ants.com www.elance.com	*The opportunity for independent professionals and freelancers to bid on projects in a variety of fields. Ants.com also offers a commission program for referrals: If you refer friends and they get placed in jobs, Ants.com pays you a percentage of the fee it earns from the hiring employer.*
Information Technology specialists	www.dice.com www.brainpower.com www.computerjobs.com	*Jobs for computer professionals in Information Technology (IT). Though many of the jobs are full-time, there are some part-time, project-based, and telecommuting positions listed. At Dice.com, you post your resume and employers bid on your services.*

SPOTTING A SCAM

While the Web can be a great resource for finding work-at-home jobs, it's also a gold mine for scammers who prey upon moms hungry for home-based options. Here's how to make sure you don't get ripped off.

Beware of Starter Fees

Scammers often ask you to pay upfront for starter kits, software, equipment and supplies, or lists of hiring companies. You shouldn't have to send in money to receive information about how to get a home-based job. Reputable companies will require you to send in a resume and prove that you are qualified for the position. You should feel as if the company is discerning about who it is hiring.

Watch for Inflated Claims

Be suspicious of any job description promising overnight success or using phrases like "effortless," "no experience required," "easy money," "hidden job market," "earn money fast," "earn hundreds or thousands a week." If it sounds too good to be true, it usually is.

Do a Background Check

Before getting involved with any work-from-home opportunity or job resource, check out the company with the Better Business Bureau (www.bbb.org), Scambusters (www.scambusters.com), the National Fraud Information Center (www.fraud.org), and WebAssured (www.webassured.com; click on its "Watch List" to view complaints about various companies). You can also type in the name of the company on different search engines to view any articles that may have been written about them.

MEDICAL BILLER TELLS ALL!

Can a mom make a living at medical billing without being scammed? Yes, says medical biller Sandra Swies-Sahnoun, *if* you have proper training and enough money to invest in the right software and equipment. But don't believe the ads you see promising that you can make a bundle easily without experience, she warns. "Medical billing is not a field you can enter rashly," emphasizes Swies-Sahnoun, who runs her own medical billing firm, SES Physician Management, Inc., from her Chicago home. Here's what you really need to be successful at medical billing.

Training

You must have a thorough knowledge of medical billing before you get started. You can get the skills by taking classes in medical billing, coding, and terminology at local colleges or through home study courses. For suggestions on reputable home study courses, check the National Electronic Billers Alliance (www.nebazone.com). You can also learn through on-

Common Internet Scams

Proceed with caution if sales pitches like these wind up in your e-mail box.

The Plea: Make money stuffing envelopes or sending bulk e-mail.
The Promise: You'll get the contacts and supplies you need to launch a lucrative mailing list business.
The Lowdown: You're asked to pay around $20 upfront. Instead of envelopes and names, you receive the same ad you answered, with instructions to send it to your own contacts at your own expense. Be aware that sending nonsolicited bulk e-mail violates the terms of most Internet Service Providers.

The Plea: Learn the secrets of making money on the Internet.
The Promise: Discover this unique business opportunity. No sales experience needed!
The Lowdown: Many of these are illegal pyramid schemes. Often you're invited to an "informational" seminar, where you will be pressured to buy costly business opportunity packages. Sometimes you're asked to e-mail or call for additional information, and then asked for your name and phone number so a salesperson can call you back with a high-pressure pitch.

The Plea: Assemble crafts from home.
The Promise: Earn hundreds weekly: An inexpensive starter kit enables you to assemble crafts that the company buys back from you.
The Lowdown: After plunking down anywhere from $40 to $200, you receive hard-to-follow directions for crafts that take hours to make. When you complete them and send them back, you're often told they don't suit the company's standards.

The Plea: Submit medical insurance claims; no experience necessary!
The Promise: Make a bundle by submitting insurance claims for doctors eager to out-source. With a purchase of software, you'll receive training, tech support, and a list of health care professionals needing your services.
The Lowdown: The software can cost thousands. Many doctors and dentists do billing in-house, or through large firms. But if they do outsource, they depend on medical billers with extensive experience. (See "Medical Biller Tells All!" page 89.)

The Plea: Make money with your PC: Home typists wanted.
The Promise: With the purchase of a diskette featuring sample work, you'll receive a directory of businesses that use home typists.

Common Internet Scams, continued

The Lowdown: You're asked for around $5 to $20, and sometimes for a sample from your printer to make sure you qualify for the jobs. You do get a diskette, but the businesses listed are frequently bogus, or not interested in home typists. Diskettes often mention other work-at-home opportunities—all of which require you to send in money for more details.

The Plea: Read books for pay.
The Promise: Purchase a "resource directory" listing publishers who hire home workers to read manuscripts for up to $100 an hour.
The Lowdown: After shelling out $50 or more, you receive a directory and instructions to send letters to publishers seeking work. But the list of publishers often has incorrect addresses, and the companies listed are usually not hiring.

the-job experience at a doctor's office or medical billing firm. Swies-Sahnoun worked for 13 years as an office manager at a nursing home and in a doctor's office before launching her business. In addition to basic training, you'll need to attend insurance seminars throughout the year (which can cost anywhere from $75 to $500) to keep up-to-date with the frequent coding policy changes.

Equipment

You'll need to purchase good medical billing software, which costs at least $500, says Swies-Sahnoun, who cautions moms to beware of anything that sells for less. She was scammed when she ordered faulty software from one of those medical billing ads in the back of a newspaper. Software by Lytec (www.lytec.com) and Medisoft (www.medisoft.com) are preferred by most medical billers, she says. You'll also need coding books, HCFA forms (the claim form needed to submit bills to insurance companies), and envelopes (both standard and window types).

Start-Up Money

You'll spend around $3,000 to get a medical billing business off the ground, not including the money you'll need to lay out for your training and a computer.

A Knack for Marketing

It's up to you to spread the word about your services. Start by making up some professional marketing materials—business cards, letterhead, and a brochure or flyer explaining what you offer. Next, make your cold calls. Swies-Sahnoun got out the yellow pages and called local doctors and dentists, asking to talk to their office managers. She quickly pitched her services and offered to send more information about her business. A week or two later, she followed up with another call. "I got two of my first clients that way," she says. Now, most of her business comes from word-of-mouth referrals. "Independent medical billers can offer more personalized service than big billing firms, and I think doctors appreciate that," she says.

A Strong Work Ethic

Swies-Sahnoun sometimes puts in 60-hour workweeks, calling insurance companies while her kids are in school and then submitting claims at night. "It's hard work, but I love it. Medical billing helped me, a single mom, put my son through a private military high school. And nothing makes me prouder than that!"

Medical Billing Resources

Check out these helpful sites:

- **iVillage Medical Billing Board (on the Work channel).** You'll get support and advice from established medical billers.

■ **AOL's Business Know-How Forum (keyword BKH).** It features an informative Medical and Dental Billing Board, for networking with others in the field.

MORE MOM-TESTED JOBS

Mompreneurs around the nation have tipped us off to some new and exciting home-based options for those of you who want to make some money without committing to long-term projects. Here are a few ideas.

■ **Try CyberSecretaries.** This company hires experienced legal secretaries and assistants to work as independent contractors typing a wide variety of legal documents and correspondence from dictation that comes over your computer. Requires fast typing (at least 80 words per minute) and familiarity with the Internet. Candidates can take a typing test at the company's website (www.youdictate.com) to see if they're qualified. Pays $7 to $10 an hour.

■ **Make Calls for Headhunters.** Stacy Perez of Dot Com Mommies worked on commission for PeopleDot.Com (www.peopledot.com), a human resources consulting firm that hires home-based workers to do telemarketing. Her assignment was to call job candidates to determine their interest in available positions. The company offers training and the opportunity to work as little as 10 hours a week. The commission-based pay depends on the amount of time you put in, and company spokesperson Barbara Bachman says you can make anywhere from $100 a week to several thousand a year. You can apply for jobs at the company's site (www.peopledot.com).

■ **Provide Home-Based Customer Service.** Perez also worked as an independent contractor for LiveOps.com, a home-based network of customer service agents who answer calls for infomercials and other direct response advertisers. An 800 number was set up to ring in Perez's home, and she was responsible for answering the calls and reading from a company script. LiveOps.com provides extensive training, and pays from $15 to $18 an hour. For job information, go to www.liveops.com.

■ **Be a Web Fact-Finder.** Jacqueline Bazy of Marietta, Georgia, was hired by a public relations firm to do "competitive Internet research" (also called "competitive intelligence") for one of the firm's clients. For approximately four hours a day, "I had to monitor several preassigned websites for mention of various topics as it related to the client and their three major competitors," she explains. She tracked things like major contracts won, major contracts lost, acquisitions, and new products developed. She was networked into the PR firm's computer (so she didn't have to pay for access to the various wire and research services) and was paid $10 an hour. Jobs like these are often found through word of mouth or through online job boards.

CLICK CASH

Is there any scam-free way for a mom to earn a quick buck on the Web without a lot of time and effort? We've found a few you might want to try out. You won't make much, but you might earn enough to cover your ISP bill or pay for your next night out at Chuck E. Cheese.

Online Surveys and Focus Groups

How It Works: You join market research companies and review various products through online surveys or focus groups held in Internet chat rooms. Surveys can be completed in spurts, around the demands of your kids; but focus groups require sustained attention, so count on doing them while the kids are asleep or well supervised.

The Payoff: Around $5 to $30 for surveys, which take about 15 minutes of your time. Focus groups last at least an hour and pay around $25 to $100, depending on the product and the company's budget.

Tech Tip: Many market research companies find you through new-mom mailing lists, so fill out product warranty cards and consumer questionnaires whenever you can.

To Get Started: Join several market research companies, because assignments are sporadic. Get a list of opportunities at www.money4surveys.com.

Selling at Online Auctions

How It Works: You sell new, used, or handcrafted items on Internet auction sites. Post a photo, description, and opening price, and wait for bids to roll in.

The Payoff: Your earnings depend on what you sell and how often. Most sites charge about 25 cents for listings and take a small percentage of the profit.

Tech Tip: Spot what's hot. Many moms scoop up trendy holiday toys well before the Christmas season so they can auction or sell them off when they become hard-to-get. Check out the auction boards regularly so you can see what sells briskly—and more important, what doesn't. "Antiques, jewelry, and vintage clothing are perennial favorites," says Annette Graf, a mompreneur from South Milwaukee, Wisconsin, and author of *How to Sell on eBay* (www.annetteonline.com).

To Get Started: Begin with items you have around the house. Then resell bargains you pick up from tag sales, closeouts, and wholesalers. Besides the large websites, such as www.ebay.com, www.amazon.com, and www.yahoo.com, try smaller ones specializing in kids' items. Some mom-owned sites to check: www.mothersnature.com and www.momsnetwork.com.

Web Research

How It Works: Many companies and organizations need your help in finding content and links to fill their fledgling websites, and are willing to pay you for your efforts. You're assigned a topic (such as migraine headaches) and asked to search for as many website links as possible on the subject.

The Payoff: Usually around 60 cents or so for every link you send, paid in increments (at three months, six months, and one year).

Tech Tip: The faster you surf, the more you'll make. (Some researchers earn $200 to $300 a month.)

To Get Started: Log onto www.studyweb.com/about/jobs.htm and sign up to see if you're qualified.

 *Web Celeb*

Jennifer J. Johnson
Founder and Principal of Johnson & Company: The Virtual Agency®
www.joandco.com
Salt Lake City
Mom of 2

Jennifer Johnson will never forget the day in June 1997 that her dream job turned into a nightmare. As head of marketing for one of the business units of Novell, Inc., she was racing to catch a plane for a three-city whirlwind business tour. But first, she had to hand off her two young sons (then three and one) to her husband. The hitch? He was on a plane himself, returning from a business trip from Korea, and his flight was 20 minutes late. "There I was, sprinting through the airport with the kids in the luggage cart, frantic that I'd miss my flight," she recalls. When her husband finally arrived, she kissed him hurriedly, passed him the boys, and bolted for her plane, which she made just in time. "It was my moment of truth," Johnson says. Her travel schedule and three-hour daily commutes were taking their toll on the family. "I realized this craziness had to end," she says. "I wrote my resignation letter on the plane."

After leaving her job, Johnson began consulting from home for other technical companies, and had so much work that "by the end of the first month, I knew I couldn't do it alone," she says. She had noticed that a number of her colleagues were "mommy-trackers" like herself, eager for better ways to balance career and family. So she hired many of these highly talented women to join her rapidly growing enterprise.

Today, Jennifer Johnson is the boss every mom in America would love to have. As head of Johnson & Company: The Virtual Agency®, a 100 percent virtual public relations and marketing firm specializing in high-tech companies, her motto is: "Work anytime, anyplace, any way, at any pace." Everyone she hires works from home and sets their own hours. "I believe in part-time jobs and full-time lives," she says. Her staff of 17 talented professionals, most of whom are moms, work from four different time zones across the U.S. "Our website is our corporate headquarters," says Johnson, who oversees operations from her own home office in Salt Lake City.

She initially hid the fact that her employees were all working from home, because she feared it would somehow undermine the credibility of her company. But "now I wear it like a badge of pride," says Johnson, whose company was projected to bill over $3 million worth of projects in its fourth year. As e-mailing and teleconferencing became increasingly standard business tools, Johnson found that her way of doing business was a big draw, both for Net-savvy clients and top marketing talent.

Still, teleworking is not for everyone, she warns. You must be extremely well disciplined, yet flexible enough to "work on the fly." And be careful that you do not fall into the trap of what she calls "the electronic latchkey syndrome," where you attempt to work without child care and wind up being emotionally unavailable to your children, even though you're physically there. She encourages teleworking moms to use some form of child care—whether it's school programs or part-time sitters—so that kids are well supervised and stimulated while you're sitting at your computer. And above all, remember why you became a teleworker in the first place, Johnson urges. Set boundaries. Be able to close the door on your work at the end of the day. "Your home office shouldn't become your home," she says, "so don't live there! Teleworkers need to religiously protect their most important assets—family, friends, and hobbies."

CHAPTER FOUR

Time & Money:
Making the Most of Both

Sound Byte

"I'm a mom. I'm also a businesswoman. For the most part, I wear both caps at the same time. I've learned to leap tall buildings in a single bound and cook dinner while the files upload. Like most work-at-home moms, I get to work half days . . . either the first twelve hours or the last twelve hours! Did I mention I wouldn't have it any other way?"

Linda Caroll, Mother of three; Mississauga, Ontario, Canada
Owner of *LindaCaroll.com* business development *(www.lindacarroll.com)*

OK, we admit it. Both of us have been known to fritter away our work time answering countless e-mails, Instant Messaging our friends, and trolling new websites (some of which are totally unrelated to our jobs). After all, the Internet is speedy, convenient, and oh so addictive. Even when we're Web-surfing for business purposes, it's hard to stop at just one link. We often find ourselves still clicking away hours later as we marvel at what's available.

But we've learned that too much unfocused Web-surfing can sabotage our bottom lines. After all, time is money, as the saying goes. As work-from-home moms, we must always keep a close eye on our productivity and our profits. We must work as efficiently as possible, so that we can earn the income we need and achieve the family balance we crave.

Yet sometimes we're a bit too efficient—working round-the-clock when we'd really prefer doing something fun with our children. We're finding it harder than ever to turn off our business brains. Technology enables us to work anytime, anywhere—on occasion we've even lugged our laptops and cell phones on family vacations, so we wouldn't miss important e-mails or client calls.

Of course, all mompreneurs have crunch times once in a while, but mixing too much business and pleasure can be detrimental to both your family and your enterprise. You'll be a smarter businesswoman if you allow yourself time away from the computer screen. And your family will appreciate it too! When our work schedules reel out of control, we remind ourselves of why we started home businesses in the first place: to achieve better balance over our professional and personal lives. That (along with the glares from our kids and husbands) is usually enough to bring us back to our senses and more reasonable hours.

If you always keep your work/family goals clearly in sight, you'll be able to successfully balance them.

DATA BANK: *What Do You Like Least About Your Internet Business?*

Can't get away from it!/ It's 24/7 . . . . 25%
Isolation 20%
Dependence on technology 16%
Accounting/Financing issues 12%

TIPS FROM AN ONLINE PLANNER

"You need a game plan for your dot-com business if you expect to be profitable," says Deborah Polydys, a Connecticut mompreneur who runs Strategic Management Resources, a consulting firm that helps entrepreneurs build successful online ventures. Even if you're happy making just a few thousand dollars a year, "approach this as a business, not a hobby," she stresses. Here's how to get into that mind-set:

■ **Identify Your Reach.** How big do you want your Web biz to be? Will you market your product or service globally, or target a smaller local audience? When you set up your website, make sure your home page identifies where you're located and the geographical areas you service.

■ **Have a Marketing Plan.** Don't just put up your website and wait for people to come. Use a "push-pull" marketing strategy. Direct visitors to your website by linking with compatible sites; then draw visitors back again with periodic announcements of special offers or events. When people visit your site, have a method for capturing information about them—like a survey, giveaway, or free newsletter—so you can build a database of visitors to contact again later. (See more on Web marketing strategies in Chapters 5 and 7.)

■ **Set Earning Goals.** Figure out your approximate monthly overhead expenses (see "How Much Will Your e-Biz Cost to Run?" on page 109); then determine how much you'll need to earn to cover those expenses plus make a profit. It might take a year for your business to become a moneymaker, but you should be working toward your earning goal every day. Ask yourself: What did I do today to move my business forward? Whether you're making cold calls, sending out press releases, or creating an online newsletter, you should be doing something to increase the visibility and profitability of your business. Evaluate your efforts monthly, to make sure they are paying off. Are you spending too much time surfing from one similar site to the next? Then consider hiring a teen to do that for you. Sometimes you need to try new strategies and delegate the time-consuming tasks before you can bring your company into the black. "A dot-com business takes an enormous amount of time to market," Polydys says. "If you're going to invest that kind of time, you should be making money!"

PROGRAM YOURSELF FOR SUCCESS

Only you can control how much time and energy you spend on your business.

Don't "Byte" Off More Than You Can Chew

"Be honest about the amount of work you can comfortably handle," advises Internet career coach Nancy Collamer of jobsandmoms.com. "Don't be afraid to slowly phase yourself into your business," she says. "I see many moms who are looking for something challenging and interesting that they can grow over time. For them, the money is almost secondary."

Decide how many hours you want to work. Many moms with young children aim for 10 to 15 hours a week, and then expand their businesses as their children grow. Because her boys are just five and six, virtual assistant Kathryn Goldman only takes on about 80 hours of work per month. "I am in the early stages of setting up my client base," says the New Berlin, Wisconsin, mom. "I will eventually add clients, but working more hours now would make it difficult for me to be available to my boys." She enjoys the freedom of working around their soccer, swimming, and T-ball schedules. "My clients also deserve my undivided attention," Goldman says. Limiting the number of projects she takes helps her meet the individual needs of her clients and her sons. She can step up her pace—and her profits—when she's ready.

BZ Riger-Hull of Charlotte's Gardens (www.charlottesgardens.com), a gourmet food and botanical gift shop, says keeping a work and personal plan are essential for keeping her business and family running smoothly. "Keeping appointments for playtime is just as high a priority as business events," the Martha's Vineyard, Massachusetts, mom says. "I review where I am and where I want to be. If they don't match or things have gotten out of hand, I set a new plan and work toward the balance I want to achieve."

Stick to a Schedule

Don't try to wing when you'll work. You'll be much more productive (and a lot less stressed) if you set aside certain hours for business every week.

Even though she works without any child care, Paula Polman carves out special times of the day to devote to Mossberry Hollow Natural Care

Products (www.mossberry.com), the bath and body care company she runs from a tiny trailer home in Canada's remote Yukon region. She works around her toddler's routine, tackling major tasks when James sleeps and doing less intensive things like list-making and brainstorming while he plays quietly. "I know when I can work, and when it is time to go to the park and play," Polman says, and her to-do list keeps her on track. "Of course, you must expect those days where you'll get no work done," she warns. "My motto is: 'Plan for work, but prepare for chaos!' "

Public relations consultant Hannah Brazee Gregory works while her two-year-old is in preschool four mornings a week, and then again during naptimes. "But when he wakes up at three-thirty, I turn on my voice mail and I am all his," says this Kansas City, Missouri mom. "Once a week I have a baby-sitter (a neighbor girl whom he loves) come to play with him. I use that time to clean my house."

Susan Barone of Smithtown, New York, has full-time in-home child care, which enables her to be available for meetings in New York City with fashion industry players as she markets UniquelyMe.com her website for plus-sized women. But she takes almost every Thursday off so the kids can have a "Fun Day with Mommy."

When planning your office hours, consider your business tasks, your available time, the kids' commitments, and your temperament, work style, and stamina. (See "What's the Best Schedule for You?" page 104.) If you're planning on regularly logging late nights and rising before dawn, make sure you can handle that pace. Renee Hogan, owner of Reneebarry.com an e-commerce site that sells home décor and collectibles, enjoys getting up early and handling the sales that came in through the night. She logs off when her four- and eight-year-olds wake up, then goes back online midday to check for more sales. Later, the Marion, North Carolina, mom has her kids help her pack boxes for shipping and carry them to the van. At night when the house is quiet, she's back at her computer, updating the site with new inventory.

Understand that working nights and weekends will be a fact of life if you're determined to run your business without any child care. "I find it difficult to maintain a workable daytime schedule, because I can only work bits and pieces here and there," says Mia Cronan of Mainstreetmom.com. "Just when I get involved in something, I usually have to step away to take care of someone. So I work during the wee hours of the night once a week or so. It's hard on the body, but I can get so much more done that it makes it worthwhile to be a little tired the next day."

Make Business a Family Affair

Discuss your schedule with your husband or significant other (and your kids, if they're old enough). "I've found that when I'm not communicative about what deadlines are looming, my husband feels out of the loop and resentful of my computer time," says Melanie Wilson of *Vegetarian Baby and Child Magazine* (www.vegetarianbaby.com). "But when I am open with him about what's going on, he is part of the process and we work as a team to keep the family going. Verbalizing my schedule helps me see things more objectively, prioritize better, and put aside tasks that aren't truly pressing," she says. (Even family members can become involved. Your parents might provide some backup child care; your sister the attorney can offer legal advice; your investment banker husband might offer financial input.)

Explain your job to children in terms they can understand: "Mommy needs to work at the computer so she can make money to pay for our trip to Disney World." Give kids jobs so they so they can feel like they're contributing, too. "Caroline provided the mouse click that launched our site on the Internet," says Lynne Bruce of MommyShop.com. The four-year-old also helped mom design the home page, was very active in the product selection process, and even helps ship packages. "She and the UPS drivers are on a first-name basis!" says Bruce, laughing. Older children can handle even more responsibility. Catherine Wald, a Shrub Oak, New York, writer who runs rejectioncollection.com, "the writer's and artist's online source for misery commiseration and rejection letters," paid her son $5 to help her set up her new computer. "It was the best five dollars I ever spent," she says, "and he was thrilled to be of help."

Gestures like these help cultivate mutual respect. "It took a long time for my family to realize that this business of mine is not a hobby," says Donna Snow, the San Jose, California, mom of six and owner of Anything

What's the Best Schedule for You?

To determine your peak times to work, answer these questions:

* What can you realistically get done with the kids around? British Columbia mom Christine Nicholls, who runs a crafts subscription business called Creative Kids at Home *(www.creativekidsathome.com)*, develops crafts ideas at the kitchen table with her daughter and does marketing research on the Web while she breast-feeds her son.

* Which work projects demand your full concentration and are difficult to accomplish with kids underfoot (for example, phone conferences or client meetings)? When can you attend to these? If it will be in the daytime, who will supervise your kids?

* If you share the computer with the rest of the family, at what times will you be able to use it without interruption? (Do school-age kids need it for homework in the afternoons?)

* Do you have the energy and the type of job that allow you to work early mornings and late nights? Are you willing to work weekends?

* What times will you save exclusively (that means no work allowed!) for your kids and husband? Web developer Linda Caroll actually "books" slots on the calendar for special family time. "For example, I might take one afternoon for a mother-daughter shopping and lunch date, and another afternoon to take the boys fishing."

   Now look at the answers to your questions and select the blocks of time during the day or night that you'll devote to different business tasks. Keep in mind that your schedule will change frequently over the years as your children grow and your business evolves.

Business, which provides small business coaching and writing services. "But once they realized just how important it was for me to be at my computer, they started to work together to give me that needed time. And that gave me the freedom to sit down to our family meals without worrying about the unfinished project on my desk."

Safeguard Couple Time

The majority of married mompreneurs we interviewed credited their husbands with giving them the moral and physical support they need to keep their businesses and families running smoothly. (And we agree! Without our husbands' help with the shopping, cooking, laundry, and child care, this book never would have gotten written!) Yet sometimes we mompreneurs put so much focus on balancing our work time and kid time that our husbands wind up feeling a little neglected. Consistently working weekends and nights can sap your energy and strain your marriage, if you're not careful. "There are times when my husband and I feel like two ships passing in the night," laments Corrie Pokrzywa of Rochester Hills, Minnesota, who runs Babyeshop (www.babyeshop.com), an online mall featuring upscale children's specialty boutiques. "He comes home from work, watches the kids, and eats dinner. Then we put the kids to bed, and he and I each turn to a PC and work till the wee hours. Sometimes, I'd just like to kick back and watch TV together, or actually go out somewhere," Pokrzywa says. She stresses the importance of involving your spouse or partner in the business so you can have "a point of connection." Her husband offers tech support and she handles the sales and creative end.

But don't make your relationship all business. If you are intending to work primarily on nights and weekends, you and your spouse need to establish the time you will set aside for each other. Find creative ways to carve out couple time. "I enjoy lunch with my husband every day," says Jill Shortreed, who runs her children's party planning service, Celebrated Times (www.celebratedtimes.com), from her home in Point Pleasant, New Jersey. "It's our time together."

Lose the Guilt!

It puts a real damper on productivity! "When I first started, I found that if I was playing with the kids, I'd feel guilty that I wasn't working on my business," says Sherri Ingram Breetzke, who runs an Internet gift boutique called the Creativity Zone. "But when I was working, I'd feel guilty that I should be spending more time with my kids. I learned very quickly that I wasn't able to perform either task at a hundred percent when I was constantly feeling guilty." She established distinct hours for devoting to work and family and decided that her business would have to grow at a slower pace than it might if she didn't have kids. And, she realized that she was a role model for her children, providing them with great lessons on how to successfully balance business and family. "Once I reached those conclusions, I was able to give a hundred percent to work when I was working, and a hundred percent to my children when I was with them—all without guilt," says the Melbourne, Florida, mom of two.

Learn to Laugh

Life as a work-from-home mom is never boring! For example, never in the "traditional" work world would you get drenched by a Super Soaker water gun that your 11-year-old aimed at your open office window. (Yes, this actually happened to Ellen.) And "phantom" computer voices don't bellow spooky warnings like "You have made a fatal error and your system is about to melt down!"—unless, of course, your teenager is pulling a prank on you. (Pat's son Josh and a buddy were responsible for this practical joke!) And what about the time Liane Hetherington-Ward's little girl removed her diaper and proceeded to poop in the middle of her mom's office floor? The environmental policy consultant will also never forget the day she told her biggest client, "Mommy will have to call you back!" At times like these a little laughter goes a long way in diffusing tension (and in our cases, helped prevent us from losing our tempers!). So next time a crisis or yet another annoying interruption invades your work time, LOL (laugh out loud). Better yet, ROTFL (roll on the floor laughing). Good humor does make all things tolerable (and we don't mean the ice cream, although that helps too!).

DATA BANK: *What's Your Best Trick for Juggling Work and Family?*

Work while the kids sleep, or around their schedule 33%

Stay organized 18%

Accept support from my family 11%

Set specific work hours 9%

Involve my family in the business 9%

Remind myself that I'm doing this for my children 7%

PROTECT WORK AND FAMILY TIME

- Plot work/family events on the same calendar to prevent scheduling a client conference and a pediatrician's appointment on the same day.

- Choose different e-mail addresses for work and family correspondence.

- Get a separate phone line for business calls.

- Use Caller ID so you can tell when important clients are getting back to you.

- Activate voice mail during dinnertime, story time, and other precious moments.

- Leave a message on your voice mail that tells clients and customers your office hours and the best time to reach you.

- Warn clients and customers well in advance when you'll be out of the office for extended periods; and leave a message on your voice mail letting clients know that the office is closed and when you'll be back.

- Delegate someone to keep things running when you're away for extended periods.

- Leave the laptop home on family vacations (or at the very least limit the time you work while away).

 *Mother of Invention*

Jamie Elliott Greene of Henderson, Nevada, wanted to keep her infant daughter entertained in her car seat. "I worried that she was getting bored just staring at the seat in front of her," says Greene, now the mom of two girls. So she designed the Smart Babies! Blanket, a brightly colored blanket that is tossed over the backseat in full view of babies to give them something interesting and stimulating to gaze at while riding. Coming up with the concept was the easy part; manufacturing and marketing it has been more challenging, says Greene, who will continue to work full-time outside the home for her local school district until her invention takes off. Learning how to market on the Web takes an enormous amount of time, she points out. And when you're juggling a full-time job and a business, along with the needs of two little girls, there's not a lot of time to spare. Through trial and error, Greene learned shortcuts to help streamline her start-up process. Here are her speedy and cost-effective strategies.

THINK TIME-EFFECTIVELY. Originally Greene planned to sell her blankets through face-to-face sales. Then she realized that would be much too time-consuming. "I didn't want to be driving all over Las Vegas to meet with customers," she says. "The Internet is the fastest and cheapest way to reach a vast amount of people." She set up a website called Smart-Babies.com, at Yahoo! Shopping, because it was easy to master and didn't require a knowledge of HTML. (See Chapter 5 on setting up a website.) To encourage return customers and build a sense of community, she broadened the site to include other developmental baby products, a gift registry, and resources and links.

PRICE OUT YOUR DREAM. Greene envisioned selling several versions of the baby blanket in different fabrics, so moms could have choices. "But I quickly learned that wasn't economical," she says. Instead she offers two styles: a two-sided multicolored blanket, and one that's multicolored on one side and black and white on the other, colors proven to stimulate baby's vision.

TACKLE ONE CHALLENGE AT A TIME. First Greene concentrated on finding a manu-facturer who could make the blanket in mass quantities without charging her a fortune. Next she focused on packaging. Her goal is to get into stores like Wal-Mart and Target. "I try to break tasks into achievable chunks, so it's not so overwhelming," she says. "It's amazing how things just fall into place when you don't push. I've learned that everything hap-pens in good time. If you keep that in mind, it takes away a lot of the stress and anxiety of worrying about how to grow the business."

DELEGATE. Hire professionals to handle tasks beyond your expertise—especially if they're vital to your site. Greene hired a Web designer (for around $50 a month), who not only designed the site, but regularly submits it to search engines and makes sure Greene has the highest ranking possible. "There's no way I could keep up with the search engine submissions myself," Greene says. (See Chapters 5 and 7 for search engine submission tips.)

INVOLVE THE FAMILY. Greene's little sister, a mom herself, volunteers two hours of her time every night to marketing the website. Greene's five-year-old daughter, Aime, modeled for pictures for the site and is Mommy's best spokesperson. She often tells other parents about the Smart Babies! Blanket, and calls herself CEO of the company. "Even if I don't make a million bucks, I know I've succeeded, because my girls watch me build this business," she says. "I have never felt so proud of myself! What a legacy to leave my daughters!"

How Much Will Your E-Biz Cost to Run?

Use these handy charts to track approximate start-up costs and overhead expenses.

START-UP COSTS

These include basic equipment, installation fees, consultations with your lawyer and accountant, and other money you'll need to lay out in order to set up shop.

ITEM	COST
Computer (with the speediest modem you can afford)	_____
Printer	_____
Fax machine	_____
Software (word processing, spreadsheet, antivirus, etc.)	_____
Office furniture (computer desk, chair, lamp, file cabinets, etc.)	_____
Phone system (preferably a two-line phone)	_____
Line for business phone	_____
Line(s) for modem/fax machine/or DSL or cable modem	_____

Phone line installation fees   _____

Answering machine or voice mail system   _____

Manufacturing equipment   _____

Other optional equipment
    (such as cell phone, laptop, or personal digital assistant)   _____

Equipment service contracts   _____

Tuition for any necessary technology education
    (such as Web design or learning HTML)   _____

Fee for registering domain name   _____

Marketing materials (letterhead, business cards, etc.)   _____

Advertising costs   _____

Web design costs   _____

Permits/Licenses   _____

Trademark/Patent fees   _____

Business name registration fee   _____

Business opportunity start-up fee   _____

Franchise start-up fee   _____

Direct sales sample kit   _____

Accountant's fee   _____

Attorney's fee   _____

Other   _____

Total Start-Up Costs   _____

OVERHEAD EXPENSES

These are the costs you might incur on a regular basis (not all of these apply to every business).

ITEM	COST
Internet Service Provider (ISP) fee	_____
Web hosting	_____
Web design maintenance fees	_____
Telephone/Fax bill	_____
Merchant account fees	_____

Child care   _____

Insurance premiums (health/home owner's, and liability,
   if needed)   _____

Credit line and/or loan charges   _____

Manufacturing supplies   _____

Warehouse rental   _____

Office supplies   _____

Postage for shipping   _____

Marketing/Advertising   _____

Business checking account   _____

Employee salaries and benefits   _____

Taxes   _____

Dues for networking organizations   _____

Subscriptions to business publications   _____

Franchise royalties   _____

Other   _____

Total Overhead Costs   _____

MONEY-WISE ADVICE

$ Buy as You Grow

Don't invest in every gizmo and gadget. You don't need top-of-the-line equipment from the get-go. Laura Brown started her virtual office and travel services business on a 486 computer system. "And boy, was it slow!" says the owner of Aah, "It's Done!" Virtual Office and Travel Services (www.aahitsdone.com). "But thanks to the fact that the government has finally realized that single parents have a hard enough time surviving, my tax return gave me the opportunity to buy a new computer. Thanks, Uncle Sam!"

$ Have Multiple Streams of Income

Generate revenue from a variety of sources—like affiliate programs (you'll learn more about these in Chapter 7)—so you still have some money coming in if other areas of your business are slow. Career consultant Nancy Collamer earns money three different ways—by providing telephone counseling, teaching teleconferences, and writing freelance articles on careers for moms. Besides running her medical transcription business, Connie Koerth of Office Wizard (www.officewizard.net) provides resume services, word processing, and a very special service in which she produces family cookbooks to help you preserve favorite recipes.

$ Have a Financial Cushion

It can take up to a year for your business to become profitable—more than that if you're launching a product—so it helps to have a nest egg set aside to cover unexpected expenses and help you and your family through the lean months.

$ Barter Services With Other Mompreneurs

Instead of paying someone to design your website, for example, strike up a deal with someone in that line of work. Offer to "pay" her with your service or product instead of cash.

$ Be Aware of International Currency Issues

When Canadian soapmaker Paula Polman launched her bath products e-tailing site, she felt it was important to offer sales in both Canadian and U.S. currencies. "Trying to set up a secure shopping cart and payment system with this dual currency, while keeping my costs low, has been a huge task," she says. "I ended up needing to create two separate shopping carts with two different providers. There are many services out there that offer free shopping carts and order processing for a small transaction fee or percentage of sales. But they are all in U.S. funds only and are not easy to use by international clients who do not have access to American bank accounts. I finally found a shopping cart that allows me to choose a different currency, but I can't use their order processing. So I have to have my own merchant accounts and link them up accordingly. It was triple the work to set up, but once done, both methods should be relatively easy to maintain."

$ Develop a Payment System

Kristie Tamsevicius, who offers website development, hosting, promotion, and writing services through Kristie's Custom Design (www.kcustom. com), recommends billing clients in installments throughout the project. "I bill clients a third upfront as a deposit, a third halfway through the project, and a third with delivery. That way I know I won't get taken for a ride," she says. Before designing invitations or announcements for clients, Andrea Milrad of Little BIG Man requires a deposit to cover all of her costs and part of her time.

$ Buy Wholesale

When looking for supplies for her crafts kits, Terri Bose of MakingFriends.com says, "I find out who made the product I want (it's usually printed right on the package) and I call them for a distributor. Then I call and ask if I can buy wholesale." You can also do an online search, by listing the item you want and following it with the word "wholesale" (for example, "chocolates, wholesale"). Then contact manufacturers directly. Keep in mind that many manufacturers require you to have an Employee Identification Number (EIN), commonly referred to as a tax ID number, before allowing you to buy wholesale. (To apply for an EIN, contact your local IRS office and ask for Form SS-4. You can get more information on EINs in Chapter 6 and on the IRS website at www.irs.gov.)

$ Find a Business-Friendly Bank

"Usually, local banks (though not large national ones) are willing to waive corporate fees for a small business account," notes Deborah Elias, a scientific writer and consultant (www.eliasconsultants.com). "They will also often accept checks made out to your name, even without a business account," she says.

GETTING THE BUCKS TO BACK YOUR BUSINESS

With over 9 million women-owned businesses in the U.S. today, female entrepreneurs are finally getting the credit they deserve. No longer is it necessary to deplete your savings account to build a website, max out credit cards to purchase equipment, or beg family members for start-up money. There are a number of more appealing sources for mompreneurs to explore, most of which are just a mouse click or two away.

The U.S. Small Business Administration *(www.sba.gov)*

The *LowDoc* program helps you secure loans of up to $150,000; *SBA Express* provides revolving lines of credit of up to $25,000. Larger SBA-backed loans are also available through many banks. The SBA *Women's Loan Pre-Qualification Program* helps you put together a solid loan application and backs you with a prequalification letter to take to banks. It's especially helpful for tough-to-finance home or service-based businesses, which have no product or corporate suite to prove they're "serious."

Microloan Programs

Many state and local agencies, such as ACCION International (www.accion. org), offer small loans (sometimes just a few hundred dollars) to qualifying women- and minority-owned businesses. Check with state economic development agencies in your home state to see what microlending programs might be available, or go to the SBA's site (www.sbaonline.sba.gov/financing/microparticipants) for lists of other participating agencies. The Association for Enterprise Opportunity (www.microenterpriseworks.org) also has a list of microloan programs. The SBA online women's business center (www.onlinewbc.org) or small business development centers, often found at colleges and universities (www.asbdc-us.org), can help you locate resources, too.

The Amber Foundation *(www.womensnet.net/amber)*

This nonprofit organization has a monthly contest in which it offers $500 grants to women entrepreneurs who submit winning business plans. The business plans are judged according to completeness, originality of concept, and long-term prospects for success.

Count-Me-In *(www.count-me-in.org)*

To encourage women's economic independence, Count-Me-In has established a national loan fund for potential or current women business owners. Business loans, ranging from $500 to $10,000, and scholarships for business training and technical assistance will be given to qualifying women. You can apply online.

Forum for Women Entrepreneurs E-Scholarship Award *(www.fwe.org)*

The Forum for Women Entrepreneurs (FWE)—a membership organization for women who own technology companies—partnered with Hewlett-Packard to offer scholarships valued at over $150,000 in hardware, software, and services. Available to FWE members.

Self-Employment and Enterprise Development (SEED) Programs

In some states, loans are available to unemployed workers to start up a business instead of collecting unemployment insurance. Counseling, training, and technical assistance are also part of the deal. To find out if your state offers one, call your state government or the United States Department of Labor in Washington, D.C. (www.dol.gov).

Passions and Dreams Funding, Inc. *(www.passionsndreams.org)*

Created by a Beverly Hills woman entrepreneur, this organization lends sums of $5,000 to $25,000 to women who don't qualify for SBA financing. The loans are offered at 9 percent interest with no payments required for the first six months, but you must have or obtain business training and allow your business to be monitored monthly for the duration of the loan.

Venture Capital Firms

Venture capital firms specializing in women-owned businesses are cropping up across the nation and can be good sources of money for growing an established business. These firms may invest anywhere from $500,000 to $2 million in your business. Viridian Capital Partners (www.viridian-capital.com) is a women-run firm specializing in start-ups in the technology and health care fields. Women's Growth Capital Fund (www.womensgrowth-capital.com) invests in businesses in their early stages (you must be in business at least a year and making a profit) or expansion phases (you must be in business two or more years and growing in revenue by more than 20 percent each year).

Angel Funding

You'll be bankrolled by wealthy individual investors who help finance start-ups in return for an equity stake and a say in how the business is run. Word of mouth is sometimes the best way to find your "angel," but you can get leads at the SBA's Angel Capital Electronic Network (www.ace-net.org) and AngelMoney (www.angelmoney.com). And local businesses can seek help from regional angel networks run by and for women that are popping up in several metropolitan areas. These include Seraph Capital Forum (www.seraphcapital.com) in the Pacific Northwest; Women First Capital Fund (www.womenfirstcapital.com) in the Northeast; and WomenAngels.net (www.womenangels.net) in greater Washington, D.C.

Small Business Development Centers

These are springing up at community colleges and universities. While they don't usually offer loans, they have well-stocked libraries and experts who can guide you toward potential lenders. For a center near you, contact the Association of Small Business Development Centers (www.asbdc-us.org).

Banks That Believe in Women

Mompreneurs with a solid business plan or an up-and-running business needn't be afraid to go directly to a bank for a loan. More and more of these staid financial institutions are opening their arms—and their coffers—to women.

■ **Fleet Boston Financial Corporation Women Entrepreneurs' Connection** (www.fleet.com) earmarks loans to women-owned businesses in the Northeast. It also offers a "Partners in Technology" program, which loans computer equipment to women business owners.

■ **Bank of America** (www.BankofAmerica.com/community) makes loans and equity investments available to minority- and women-owned businesses, providing between $50,000 and $500,000 to companies with annual net incomes of less than $2 million.

■ **Wells Fargo Bank Women's Loan Program** (www.wellsfargo.com) offers loans from $5,000 to $100,000 nationally. To qualify, you must be in business at least three years, be profitable, and have satisfactory personal and business credit.

■ **Your Personal Bank** may be more generous than you think—especially if you've been doing business there for some time. Check it out for loan possibilities, too.

HOW MUCH CAN YOU MAKE?

Your earning power depends on your type of business and the number of hours you're willing to devote to it. Because the Internet is still in its infancy, many of the moms we interviewed for this book were just starting up their Web businesses and not taking in sizable incomes. Yet we've also met a good number of dot.com moms who are earning six-figure salaries. The good news is that there's no glass ceiling in cyberspace. Once you get your business up and running profitably, there's no limit to what you can earn. Of course, "You won't get rich overnight," emphasizes Wendy Harris of the National Association of Medical Billers (www. billersnetwork.com), where she offers billing training, information, and support. "But if you stick with it and work hard, the profits will come," says this mom of two from Valley Falls, New York.

HOW MUCH SHOULD YOU CHARGE?

Unfortunately, there's no standard answer to this question. When pricing your product or service, you must consider the type of business you're in, your location, your competition, and the current economic climate. To get an idea of what's fair, network with other moms in your field and ask them about their rates or prices. Online message boards and chats are a great place to start, and you'll find that as long as you're not a direct competitor, mompreneurs are very willing to share their advice and strategies. You also need to assess what your competitors charge. Log on to the websites of businesses with products and services similar to yours and check out the fees and pricing policy. If the information isn't available, e-mail or phone the company, as if you're a potential customer, and ask what it charges. Then set your prices or fees competitively. While you don't want to price yourself out of the market, don't go too low, either. Bargain-basement pricing can backfire and actually scare customers and clients away.

To make sure you're charging enough to cover your time and expenses: Roughly estimate how many hours you devote to your service or product; then determine how much you'll have to charge to cover your time and costs while still making a profit. If you're a product inventor, craftsperson, personal chef, or in another business that requires cash outlay, include material costs, overhead, and retail margin. Don't forget to add in time you spend on e-mails, travel, and brainstorming sessions. What about thinking time? "My mental wheels are almost always turning," says Joy Rotondi-Cann of www.foodies.com, a company that builds custom websites for food-related businesses. "If I come up with a brilliant website navigation system while doing the dishes, does that count as hours?" asks the Marblehead, Massachusetts, mom. We say absolutely. Some of us come up with our best business ideas in the shower or on the treadmill! If you don't factor in that "creative" time, you'll be shortchanging yourself.

ARE YOU SPENDING YOUR TIME PROFITABLY?

It's so easy to get stalled in cyberspace. There's always one more e-mail to answer, one more search engine to register on, one more tweak you can make on your website. Before you know it, hours have passed and you've got little to show for your efforts. And though marketing your Web business is absolutely key to future financial success, it can be a full-time job in itself. So, it's an ongoing challenge to split your time between promotional efforts and those projects which generate an immediate income. Shelley Sampson of HerWebBiz.com sets aside at least five hours a week to promoting her site and attracting traffic.

If you want to reach your moneymaking potential, you need to figure out the business tasks that matter most and be aware of how you spend your time when working, so you can put your energies where they'll earn the biggest payoff.

TIME TRACKER

To see if you're working at top efficiency, it's helpful to keep a log of just how much time you are spending on various work tasks. Warning: This can be quite an eye-opener! Ellen was shocked to see that she was spending nearly a third of her workday answering e-mail and chatting on home-based business message boards. By limiting how many times she logs online and checks her e-mail box (she aims for no more than three times a day), Ellen actually gained hours to spend on writing articles and lining up new work.

These tips will help you make the most of your work time.

1. **Assess Your Workload.** Think about all the tasks that are essential for running your business—from creating and developing projects or products to maintaining and marketing your website to answering e-mail to processing bills to networking with clients and customers. Jot these down on paper, and then prioritize them by estimating how much time you think each task deserves.

2. **Evaluate Volunteer Efforts.** Make a list of your professional and personal volunteering projects. Make sure you are only committing to the ones that are most important and meaningful to you. Most of us treasure the opportunity to be available to help out in our children's schools—yet that doesn't mean we have to be on call for every fund-raiser or class party. The same goes for professional organizations: Be selective and only choose projects that won't zap too much of your work time.

3. **Make a Daily Log.** Monitor your work time for at least a couple of weeks to see exactly how you are spending it. For every work project you've been involved in, list the business tasks you attended to and how much time you devoted to it each day. Also track the time spent on any volunteer efforts that cut into your workday. And if you interrupted your office hours to tend to a routine household chore or entertain a chatty neighbor, note it on your log. You'll get a good look at your work style and the tasks and interruptions that gobble your time. Then you can adjust the way you work, if necessary, and come up with strategies for preventing non-kid interruptions. The log also helps you gauge the value of your time—an important factor when setting prices and fees.

4. **Review Your Profitability.** Compare your daily time log with your prioritized list of business tasks (done in step one). Are the tasks of most importance getting completed in an efficient manner? If not, why? Which could you easily and inexpensively delegate? Are household tasks conflicting with work time? (Be honest now! Did you really mean to bake those cupcakes when you should have been finishing up your client's proposal?) With a few little adjustments, you can improve your bottom line!

MAXIMIZE YOUR EARNING POWER

Here's how to maneuver around those speed traps that stonewall productivity and profitability.

*TIME TRAP: **Wheel-spinning.*** You have so many things to do, you just don't know where to start.

*TIME TRICK: **Have an Action Plan.*** Soapmaker Paula Polman makes a daily to-do list while her toddler eats breakfast. "I get the most accomplished in a day that way because I know what needs to get done and which things I can do while my son is awake," she says. Nancy Hayes, owner of Accurate Office Services in Arnold, Missouri, e-mails clients with any questions before she starts their projects to prevent wasted time and hassle later.

*TIME TRAP: **System Failures.*** Your computer crashes, and after several hours you finally get it up and running again. Then the server goes down. And you haven't finished any "real" work all day.

*TIME TRICK: **Protect Your Equipment.*** You can't eliminate tech problems, but you can minimize them. Make sure your computer isn't overloaded with unnecessary software that might be hogging up RAM and leading to slowdowns and crashes. You'll need all the room you can get on your hard drive anyway, for the antivirus software you'll need to install and run regularly in order to keep your computer free of bugs.

To keep from losing access to her computer, printer, and fax during storms and blackouts, environmental consultant Liane Hetherington-

Dot.com Disasters

Cyber-Crisis: Your toddler shoves a baseball card into your floppy disk drive.
Crisis Prevention: Childproof your work station by putting tape over the openings of disk drives, keeping sharp objects out of your child's reach, and setting aside a kid-friendly corner for him or her to do projects with crayons, or other no-mess materials.

Cyber-Crisis: A new and powerful e-mail virus crashes your hard drive.
Crisis Prevention: Safeguard your system with a powerful antivirus software and update it regularly. Avoid opening e-mail attachments from people you don't know.

Cyber-Crisis: After getting a nasty letter from a dissatisfied customer, you hastily compose an angry reply and e-mail it. Five minutes later, you can't imagine how you could have done such a stupid thing!
Crisis Prevention: Think before you click "send." If you do draft a hasty e-mail note that's angry or potentially offensive, file it in the outbox for sending later. That gives you time to cool off and read the note again before you burn any bridges.

Cyber-Crisis: You're having an Instant Message conversation with a demanding client when your sister Instant Messages you. "Can't talk now, Sis . . . I'm on with Dracula and he wants more blood," you say. "Who's Dracula?" Instant Messages back your client, and you realize in horror that you answered the wrong person.
Crisis Prevention: Never bad-mouth a client or customer online—you never know when an e-mail or Instant Message will go astray!

Ward plugs her equipment (and a lamp) into an uninterrupted power supply/surge protector (a battery backup that keeps things running a while after power outages). Use regular surge protectors for the rest of your office equipment. And be sure to frequently (several times a day at least) save your work onto a disk to prevent losing valuable data. There's not too much you can do when your server goes down, but if you find that your ISP fails you too frequently, consider switching to one that's more reliable.

TIME TRAP: Lost In Cyberspace! Web-surfing is taking over your life!
TIME TRICK: Surf Selectively. Before you log on, have a list of what you need to accomplish while online, and give yourself a time limit. Kathy Burns of

SasEz! Palm Pilot Files (www.palmpilotfiles.com) actually sets an alarm to keep herself from getting sidetracked. You can also streamline hunts on search engines by surrounding the phrases you're looking for with quotation marks or parentheses.

TIME TRAP: *Housework.* You didn't get your proposal done, but you did vacuum every room in the house and cleaned out the kids' closets!

TIME TRICK: *Bust Dust During Nonworking Hours.* "I do not even put a spoon in the dishwasher during work time," says Joy Rotondi-Cann of foodies.com. Of course, you may be able to sneak in little things (like throwing the laundry in the dryer or marinating the chicken for tonight's dinner), but don't try to tackle big chores. Instead, find ways to streamline the housework. "I pick one day a week to do all of the chores like shopping, cleaning, and cooking," says Vicki Andrews of A Few Good Women (www.afewgood-women.com), a consulting firm which helps elementary school teachers and students integrate technology into their learning. Michelle Litel, owner of Tisket-a-Tasket Custom Gift Baskets, cleans her house whenever she can (when she's not working, of course!), so dirt doesn't build up. But Litel also pays a friend to clean her house once or twice a month. "When I get to the point where I am able to only work from home, the schedule will be a lot less hectic," says this single mom from Carmel, Indiana, who still works full-time outside the home while she builds her basket business.

TIME TRAP: *Work/Family Collisions.* Your baby comes down with a terrible ear infection the day before a killer deadline. As you pace the floors trying to rock her to sleep, you wonder how you'll ever get your project done.

TIME TRICK: *Have a Safety Net.* Because sickness comes with the work-at-home territory, and your children are inevitably stricken at deadline time, you must build extra time into your schedule. It's a good idea to aim to finish projects a few days before they're really due, just in case. Writer/consultant Robbye Fox of Olney, Maryland, builds a cushion into deadlines and always saves a free block of time on her calendar for crises and last-minute assignments.

You've Got (Too Much!) Mail

Is e-mail eating up too much of your time? Try these tricks.

* Consolidate work-related e-mail boxes so that all your business mail comes into one.

* Prioritize e-mail by scanning addresses and headings and responding only to those that seem most pressing.

* Delete spam and other junk mail without reading it. (Don't make the mistake of writing back; you'll only confirm your address and encourage even more spam.)

* Block spam by activating the junk mail filter on your e-mail program. You can also use free spam-proofing services such as Brightmail *(www.brightmail.com)*, which separates potential spam from the rest of your e-mail so you can view it (or delete it) later.

* Use an auto-responder (available on some e-mail programs) to send electronic form letters telling clients when you're out of the office.

* Have prewritten answers to common customer queries filed in your word processing document folder, so that you can cut and paste them into personalized e-mail responses.

* Keep your e-mail notes brief, to encourage brief answers.

* Set certain times of the day for reading and answering e-mail. If you check your box too often, you'll soon be spending almost all your time responding.

* Pick up the phone. Sometimes a call can be quicker and more time-effective. And it establishes a personal connection, reminding clients and customers that there's a real person behind that screen!

TIME TRAP: Too Much Multitasking. There isn't a mompreneur around who hasn't mastered the art of changing diapers while talking to clients on the portable phone. And we're whizzes at breast-feeding and answering e-mails simultaneously. While we couldn't survive without multitasking, doing too many things at once can compromise work quality and sabotage productivity. And it can send the wrong message to your family. If you're conducting conference calls from the sidelines of your child's softball game or taking your laptop to bed every night, your kids and hubby are bound to think your business is more important to you than them. They may even grow to resent your business.

Speedy Strategies

These shortcuts are guaranteed to boost your productivity and bottom line.

1. Send invoices by e-mail.

2. Order office supplies and stamps online. Check out sites like: *www.stamps.com; www.simplypostage.com;* and *www.smartship.com.*

3. Store all your business and family data on a Personal Digital Assistant (such as a Palm Pilot) to minimize paper-shuffling.

4. Get a DSL or cable modem line to speed up Internet connections.

5. Combat cyber-clutter. Instead of wading through the hundreds of favorite websites you've bookmarked, use a bookmark manager to categorize them. Available free at: *www.clickmarks.com; www.blink.com; www.backflip.com;* and *www.hotlinks.com.*

TIME TRICK: *Juggle With Care.* Review your business tasks and decide which ones need your total concentration and which can be done with the kids underfoot. Understand your multitasking threshold. Only you know how many things you can juggle at once before you get frazzled.

TIME TRAP: *Working 24/7.* When you work on the Web, "it's easy to be a workaholic," says Kristie Tamsevicius of Kristie's Custom Design (www. kcustom.com), which offers Web development, hosting, and promotion services. But if you do this regularly, it will certainly take its toll, leaving you so tired you may not be able to work up to your full capacity. You're likely to get cranky with kids and clients and be more prone to making business mistakes.

TIME TRICK: *Give Yourself a Time-Out!* Limit your late nights. You can't work effectively if you're always bleary-eyed. "I have a hard time walking away when I know there is more work to be done, but I do much better when I have set hours and can shut the door when work time is over," says Milwaukee mompreneur Amy Schlicht of MyPerfectCandle.com. "It helps to have a way to close off your work area," she adds. Instead of consistently working every night and then flopping into bed, end your day with a special treat. Whether it's curling up with a good book or sitting on the

Are You A Multitasking Maniac?

Don't: Make cell phone calls to clients while carpooling the kids or you're jeopardizing everyone's safety.

Do: Wait for downtime to make calls—such as when you're waiting for your son to get out of karate class.

Don't: Tackle a client's Excel spreadsheet or PowerPoint presentation while helping your daughter with her math homework—it could lead to big errors on both!

Do: Save complex, detail-oriented jobs for when the kids are asleep or otherwise occupied.

Don't: Get so wrapped up in tinkering with your website that you don't notice that your toddler has jammed all your backup disks into the VCR.

Do: Squeeze in short and simple jobs when the kids are underfoot—like reading e-mail. But make sure that you check on children frequently to make sure they're not roaming into dangerous territory.

Don't: Run to answer your business phone during dinnertime.

Do: Drop your multitasking mind-set at certain special times of the day to focus totally on your family.

porch with your honey and gazing at the stars, "it will rejuvenate you," says Brigitte Thompson of Datamaster, a service that provides accounting and tax services.

Even when daytime business tasks get overwhelming, a short break can be just the ticket to feeling in control. "I want to give praise to the person who invented the jogging stroller," says Cecilia Ekberg, creator of Swedish Blondes and Nutty Blondes cookies. "When business gets too hectic, I put my son in it and take a nice long walk to clear my mind," she says.

TIME TRAP: Constant Interruptions! It's becoming impossible to meet deadlines with the kids underfoot. You're frequently feeling frustrated by your children's demands, and constantly snapping, "Not now, Mommy's working!"

TIME TRICK: ***Don't Feel Guilty About Child Care.*** Give yourself permission to use it when necessary. "Too many new mompreneurs start businesses without any child care backup, and then wonder why their business is not thriving," notes San Jose, California, mom Donna Snow of Anything Business (www.anything-business.com), who provides small business coaching, writing services, and virtual assistance. Though your baby may be a long and reliable napper now, allowing you long stretches in which to work quietly, it won't last. It becomes tougher to work without child care as your children grow more active!

Part-time child care buys you chunks of time so that you can give both your children and your business your undivided attention. After all, what's the point of working from home if you're constantly feeling flustered? That's not healthy for you, your children, or your venture.

You also need to be honest about just how much attention you are really paying to your children if you are trying to work with them underfoot. It's so easy to get caught up in cyberspace while your kids watch videos for hours. But surely that's not what you had in mind when you decided to start your business. If this is happening too often, it's much better to hire someone who can play with them, keeping them stimulated and well supervised.

If you're worried about the cost, take heart: Mompreneurs have many more low-cost, part-time child care options than mothers in the traditional workforce.

DATA BANK: *Do You Use Child Care?*

Yes 58%
No 42%

REAL-LIFE CHILD CARE SOLUTIONS

Here are some of the most creative and cost-effective child care choices used by mompreneurs.

Soul Snacks

Feeling frazzled? You're not alone. Dot.com moms have three jobs: mommy, business-woman, and marketing maven (the responsibility of marketing your website is a full-time job in itself!). "But fifteen minutes is all you need to refresh your mind and body," says Susie Cortright, mom and founder/publisher of Momscape *(www.momscape.com),* an e-zine devoted to nurturing busy mothers. Her "soul snacks" are guaranteed to calm your jitters and recharge your batteries.

* **Affirm Your Success.** When you're having a bad day (or week!), write down all the great things you have accomplished (both professionally and personally). You'll feel a lot more competent when you see successes on paper. Also try hanging motivational quotes and any awards or positive notes you've received on a bulletin board by your desk, to keep you going when the going gets tough.

* **Use Creative Visualization.** Close your eyes for a few minutes and imagine yourself going through a typical day with an inner peace that nullifies real-world pressures. Visualize yourself as cool and confident.

* **Indulge in Small Luxuries.** Furnish your home office with reminders that you are tak-ing care of yourself. Buy yourself flowers and put them on your desk. Treat yourself to a tube of sumptuous French hand cream. Keep an electric kettle and your favorite herbal tea nearby—it's particularly relaxing when you're doing something tedious like checking your Web links or changing meta tags.

* **Exercise.** Go for a walk, or run, or work out to your favorite video. You'll clear your mind, energize your spirit, and strengthen your body.

* **Brainstorm Your Own Soul Snacks.** If you had 15 or 30 minutes each day just for you, how would you spend it? Now set aside this time on your calendar every day, and treat yourself to "me" time—even if you spend that time staring out the window, it's essential to give yourself some downtime every day. You'll feel more productive and less frustrated.

Work the School Shift

One of the most popular options for moms with kids preschool age and older, this one allows you to work for long stretches of uninterrupted time. And "you must have some uninterrupted time to work in order to build your business," says Snow. Five of her six children are in school full-time, and she'll be putting her preschooler in a part-time program soon.

Keep in mind that your business cannot shut down during school breaks, so you must have a supplemental plan. "The first day of summer vacation was a disaster last year!" says economist Anne Ramstetter Wenzel (www.econosystems.com). "I thought my seven-year-old would entertain himself for a few hours in the morning while I worked," says the Menlo Park, California, mom of four. "But after being interrupted numerous times, it dawned on me: He's used to interacting with a teacher and seventeen other students every morning, while I'm used to peace and quiet! I arranged to have him go to a nearby Montessori school three mornings a week. On other mornings, I'd invite one of his friends to come over and they'd play quietly while I worked within earshot."

Form Parent Partnerships

Convenient and cost-free, you exchange child care duties as needed with a friend or through a baby-sitting cooperative run by neighborhood parents. Dawn Vaughan, a home-schooling mompreneur from Picayune, Missisippi, partners up with a pal who also home-schools. "She teaches my children along with her own three days a week, so that I can have some time to meet with local clients and be able to work during the day without distractions," says Vaughan, who designs custom homes for clients via the Internet through her firm, Vaughan's Home Design (www.vhdesign. com). "Before we worked out our arrangement, I survived on three hours of sleep a night, which was definitely not healthy," she says.

Michelle Donahue-Arpas of GeniusBabies.com in Charlotte, North Carolina, belongs to a playgroup which meets three to four mornings a week. She and the other moms take turns watching the kids, so each gets some time to herself.

In Connie Koerth's small town of Brillion, Wisconsin, they have something called the "Time-Out Baby-sitting Co-op." "We use cards instead of money and trade the cards for watching each other's kids," says Koerth of Office Wizard (www.officewizard.net), which provides medical transcription services to hospitals and clinics. You can find baby-sitting co-ops through community groups, local Ys, and MOMS club chapters.

Get a Mother's Helper

Perhaps there's a trustworthy young neighbor in upper elementary or middle school who can come to your home for a few hours in the afternoon and play with your children while you work. You'll get lots done this way, yet still be within earshot in case the kids need you. This is a great option for school breaks, when preteens are desperate for jobs.

Trade Off With Daddy

If your husband has nontraditional hours or a flexible job schedule, share the child care. "My husband has adjusted his schedule so that he works in the early morning hours while I enjoy the children," says Brigitte Thompson. "Once he is home, I work the second part of the day while he spends time with the kids. It works out great for all of us."

Recruit Grandma or Grandpa

(Or Aunt Sue or Cousin Ed, or any other family member you're lucky enough to have living nearby.) "My mom and dad watch the boys for me as often as I need them to," says Kathleen Driggers of Bremerton, Washington, who runs a webhosting business that specializes in women's enterprises (www.herwebhost.com). "Being a single parent raising two handicapped children and running my own home business, having child care help is absolutely essential," she says.

Hire Part-Time Home Help

If you have a baby or toddler and no family members live nearby, consider hiring an in-home sitter a few times a week. Your best bets: a high school or college student who can work around his or her class schedule. Or consider a retired neighbor—senior citizens are often anxious to feel useful and earn some extra money.

Utilize Tot Drops

Local churches, synagogues, and community centers often have drop-off child care programs known by names like "tot drop," "stay and play," or "PDO" (parents' day out). You can drop your children off on a per-needed basis and they get to socialize with other kids their age.

Find Flexible Family Day Care

Many family day care providers are willing to take your children just one or two days a week; some will even consider half days. The best way to find them is by networking with other moms, since family day care providers usually don't advertise.

Go Mobile

Pack up your laptop and cell phone and head somewhere the kids can be safely supervised. "I just started taking my boys to the library after school for an hour or two," says Lorrie Morgan-Ferrero, a virtual assistant and Internet marketing specialist from Studio City, California. Her sons (who are 8 and 10) get their homework done, while she tends to the administrative tasks of her business, Cyber Staff Services (www.cyberstaffservices. com).

Each week, Susie Cortright, owner of Momscape.com, drives 80 miles from her Breckenridge, Colorado, log cabin to her parents' or in-laws' home. The grandparents alternate taking care of her 18-month-old daughter, Cassie. "Cassie gets her grandma time, the grandmas get their baby fix, and I get lots of work done," says Cortright. "The arrangement works wonderfully!" Wireless gadgets are lifesavers for times like these. Shannon Rubio of TheSmileBox.com bought a special attachment for her Palm Pilot so she can check on her gift box orders anytime, anywhere. This handy tool allows her to dial a special number, hold her Palm Pilot up to any phone, and download e-mail from her home PC. "I've even checked orders from the Burger King drive-through!" she admits.

Mix and Match

Over the years you'll discover that just one child care strategy may not be enough to give you the coverage you need for your growing business; you'll learn to use a combination of plans that best suits the ages of your children. Diana Cant, owner of WebCob Enterprises (www.webcob.com) a Canadian Web hosting business, sends her preschooler to nursery school for two and a half hours twice a week, and also has a babysitter who comes three times a week for two hours at a time. Kathryn Goldman, a virtual assistant from Berlin, Wisconsin, has a number of options for her five- and six-year-old boys. Her husband, an air traffic controller, has a different schedule every day, so sometimes he's home until 2 or 3 in the afternoon and she's able to work till then. On days he's not around and she has meetings or deadlines, she has a friend down the street take the boys for a few hours. In the summer, a friend's daughter helps Goldman out, taking the boys to the park or occupying them quietly indoors.

CHILDPROOFING YOUR WORK TIME

When you're a mompreneur, every day is "Take Your Children to Work Day," whether you have child care or not. Here's how to work successfully when the kids are underfoot.

■ **Work in Spurts.** "I work a couple of hours in the morning, then break for a couple of hours, and I repeat this all day long," says Tina Jacks of At-HomeWorks.com (www.at-homeworks.com), which provides work-at-home resources and Web development. "I get my work done, and my three-year-old doesn't feel left out or neglected," says the soon-to-be mom of two from Kirbyville, Texas. "Sometimes the house isn't as neat as I'd like, but thankfully I have a very understanding and supportive husband who is as tickled about what I'm accomplishing as I am," she says.

■ **Create a Kid-Friendly Work Station.** Set aside a corner of your office space for your child to do her "work" beside you. Furnish it with kid-sized chair, table, or desk, toy computer and phone, and "office supplies" like crayons, pencils, stickers, and paper. Old briefcases, clipboards, business cards, and stationery will help your child feel like she's the president of her own company, too.

■ **Make Tedious Tasks Fun.** Wendy Harris pays her two sons to assist with her medical billing and training business by stamping and stuffing envelopes and drawing graphics. "They like using the money to buy trading cards," she says. Michelle Donahue-Arpas of GeniusBabies.com makes packing boxes a game for two-year-old Trishie. "She scoops the pink packing peanuts into the boxes," says Donahue-Arpas. She also involves her husband, who she says has become "an excellent gift wrapper"!

■ **Reward Kids with Quiet Toys.** "I was having a hard time getting my phone calls done without interruption from my little girl, who's three," says Lori McGuire of Wilsonville, Alabama, a party consultant. So she made a "treat basket," filled with special things like individually wrapped candies and gum, stickers, and bubbles. "When I need to make a call, I tell her that if she can be quiet she may have a treat from the basket when I'm done. It works like a charm. Even if she tries to interrupt, all I have to do is point to the basket and she remembers our deal," says McGuire.

Believe it or not, there will come the day when you won't need to resort to tactics like these anymore. "I've been an entrepreneur long enough that my children are pretty good about letting me get a project completed if I tell them it's a high priority," says Donna Snow of her six kids, who range in age from 3 to 15. "Every day is a challenge, but at night when my head hits that pillow and I drift off to sleep, I realize that I've gotten one step closer to my dream."

 *Web Celeb*

Eugenie Diserio
Founder, Vice President, Creative Director of Astronet
  (www.astronet.com), AOL keyword: Astronet
New Canaan, Connecticut
Mom of 2

You might say Eugenie Diserio's planets were in alignment the day she closed her cyber-deal with AOL in 1995. The online giant was looking to fund the content companies of new "infopreneurs." Former rock musician Diserio proposed Astronet, a site focusing on astrology—a subject she's been passionate about since her teenage years. The single mom had recently lost a marketing job and was living in her parents' house with her six-year-old son, Jake, when she hit upon the idea to offer horoscopes, computer-generated charts, and live readings over the Internet. Just as her unemployment insurance was about to run out, Diserio's persistence paid off—AOL gave her business plan the go-ahead, and Astronet became an original America Online Greenhouse Partner. "At the time, I was trying to reinvent my life, and this 'virgin frontier' had no glass ceiling and didn't require years of business experience," she says. "In fact, 'oddballs' and risk-takers were better at making the leap into cyberspace than corporate types."

With $150,000 in seed money and plenty of entrepreneurial spirit, Diserio set up shop in her parents' basement. Behind the screen name of "Genie Easy," she read charts, wrote a daily column, and recruited a team of talented expert astrologers and writers to her new site. Traffic was brisk from the start, especially among women. "Nobody else was offering electronic horoscopes at the time," Diserio remembers, "and visitors loved the Genie Easy persona. My 'team' helped too—they talked up the site in their magazine columns and radio shows." Astronet became so popular, it was voted an AOL Members' Choice Award winner four times.

After another round of funding, Diserio was able to move into office space in town. She hired several executive managers and soon launched www.astronet.com on the Web, expanding the brand beyond AOL. "Even though we were successful from the start and always ran the business 'lean and mean,' an astrology site still wasn't considered mainstream enough by many investors," says Diserio. "And Astronet was too specialized to go the IPO route." But after more creative financing and exponential traffic growth, Astronet's success began to attract attention from the merger and acquisition bigwigs.

Late in 1998, Hearst New Media acquired Astronet (for a reputed high seven figures), and two months later, merged it with Women.com. But "Genie Easy" is still the "mayor and mom of Astronet!" Diserio says, with a laugh, and its guiding inspirational guru through her columns— "Genie's Day" and "Ask Genie." She's also the mayor and mom of the company's office headquarters—still in town so Jake can drop by after school, and still home to its staff of 15 full-time employees. (About 75 freelance writers and readers connect from their own computers.) Even the most skilled psychic might not have predicted that this astrology buff would achieve such success and be able to live what amounts to the "reinvented life" she envisioned. Besides building a booming e-Biz, Diserio has since married and given birth to Jake's baby brother, Luke.

Although the stars may have been shining in her favor, Diserio knows that her incredible drive also had a lot to do with her good fortune. "I had to make this business work for me and Jake—it was our survival," she says. Her secret? "Have the discipline and confidence to keep marching on, setting your radar on the end result. Procrastination is your worst enemy."

Even though Diserio pushed herself hard, there was never a question that Jake came first. Mom was always available for meals, snuggles, and sporting events, working on Astronet around her son's school schedule and after he was asleep for the night. The close proximity of her family and their emotional support helped tremendously. So did Diserio's ability to seek balance in her life—she is, after all, a Libra! "Understand your limits and be able to switch gears to rejuvenate, refresh, and do something for yourself," she advises. "The development of your spiritual life and health are very important, too."

Now that she's financially secure and happily married, the future looks very rosy indeed. But Diserio has not forgotten her years of struggle, and is constantly working to empower other women to achieve their goals. She continues to oversee the vision and high-quality content of Astronet and is looking to expand her Genie Easy persona into other media. Her latest endeavor is a book titled *Roadblocks on the Highway of Life, or How to Clear Out Obstacles and Get What You Want.* Diserio offers this advice for *all* mompreneurs, whatever your horoscope may read: "The quality of your relationships and family life will impact on the success of your business."

CHAPTER FIVE

Web-Wise:
Building a Winning Website

 Sound Byte

"My biggest challenge was creating an inviting and user-friendly website on a small budget. I worked with a friend who was starting her own Web design firm and I became one of her guinea pigs. Our goal was to have my site reflect the vision and personality of my company—and it does!"

Vicki Mote Bodwell, mother of two; New York City
Founder of Warm Biscuit Bedding Company *(www.warmbiscuit.com)*

While "site-seeing" to research this book, we surfed the Net until our fingers grew stiff from clicking. What we found were some pretty amazing Web pages developed by and for mompreneurs. It made us glad that we had waited to build our website. We learned so much by visiting other sites and were so inspired by the talents of these Web-wise women that our site turned out much better.

The motto of our story is: "Do your homework before you forge ahead into the world of the Web." Of course, we reserved our domain name several years ago—that's something that must be acted upon as quickly as possible. (See page 138 to learn how.) But it's also important to research other sites, attend a Web design workshop or two, read a book, participate in online discussions, and even consult with some Web developers before you rush into construction. (See Dot.Com Directory for resources.)

Luckily, you can always go back and "renovate" your site—unlike a home remodeling job, a website design is not irreversible. In fact, it's smart to start small and "add on" as your business grows, suggests Web developer Joy Rotondi-Cann. And it's a lot cheaper and easier to update a website than a kitchen or bathroom!

DATA BANK: *What Was Your Biggest Internet Business Challenge?*

Designing/Maintaining/Marketing my website 54%

WEBSITE FAQS

To cut through the confusion and get your site construction under way, we compiled the most frequently asked questions about bringing a business to the Web . . . and found out the answers for you.

Q. Where do I start?

Choose a *domain name*. Most mompreneurs go with something close to the name of their business, product, or service for easy access. For example, Jennifer Balog of Verona, Wisconsin, selected magicalgift.com for her gift basket business—short, sweet, and to the point. Avoid a name that's too lengthy—it takes longer to keyboard into the search engine.

Q. How do I reserve a domain name?

Even if you don't plan to build a site for another year or two, it's imperative to reserve at least one domain name before someone else grabs it. This will become the root of your *URL* (Uniform Resource Locator)—your website's home page address on the Internet. For one-stop shopping, go to www.networksolutions.com—you can find out if the domain name you want is available and then immediately register it; BuyDomains.com, enom.com, and register.com are other registration sources. Fees run about $35 per year. The URL for an e-Business usually includes the dot.com suffix, but it may be wise to also register the dot.org, dot.net, dot.biz, or other options so you won't have to "share" with another website. (See Chapter 6 for more information on selecting and protecting your domain name).

Q. What's a host and how do I choose one?

A Web *host* (sometimes used interchangeably with an *ISP* or *Internet Service Provider*) is actually a computer that stores your website and makes it available for viewing. That computer is called a *server*—a virtual "home" of sorts for your e-Biz. When you're looking for a place to live, it's important to find the community and house that best matches the needs of your family and budget. The same goes for your hosting service and your website. You can sign up with a wide range of hosts offering a wide range of services at a wide range of prices. We compare the pros and cons of each in "The Host(ess) With the Mostest" Chart on page 143.

Q. What should I look for in a host provider?

High-speed connections and reliable tech support are essential. You want your Web pages to load quickly so viewers don't get antsy and flee to another destination while waiting for your site to come up on the screen. The time it takes for pages to load depends on the *bandwidth* your host is offering. It's smart to go with the most bandwidth that fits your budget. In more remote areas, Web hosts may offer the minimum bandwidth only. Virtual assistant Michelle Storrusten, owner of galfridayenterprises.com in Great Falls, Montana, overcame this problem by setting up two alternate Internet access options on her computer. As far as tech support goes, you want 24/7 assistance year-round. If you're filling an order or completing a job at 4 A.M. and you hit a glitch, you'll need a troubleshooter immediately! That means someone who can "hold your hand" and talk you through the crisis—not an e-mail auto-responder.

Q. What about e-commerce capabilities?

Look for more than bandwidth and tech support from your host if your business is an online store—you're going to need specific services that will generate sales and keep visitors coming back to buy more. Absolutely necessary is a secure server to take orders, process credit cards, and encrypt card numbers over the Internet (see page 160). In the long run, you'll need a host that offers an electronic shopping cart, easy-access product database, site and traffic analysis reports, order forms and form mail, multiple e-mailboxes, and an interactive area for customer communications. And make sure the host's server has enough space for future expansion of your website.

Q. How can I catch the attention of Web surfers?

Make your home page and website user-friendly. With all the competition out there, cyber-cruisers are stopping at sites that load quickly, have a clean, uncluttered look, use small, colorful graphics, and are easy to navigate. Too many bells and whistles (not to mention video clips, animated images, pop-ups, and other razzle-dazzle!) can slow the loading time, overstimulate viewers, and even chase them away! Pay attention to the content, too. "I wanted a website that promoted my work," says Debra Haas, a public policy consultant specializing in education and finance issues, "but I didn't want it to sound like I was bragging too much." (See "Web Dialog" box, page 150, for more tips.)

Q. Do I need to know any special programming language or have graphics skills to launch a website?

It depends on how much you plan to do yourself. Several of the hosting companies offer free Web page templates—you provide the text in plain language, select graphics from a clip art or illustration program, include the links you want, and they do the rest. To build a site that's a notch or two up in personalization, go with an ISP hosting service that offers website packges or purchase the software yourself. Beginners may be better off with one of the *WYSIWYG* (What You See Is What You Get) packages that allows you to plunk text and graphic elements down on your Web pages without knowing a thing about *HTML*. To input illustrations or photos that you've scanned or *digitized* into your hard drive, familiarity with a page layout program is helpful, but your computer's mouse, keyboard, and Web browser can usually take care of the bulk of the construction.

For a more professional, customized look, a knowledge of *HTML code* will give you an edge (see "Breaking Ground in Cyberspace," page 147). If you're designing your own Web pages, you'll need to know how to use an *HTML editor* and *FTP* (File Transfer Protocol) software to upload your site to your ISP. *Javascript* provides interactivity and other special effects, but it's not necessary to know the program; there are many cut-and-paste applications available on the Web. Also accessible for downloading are free images, photos, icons, and backgrounds for your Web pages if you don't want to master a graphics program like *PhotoShop* or *Adobe Illustrator*. For the most part, however, the more unique you want your website to be, the more techie stuff you should learn (or delegate). If you start to feel overwhelmed, it may pay to hire a professional to save time and money down the road—especially if your business revolves totally around your website. (See "How to Hire a Web Designer" on page 154.)

Q. How large a website do I need?

That depends on what you hope to accomplish through your site. Is your main goal to establish a Web presence and provide information? Text doesn't take up as much "room" as graphics, but it's nice to have an appealing balance. Do you also want to get feedback from visitors who stop by? Then you'll need to add some interactive features on your site. Are you planning to sell products or services? A virtual store stocked with merchandise requires more e-commerce capabilities than a service-based business, but both must supply necessary payment options and other forms. The more tools and pages you add to your site, the more bytes of space you'll need on the server. Some hosts limit the amount of space they offer; others simply charge more. For a home business website with basic e-commerce features, 5 MB of space is a good starting point; information-only sites can be smaller and large e-tailers may require more.

SET YOUR SITES ON SUCCESS

For many mompreneurs who are prospering on the Net today, the biggest hurdle was developing a website. "I didn't have the money to pay someone to do my site for me," remembers Jeannie Rigler, owner of Brides and Babes, a calligraphy service, "so I bought an inexpensive construction kit and was on my way. It was one of the biggest learning experiences of my life." After she'd gone through much frustration and elation, www.bridesandbabes.com was up and running.

Melanie Wilson, founder of www.vegetarianbaby.com, is another mompreneur who "started out cold," turning to a cyber-support network for help. "Early on, I joined an e-mail list of women who owned businesses on the Web," she says. "The members of this group have acted as mentors, technical advisors, shoulders to cry on, and much more." Wilson recommends this route to all Internet newbies, and adds, "Don't be afraid to ask questions!" For a helpful list, check out www.digital-women.com.

Elizabeth Roy, a craftswoman in rural Quebec, Canada, found support on the Net too. "I got wonderful advice from the women I met in the iVillage Work-From-Home chat room," she says, "and help in building my Web pages from About.com."

Surfing the Web for appealing sites is also a way to get the job done. During her cyber-travels, Suzanne Boyd, who operates an online consignment shop, happened across a website that looked warm and inviting. "I contacted the webmaster and found out the site was designed and scripted by the husband-and-wife team who owned the business," she explains. "They were just getting into Web development, and I ended up with a great deal. To me, that was an omen that www.kindercloset.com was meant to be!"

And what about Vicki Mote Bodwell? She decided to go with a Yahoo! Store. "I researched all the ways we could put Warm Biscuit Bedding Company on the Web, and realized that this was the best option for our budget," she says. "I also recognized that Yahoo's built-in shopping search engine would drive a tremendous amount of target traffic to my site." Bodwell's Web developer spent some time modifying and customizing Yahoo's design templates to reflect Warm Biscuit's mission—to create rooms that inspire big dreams for both parents and children. The site now has a lot of personal flavor *plus* the marketing clout of Yahoo!.

These moms ultimately made a home on the Web and are now reaping the rewards. You can too—whether you choose the easy-to-use website tools available online, are ready and eager to master HTML (Hypertext Markup Language) and build your own site from scratch, or simply want to learn the "tech talk" so you can communicate intelligently with a website designer.

The Host(ess) with the Mostest

The genial hosts out there in cyberspace are all vying for your website. Take a look at the options and weigh the pros and cons.

Host type: Large Community Hosting Service
Examples: Yahoo!'s GeoCities, America Online's AOL Hometown, Lycos' Angelfire and Tripod, iVillage Home Pages
Cost: Free
Net Gains: Templates and clip art for quick creation and launch of Web pages
    No monthly fee
    No special software or programming needed
    Low-tech
Net Losses: Prefab, cookie-cutter look
    Most use a subdomain name rather than a top-level domain name *(www.tripod.com/biz/mompreneursonline.com,* for example, instead of *www.mompreneursonline.com)*
    No unique identity
    No control over banner ads
    Limited amount of space
    Products can't be purchased online

Host Type: Commercial Service Providers
Examples: BigStep, eCongo, FreeMerchant, Homestead
Cost: Free
Net Gains: Predesigned site-building elements

Catalog of products, online ordering, and basic e-commerce elements

Foolproof design and setup

Net Losses: Must make separate merchant credit card arrangements

May be hidden costs (credit card processing, shopping cart, adding products to database)

Some use subdomain name, not a top-level, registered domain name

Banner ads from the host

Little or no promotion or marketing support

Host Type: All-in-One Hosting Services (Electronic Storefronts)

Examples: Yahoo! Store, eBiz Builder, iCat, One-Stop eStore

Cost: From $10 to $300/month, depending on number of items offered

Net Gains: No HTML programming knowledge required

Quick and easy setup through Web browser

Some freedom and flexibility to personalize site

Full e-commerce services (catalog of products, shopping cart, online order form, product database, merchant credit card setup, secure server)

No unwanted banner ads

Traffic building help/shopping search engine

Some offer frills such as gift certificates, personal shoppers, gift reminder services, and more

Net Losses: No product reviews or news

No chat rooms or message boards for customer feedback

Fees based on number of products for sale; limits imposed

Limited number of e-mail accounts

Host Type: Dedicated Web Hosting Services, ranging in scope from mom-and-pop operations, to servers run by website developers, to super-sized ISPs for handling high-traffic sites

Examples: Go to *www.TopHosts.com* for a ranked list or ask other people for recommendations

Cost: $20/month and up

Net Gains: Maximum freedom and flexibility to personalize your site

No limit on pages

Most provide e-commerce essentials, including secure server for credit card encryption

Multiple e-mail accounts provided

Can compete with the "big players" in cyberspace

Net Losses: Need some knowledge of HTML and/or technical skill

Must design site yourself or hire a Web designer

Takes more time and money to set up

May charge additional fees for merchant accounts, secure server, and shopping cart

THE CHAT GOES ON

Still confused? "Go with stability," suggests Kathleen Driggers, owner of HerWebHost.com. She points out that free sites are great services for personal home pages, but that a business needs faster speed and a more stable image. "Free hosts pack a lot of sites on each server," she says, "and this slows down the loading time. Most paid hosts have to limit the number of sites per server." As far as image goes, your domain name is your online identity. "If you're serious about doing business on the Web, your goal should be to get your own domain name," advises Maryland mompreneur Dottie Gruhler, founder of HerPlanet.com. "It projects a more professional image than a subdomain name and makes it easier for Internet users to find you."

On the other hand, if you're not quite ready to make a financial commitment, a free site may be a good way to get a taste of cyberspace. Shirley McKinney, founder of Fantasy Cards/Cottage Row Graphics, started small and gradually moved up. "I didn't want to drain the family resources," she recalls, "so I began with a free site and when I built up my traffic base, moved to my own domain." It's also possible to reroute a subdomain name through a company like eNom.com. This allows you to bypass the free host's name in your URL and use your own domain name.

Website hosting is one of those rare fields in which the phrase "You get what you pay for" doesn't always apply. Hosts with lower monthly fees may offer the same features, tech support, and speed as those that charge three or four times as much! Bottom line—it pays to comparison-shop. Wisconsin Web designer Jean Lentz has a last bit of advice to offer: "Don't sign up with a hosting service that requires you to commit for a long period of time. Things change so often that today's good deal may become tomorrow's bad one in six months."

CLICK AND SAVE: *Mom-to-Mom Hosting*

Some of our favorite mom support networks and home business sites offer webhosting for reasonable monthly fees. To find out if these are right for your e-Biz, ask for referrals and contact other mompreneurs who are using their services.

>> *www.behosting.com*

>> *www.herwebbiz.com*

>> *www.herwebhost.com*

>> *www.homeworkingmom.com/join.htm*

>> *www.momsnetwork.com*

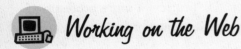 *Working on the Web*

MOMPRENEUR: Brigitte Thompson, Williston, Vermont

e-BIZ: Datamaster, LLC, an accounting service. Her website provides tax tips, a newsletter subscription, and information about her book, *The Home Daycare Complete Recordkeeping System.*

URL: www.angelfire.com/biz/datamaster

HOST: Lycos' Angelfire

COST: Free Web design, free hosting

SITE SPECS: 5 MB of space, clip art, photos, links, banner or pop-up ads

CLICK-ABILITY: When Thompson first thought about making a website, she was completely lost. Knowing nothing about the mechanics of site building or the different hosting possibilities, she went on the Internet to do some research. While online, she met a Web designer who offered to create a one-page site for her on Angelfire. "Once I got a feel for how it worked, I dove right in and created several more pages," says Thompson. "I've now built sites for other people and revised my own a few times." With Angelfire's user-friendly templates, it was simple for Thompson to design a customized website and establish links.

Angelfire charges no fees, which is "wonderful" for Thompson's small, informational site. There's a limit to the space she's allocated, but this mompreneur thinks it's generous enough. "I haven't even used one-eighth of the total space and I've uploaded hundreds of images and files," she says. Nor has Thompson found any drawbacks to the subdomain name or banner ads that come with the territory. Her site is listed with the major search engines, and the chosen ads don't bother her. However, she does suggest that before signing on with other free hosts, it's smart to check with the ISP to make sure that adult-rated ads will never appear on your site.

Eventually, Thompson wants to set up a merchant account for her business and will probably have to switch to a host that offers a secure server. But in the meantime, she's quite content. "Unless a business is completely dependent on Internet sales, I would recommend using a free host to test the waters," she says. "You can always copy and paste your site to another server as your business grows."

BREAKING GROUND IN CYBERSPACE

You've registered your domain name, lined up a host, thought up some design ideas, and are ready to take out your virtual hammer and nails and construct your site. Go ahead and start building—if you're using a prefab template and toolbox from one of the hosting companies. You simply plug in the text and graphics you select, and the Web tools handle the HTML coding for you. Be sure to keep our "Click and Save" list of online resources (page 149) close by, in case you hit a pothole or two on the cyber-highway! And don't launch the site until you're really satisfied with the way it looks (see "Web Dialog" box, page 150).

If you're acting as your own "general contractor" or are subcontracting the work out to a Web designer, it's smart to become a little more tech-savvy before you break ground. Mompreneur Linda Caroll, who specializes in designing browser- and platform-compatible sites, agrees. "With the abundance of website creation software on the market and Internet, almost anyone can design a website—often without even looking at the 'code' behind the design." But, Caroll warns, when people create sites without a basic understanding of HTML, they are often unaware of these technological trouble spots:

■ HTML code may not work the same way with all Web browsers. It's important to make sure your Web pages are compatible with the most current Netscape, Internet Explorer, and AOL browsers on both Mac and PC

■ Not all colors are available on both Mac and PC platforms

■ Not all screen resolutions are formatted alike

■ HTML fonts may not be compatible with default computer fonts, and your site won't look the same to all viewers

■ Some Web design software adds superfluous code that slows down the loading time of a site

■ Some software may not add *meta tags*—those all-important pieces of HTML code that help search engines find your site.

Knowing this much "tech talk" can help you impress a Web designer with your questions! If you plan to go that route, see "How to Hire a Web Designer" on page 154 for more tips. If you decide to be a do-it-yourselfer, your next step is to get your hands on Web design software and learn how to use it. Jean Lentz, mother of two boys and owner of White Forest Software in Wisconsin, suggests enrolling in a class (either on- or offline) and/or buying a book that teaches one of the popular website design packages. This will probably turn out to be a less expensive way to go, but "you must have the time to spare and a high frustration level. It's for the ambitious and adventurous only," Lentz adds with a laugh.

YOUR VIRTUAL WELCOME MAT

Viewers really don't "read" on the Web—they browse. Your *home page* is what will tempt them to put on the brakes and "park" in front of your domain and stay a while. You just have a few nanoseconds (about 15 to 30, say the experts) to grab a surfer's attention and get your message across. To do so, opt for a crisp, uncluttered home page that comes up on the screen quickly, clearly explains the purpose of your site, and speeds viewers toward their destinations. Choose simple words and images that will "sell" your e-Biz to window shoppers. And if you want vistors to get past your "storefront" to explore some of your offerings, your site must look and be easy to navigate. "If a website fails to provide what the visitor is looking for, the browser's back button is right there, right now," says Web developer Linda Caroll (www.lindacaroll.com).

CLICK AND SAVE: *Website Design Help*

>> *www.coolhomepages.com*

>> *www.digital-women.com/toolbox.htm*

>> *www.dotcommommies.com/webdesign.html*

>> *www.hwg.org*—HTML Writers Guild

>> *www.veryclever.com*—examples of well-designed pages

>> *www.webmonkey.com*—website design resources/tutorials

>> *www.worstoftheweb.com*—examples of poorly designed pages

>> *www.zdnet.com/ecommerce*—downloads to build Web pages

Web Dialog

We called on Caroll and other skilled Web design mompreneurs for their thoughts on how to give a site top "visitor value." They've all learned through personal experience and lots of hard work just what makes for a winning website. . . . and what doesn't.

* **Fast Loading Time:** Surfers are an impatient bunch! If your home page takes more than 25 seconds to load, many won't hesitate to move on to another site.

    What can slow down loading time? Pages filled with too many graphics, animated images, plug-ins, and/or pop-up windows. To make matters worse, many viewers are connected to the Web by super-slow dial-up modems. So keep your home page eye-catching but simple. Linda Caroll says it all: "On the Internet, you seldom get a second chance to make a good first impression."

* **Clean, Colorful Design:** "Create a good balance between graphics and text," advises Dottie Gruhler of *HerPlanet.com*. Text-heavy sites look boring and graphic-crammed pages take too long to load. "Avoid large, gaudy images, huge fonts, and garish back-grounds," adds *HerWebHost.com's* Kathleen Driggers. "The simpler the design, the more usable the site is." There are two basic image formats used on the Web—*GIF* and *JPEG*. GIFs are recommended for graphic images and JPEGs for photos. As far as layout goes, "Keep it consistent from one page of your site to another and organize the pages in a logical way," says Gruhler. And don't overrun your site with flashing icons and banner ads—too many in one place looks tacky.

* **Concise, Catchy Content:** Content is king on the Net—it's what separates a so-so website from a successful one. Viewers are looking for good information—not sales letters, repetitive catalog pages, or cute dancing images (whose cuteness wears thin quickly!). Your goal is to provide well-written (and spell-checked!) copy points about your product or service, your qualifications, and what makes your business unique. Web expert Jean Lentz, founder of *www.whiteforest.com,* warns against being too wordy. "Web pages should display kernels of information with links to other pages on your site where visitors can easily go if they need more," she says. Headlines, bulleted lists, and short paragraphs can lead viewers to more detailed descriptions.

* **Easy Navigation:** Visitors to your website are "in the driver's seat" and should be able to cruise through your pages without getting lost. "This requires intelligent use of navigational bars or buttons, icons, and menus," says Lentz, "making it possible for a visitor to get from any one page to another in a maximum of three clicks of the mouse." If navigation is confusing or complicated, visitors will drive off your site in search of others.

* **Interactivity:** Quizzes, surveys, contests, freebies, newsletters, and other interactive devices add to the "visitor value" of your site and will encourage viewers to come back for more. "At the very least, I think it's important to offer a feedback or contact form so visitors can easily get in touch with you," feels Driggers. The big bonus—these intereactive features allow you to capture e-mail addresses and other information about present and potential clients or customers for future marketing efforts.

* **Page Headings and Keywords:** Placing a *title* on each page of your website helps the search engines direct surfers to your e-Biz. For example, in our case, the home page title may read "Mompreneurs: Work-at-Home Businesses for Moms," and another page can be titled "Mompreneurs: Home-Based Jobs for Moms." The words you choose in these titles are known as *keywords*. Following the title should be a few sentences explaining that page, using the same keywords plus others that best describe your business, products, and/or services. These keywords are also known as *meta tags* and are written in HTML code.

   Meta tags are what the search engines look for and use in listing your website, so use multiple keywords and mention the most important ones first and frequently. (It's not a good idea to use the word "the" first, even if it's part of your business name.) You can sprinkle the same keywords throughout your home page—either in visible or invisible text (HTML coders know how to "hide" keywords so the search engines can see them but viewers can't). Graphics should get *alt tags*—a word or two of text that the search engines can identify and match with your site.

* **Frame With Care:** Some designers use frames to display several sections of different Web pages at the same time. "If you're not an HTML wizard, you run the risk of frames that don't display all the content, or that can't fit in the viewer's monitor," cautions Linda Caroll. "Worse yet, search engines can't index frames properly and surfers may find your interior frames listed while the navigational information is in another frame." It's important to have navigation buttons or bars on every page so they're in front of the viewer at all times. Another problem with frames is that they don't always print properly, frustrating a visitor who is trying to print a page from your site to keep for reference.

* **Updates:** Keep your website fresh. "Change the information on your site regularly so you don't bore visitors," recommends Dotty Gruhler. This can be as simple as having an updated "Timely Tip" or "Weekly Special" on your home page, or a current list of resources related to your services or products.

* **Linking:** Exchange links with other websites to help drive traffic to your site—a boost in traffic can boost your ranking within the various search engines. When visitors click

on these "live" hyperlinks, they're automatically transported to another website, and vice versa. Choose links that are related to your business or otherwise beneficial to your viewers, recommends Jean Lentz. For example, a parenting e-zine may link to an e-tailer selling childproofing gadgets. When you incorporate links into your Web design, have them open in a separate window, says Kathleen Driggers. "You don't want visitors surfing off your site and never finding their way back!" (See "Top Ten Marketing Moves" in Chapter 7 for more on linking.)

★ **Marketing Power:** Your site is part of your brand identity, and should project the same professional image as your business cards, letterhead, and other marketing materials. In turn, your URL should go on all your offline materials, including letterhead, cards, flyers, brochures, and mailing labels, as well as the digital signature file you attach to your e-mails. (See Chapter 7 for tips on creating a signature file.) "A well-designed website can be your most faithful employee," says Caroll. "It can greet your customers and clients, answer their questions, and process their orders . . . twenty-four hours a day, three hundred sixty-five days a year!"

Mother of Invention

When artist Shelly Kennedy decided to "take a serious approach to a lot of creative 'fooling around' over the years," she turned to the Internet. The result is Drooz Studio (www.drooz.com), an online gallery for the one-of-a-kind canvas wall hangings she designs for babies' and children's rooms. Kennedy creates all of the handpainted 4-by-5-foot "movable murals" and smaller customized banners in her home-based studio, photographs the results, and "mounts" them on her website.

THE INSPIRATION: When daughter Chloe was born in 1998, Mom and Dad wanted to decorate her nursery in a unique way. Unable to paint the white walls of their rented apartment, Kennedy "muraled" the ideas onto a large piece of canvas and hung it on a wooden dowel. "When we moved to our first home, we took down the well-loved mural, rolled it up, and hung it back up in Chloe's new room on the very first night. It made her feel so secure and comfortable."

Kennedy realized she was onto a business idea. Although she would have to price her heirloom-quality pieces on the high side, she felt that parents wouldn't mind investing in beautiful artwork that could easily be moved from house to house and passed down from generation to generation. Husband Marc Strang, an art director who was learning Web design, dreamed up the "ultimate job"—a website featuring Kennedy's wall hangings that would allow her to work with complete artistic freedom *and* be home for her children. (Chloe's brother Clark was born a year later.)

THE NAME: Little Chloe actually chose the business name. "At eighteen months, Chloe loved to express herself artistically but wasn't able to pronounce many words," says Kennedy. "She collectively referred to all her art supplies—crayons, chalks, and paints—as 'drooz,' so we reserved drooz.com for our domain."

THE DESIGN: Browsing through www.drooz.com is very much like walking through a real gallery, thanks to the easy navigation, welcoming design, and gorgeous images. Strang designed the site and a photographer friend took the pictures. Together, they created a feeling of childlike whimsy, very much in keeping with Kennedy's artistic themes. And since Daddy is the webmaster, it's easy to make changes to the site and update the content right from the home computer, working with their amenable hosting company, Webstream.

THE CHALLENGES: To make sure the site loaded quickly, images had to be kept small—a problem when you're trying to show off detailed, original artwork that measures 4 by 5 feet. "We tried to convey the scale of my pieces in a two-inch stamplike image, but some people missed it," says Kennedy. Strang solved the problem by inviting visitors to click on each wall hanging to enlarge it on the computer screen. Another challenge—getting listed in the search engines. Kennedy found it took forever, and then some of the listings were incorrect. "I filled out my server's form, using ten keywords—such as 'nursery decorating,' 'baby bedding,' and 'cribs'—to cover cross-merchandising possibilities, plus a brief twenty-five-word description."

THE LEARNING CURVE: It took about six months for www.drooz.com to be listed (the host server said three to twelve weeks!) and Kennedy still couldn't find her company under some of the keyword searches. Her advice—register with the search engines early and post a "Coming Soon" notice at your URL if your site isn't up yet. Kennedy realized that great customer service was key to turning browsers into buyers, so she added a bit of extra personal contact at www.drooz.com. "I now try to talk personally by phone with every client and always include a handwritten thank-you note with every purchase," she says. "I also send out color swatches when requested. These wall hangings are expensive purchases, and customers deserve a little pampering." As far as long-term survival goes, Kennedy has learned the importance of not being too trendy. To give her artwork "staying power," she uses classic, timeless themes and tries to stay away from "commercial" images.

THE REWARDS: "I love being able to reach people (or have them reach us!) from all over the world while I basically run the business from my basement floor," says Kennedy. And being home with Chloe and Clark is terrific . . . though challenging at times. She now schedules separate play sessions when everyone can paint or draw together so the kids don't get into "mommy's work," and she's learned to put important papers and supplies out of the reach of little hands. "I have to be super-organized so this week's huge order from the West Coast doesn't turn into next week's grocery list," Kennedy says, laughing.

HOW TO HIRE A WEB DESIGNER

For some mompreneurs, spending money on a Web designer is well worth it—it can save time and energy *and* result in a polished product. And it doesn't have to cost a fortune. "Check out a local school or training center to see if an instructor would be interested in using your business as a class Web design project," suggests Wendy Willard, owner of Willard-esigns.com in Maine. "Or seek out recent grads or young Web development businesses—they may be offering discounted services so they can start building a portfolio."

What if you decide to go with a seasoned pro—how much should you expect to pay? "Fees vary quite a bit, depending on the artistry, scope of the site, and degree of interactivity," says Joy Rotondi-Cann of www. foodies.com. "The initial conception, images, and navigation are the 'spendy' parts of Web design." Wendy Willard also admits that pricing is hard to pin down, but offers these ballpark figures: "If you hire an individual or a small design firm, it can cost anywhere from fifteen hundred to twenty-five hundred dollars for a small informational and marketing site to between two thousand and seven thousand dollars for an active e-commerce site," she says.

Webmasters charge a more modest monthly or quarterly fee to refresh Web content—a task that can take a big chunk of time out of your schedule. However, some mompreneurs feel it's very useful to learn how to maintain and update a site themselves. Michelle Mix, creator of the More About Me™ Emergency Information Kits (www.emoreaboutme.com), says, "My biggest mistake was relying on someone else to maintain my site. It almost put my business in jeopardy." Unfortunately, Mix's webmaster never followed through on the updates she sent him, but continued to bill her. After many months of frustration and fighting, Mix finally took control of the site into her own hands.

Of course, you can spend thousands of dollars more on a website launch if you go with a large, well-known design company, and considerably less if you get a package deal from a hosting service. What's most important is finding someone who shares your style and vision *and* fits into your budget. Word-of-mouth (or word-of-e-mail!) referrals are usually most reliable. The tips that follow, courtesy of Web designer Wendy Willard (www.willardesigns.com), will help you choose the best fit for your e-Biz.

■ Be prepared. Formulate an idea of what size and type of website you want before you talk to any Web designers. Then create a *Request for Proposal (RFP)* document outlining exactly what you want the individual or design group to accomplish. This will help assure that everyone involved is on the same page from Day One.

■ Set up a budget. Figure out how much money you can afford to allocate to the project. To come up with a realistic amount, contact e-Business owners or webmasters through their websites or in an online networking group. Then formulate a budget that covers a fairly broad price range, and expect to get bids on both the high and low ends.

■ Check the portfolio. Experienced designers all have a portfolio of websites they've developed. Ask for a roster of projects that were similar in size and scope to yours, and view them carefully. Find out exactly what tasks were performed by the Web designer, and in what time frame.

■ Contact references. A good designer should be willing to share references with prospective clients. Call at least three or four former clients, and ask if the work was done satisfactorily and within the promised time. You don't want to get involved with a designer who has walked away from projects midstream or not delivered what was expected.

■ Communicate with your designer. The more your designer knows, the more customized and effective your site will turn out. Relate details about your business, such as your major competition on the Net, your target audience, and what sets your business apart. Talk about the text, images, links, and meta tags that will enhance your site and decide who is responsible for providing what. You may even want to sketch out a rough plan with pencil and paper.

■ Sign a contract. Make sure everything is in writing, including the agreed-upon fee, date of delivery, and responsibilities of both you and your designer.

Working on the Web

MOMPRENEUR: Louise Larson Janke, Trempealeau, Wisconsin

E-BIZ: Tutor House Children's Software, an online company that reviews and offers top children's computer software programs, helping parents make informed choices

URL: www.tutorhouse.com

HOST: Adgraphics, Boston

COST: $2,800 for design (courtesy of Paragraphics in Washington State); $59/month hosting

SITE SPECS: 11 MB, logo, clip art, photos, search features, newsletter, shopping cart

CLICK-ABILITY: Although Janke is in the business of selling high-tech software, she wanted her website to look friendly and fun—more of a "help site" than an e-commerce site. Since Tutor House is totally Internet-based, Janke decided to go with a professional designer who could help her stand out in the cyber-crowd. She also realized that she "couldn't do it all," and preferred to focus on building her business instead of learning HTML at the local technical college!

To find a designer, the Wisconsin mom of two got several referrals, visited many sites, and began corresponding by e-mail with Janet Crosby of Paragraphics. "I wanted to make sure she was friendly and flexible," Janke says, "and would understand the image I wanted to convey. Through our e-mail 'conversation,' I could 'feel' that she had the right personality for the job." The two actually negotiated the whole deal, exchanged design suggestions, and divvied up tasks electronically!

Before signing on with Paragraphics, Janke researched Web design fees and found them to be "all over the place—everywhere from five hundred to twenty thousand dollars" for her size site. Crosby's initial project fee of $2,800 and her $200 monthly charge for updates seemed reasonable—especially with all the personal service she provided. The designer took care of the order forms, shopping cart, and links, and recently listed the site with various search engines; Janke periodically feeds her new written reviews and product shots. Tutor House's host provides a secure server and forwards orders, but Janke arranged for her own merchant account. And that was another lesson in itself! "I ended up paying too much for a merchant account at first because I was afraid I wouldn't be accepted anywhere else," she recalls. "Then I worked up the courage to go to my local bank, got the account, and now pay only four dollars a month, instead of forty-eight!"

E–COMMERCE BASICS . . . AND BEYOND

Have you ever been so put off by the confusing layout and unfriendly atmosphere of a brick-and-mortar store that you just turned on your heel and walked right out? On the Internet, you can "surf away" from an e-Biz without so much as a dirty look from a salesperson! This means you have to work that much harder to please visitors so that they actually make the transition from "window shoppers" to paying customers or clients—and then return for many more trips to your site. An appealing home page is the first important step (see "Your Virtual Welcome Mat" on page 149.) But make sure the rest of your website provides a hefty dose of customer service, treating visitors to all the right e-commerce essentials, *plus* a few nice frills.

$ Be upfront about security, shipping, and ordering

to make shoppers feel comfortable right from the start. Post a message on your home page explaining that your site uses a secure server for credit cards, and direct shoppers to your privacy policy (which should be included on a nearby page of your site; for more on this, see Chapter 6). Provide links to another page where customers can find a chart of shipping and handling costs so they'll know exactly what's involved *before they're ready to place an order.*

$ Merchandise goods creatively

but make them easy for shoppers to locate. Group thumbnail images (small graphics) of products on your Web pages; viewers can click on these to enlarge them for more detail. Display similar items together for smoother navigation. Keep descriptions concise but informative, and don't bury the price tags!

$ Provide a search feature

to help shoppers quickly locate specific products without scrolling through your entire database. You can organize the search by product name, category, price, and/or manufacturer.

$ Install a shopping cart

for customers to conveniently pick up items as they meander through your electronic store. Clearly state how shoppers can just as easily *remove* items if they change their minds!

$ Keep your inventory updated

to prevent out-of-stock items from being tossed into the shopping cart. Arrange for an accessible product database with your hosting service so you can easily add and subtract merchandise and change prices.

$ Make the checkout process hassle-free

or shoppers will abandon their carts and surf out of your site empty-handed. Provide a simple order form with clear, courteous instructions for completing the purchase. Use a built-in system to calculate the total amount owed—including shipping, handling, and taxes—before requesting a credit card number.

$ Set up a merchant account

for credit card customers. Choose a Payment Gateway/Merchant Bank Package so credit card approval and payment is all in one system on your site. Because the credit card business is super-competitive and the differences among rates, setup costs, and transaction fees can be mind-boggling, shop around for the best deal. If your business is service-based or has a tiny inventory, you may opt instead for an online credit card processing company like iBill.com or abanx.com. Keep in mind that these may take a larger percentage off the top. Some sellers are going with Paypal.com, which enables them to accept checks and money orders.

$ Secure credit card transactions

through your ISP or host. Make sure your webhosting service or processing center offers an SSL (secure sockets layer) server, which enables credit card information to be encrypted or "scrambled" before it's sent over the Net.

$ Offer a printable order form or toll-free number

for visitors who are hesitant about ordering over the Internet. They can have the same shopping experience, then send in their order by fax, mail, or phone.

$ Send out an e-mail confirmation

to immediately let a shopper know that the order has been received. A built-in auto-responder can take care of this task; be sure to include a complete record of the transaction (order number, item(s) ordered, shopper's name, shipping address, and total amount of sale).

$ Pride yourself on customer service

Send out follow-up e-mails (personal, if possible) showing the progress of the order and shipment. Include your customer service e-mail address and toll-free number on all correspondence. Post all your contact information—including mailing address, phone and fax numbers, and e-mail address—on a highly visible or accessible place on your website, and clearly state your return policy.

$ Personalize with perks

Extras like gift wrapping, birthday reminders, coupons, discounts, and special promotions for loyal customers are always appreciated. (See Chapter 7 for more ideas.)

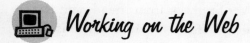 *Working on the Web*

MOMPRENEUR: Melissa Caust-Ellenbogen, Columbus, Ohio

E-BIZ: Pinultimate, a company specializing in one-of-a-kind pins crafted by artisan jewelers

URL: www.pinultimate@yahoo.com

HOST: Yahoo! Stores

COST: $100/month for "store rental"; $45/month for Merchant Credit Card

SITE SPECS: 50-item inventory limit, Yahoo's credit card vendor (BankOne), shopping cart, logo, photos, search feature, 6 MG e-mail space

CLICK-ABILITY: Zeroing in on a domain name can be an out-of-this-world experience, as Caust-Ellenbogen discovered. She began by brainstorming name ideas with her family and a few friends, and came up with 10 or 15 possibilities. After testing out the choices on various people for ease of remembering, the list was narrowed down to a few strong candidates. "I was casting about for a way to select 'the winner' when a friend unexpectedly offered me an appointment with her psychic," she recalls. "I showed him the list and asked if he had a good feeling about any of the choices. He picked Pinultimate!"

Caust-Ellenbogen took a more down-to-earth approach to her website design. She turned to Yahoo's user-friendly storefront templates and built www.penultimate@yahoo.com on her own, occasionally calling on a techie friend to come in at critical junctures. She bought a digital camera, photographed all the handmade pins and brooches herself (finally figuring out that a tripod made all the difference between amateur results and professional quality!), wrote product descriptions and artist bios, got a business license—the whole works.

During construction, Caust-Ellenbogen learned a lot by hunting and pecking around the Web, seeking advice. "Yahoo is particularly good about answering questions—they get back to you within eight to twenty-four hours," she says. "And they offer a ten-day test drive prior to the official launch, so I was able to get feedback from friends and family—including my two teenage children!" If the site didn't fly, this self-proclaimed "trial-and-error person" knew she could always go back to the drawing board.

On the whole, Caust-Ellenbogen is satisfied with her Yahoo! Store. Pinultimate is included in Yahoo's shopping directory, and at such a busy portal, this can be a big traffic-builder. A flexible month-to-month commitment and no upfront payments mean better cash flow. And automatic notifications and updates to customers eliminate some "paperwork." The downside is that if she decides to expand, Pinultimate will have to jump up to a 1,000-unit Yahoo! Store, costing about $300 a month. And Caust-Ellenbogen doesn't appreciate the lack of gift certificate processing or the fact that her site is often "buried" in Yahoo's shopping search. But for the time being, "The Pinwoman" is sticking with what she has, even though a number of smaller hosting services with lower monthly fees have tried to change her mind.

VIRTUAL STORES NEED REAL WAREHOUSES

Some mompreneurs have built successful e-shops selling jewelry, scented candles, or spice blends—products that take up little storage space. Others stock a limited inventory, like single-subject books or silk-screened T-shirts. With these kinds of goods, warehousing and shipping headquarters can be a garage, basement, or spare room of the house. Jeanette Benway's basement shelves are stacked with Cozy Rosie® polar fleece stroller blankets. Louise Larson Janke of www.tutorhouse.com stores her software programs in a small outbuilding on her property and hires high school students to help send them out during busy times. But what if you're selling hand-painted children's furniture or rebuilt computers from your website? These take up a lot more shelf space than candles or earrings!

How can you tackle the storage and shipping dilemma? Drop-shipping is one answer, if you're dealing with products made by manufacturers that offer that service. For example, a gift site selling merchandise that may be ordered from various vendors may want to contract with those that will drop-ship to customers. Terri Vincent, a partner in eStore 2000, says, "Lots of smaller companies are willing to drop-ship, but you have to do a bit of legwork to locate them." She suggests looking under "Drop-ship" on the different search engines to find these companies.

Another option is to outsource the warehousing and shipping. Fulfillment companies are popping up online and off to meet the growing demands of e-commerce. These services warehouse your products and take care of shipping, handling, and receiving. But before you sign up, check out a company by asking these questions:

- How large is the warehouse space?

- Will my merchandise be stored in its own separate area?

- How will I be billed for storage? By number of items, square footage, or another method?

- How does the company charge for receiving and shipping? By the piece or by the hour?

■ Does the service offer a choice of carriers, including UPS, FedEx, and the U.S. mail?

■ Will the fulfillment house e-mail me shipping and receiving reports? Or will I have to use another form of communication?

■ Is the warehouse fully insured for fire, flood, and theft?

To find a fulfillment service, ask for referrals from other virtual store owners and click on our resources in the Dot.Com Directory (page 271).

 *Web Celeb*

Carley Roney
Cofounder and Editor-in-Chief, The Knot, Inc. *(www.theknot.com)*, AOL Keyword:
    Weddings
New York City
Mom of 1

It was the nightmare of planning her own wedding—plus the desire to smooth the way for other brides and grooms—that inspired Carley Roney to create The Knot. "Couples who are getting married need lots of information within a tight deadline," she says. "The Internet is a perfect fit." Roney and her partners (husband David Liu and two good friends from film school) realized that their target group was perfect, too—young, Internet-savvy people who are anxious to communicate with others in the same prenuptial boat. Since the partners feel "community is what weddings are all about," they included message boards and chat areas in their website plans.

In 1996, Roney took her firsthand experience and unique vision and set out to reinvent the way couples plan their weddings. She started with the name. "Our mission was to provide a fresh take on the whole event, so we didn't want to use the words 'marriage' or 'wedding' in our domain name." Roney came up with "The Knot," and it was a go. The website's design also broke with tradition—no roses and doves to turn off trendier viewers! Instead, speed was an important element, and the site was designed to be simple and clean for fast loading. The Knot was poised for success—it had just the right blend of content and community, a round of funding from AOL, and a running start in its e-market (the bridal magazines lagged far behind)! It didn't take long for it to become the most popular online wedding resource.

Since its initial launch in 1997, the website's design and content have evolved to meet the needs of its audience. Soft colors and a clear layout project a pleasing mix of romance and practicality. The resources are much more extensive, and the content now has an inviting personal touch. "Brides wanted to know there was a face behind the site and be able to 'hear' my own story and opinions," Roney says. The interactive "Ask Carley" section delivers just that, providing a nice balance of personalization and professionalism. Here, brides and grooms, their families, wedding guests, and interested others can get expert advice on dilemmas ranging from "I'm very close to my brother's ex-wife—should I invite her and her new beau to the wedding?" to "How do I preserve the top layer of my wedding cake so we can enjoy it on our first anniversary?" Information is updated daily to keep visitors coming back for more.

The e-commerce component of the site has greatly expanded, too. In 1998, The Knot launched the first full-service gift registry on the Internet, offering top brands and tasteful choices to suit everyone's pocketbook. As of 2000, e-shoppers could find over 10,000 handpicked products using the registry's search feature. More interactivity has also been introduced. Brides can click on and view over 15,000 gowns in every style and price range; tools for guest lists, planning, and budgeting are readily available; couples can create their personal wedding album Web page; and an increasingly active community keeps the message boards and chat rooms hopping.

After Roney authored *The Knot's Complete Guide to Weddings in the Real World* (Broadway Books, 1999), traffic to the site doubled. Several more books and magazines followed, all with the goal of extending and reinforcing the online brand to an offline audience. It's a winning strategy—by 2000, The Knot was employing about 250 people and was able to stake the claim of being "America's #1 online wedding destination." That distinction caught the attention of producers from NBC's *Today Show,* and in the fall of 2000, Roney coordinated a live, on-air wedding for a lucky couple voted in by viewers. "The *Today Show* was looking for a twenty-first-century approach to weddings, and online planning is very fresh," says Roney. Choices for everything from the bridal gown to the honeymoon location were posted on the Web, and visitors logged on to pick their favorites. "Today Ties the Knot" was a major success all around.

In 1997, during one of the company's most intense growth phases, Roney gave birth to her daughter, Havana. After the crazy hours of an Internet start-up, "sleep deprivation wasn't new to me!" says Roney. "And my mother-in-law was (and still is) my number one key to success. I never had to worry at all about child care, and that's a defining factor." While Grandma watched the baby, the brand-new mom was busy launching the site's gift registry. The Knot had 60 days to get it online—an impossible feat for any small e-Biz, especially one with a four-month-old infant on board! "When we were finalizing the product selection for the registry, I was on a conference call to California and nursing Havana at the same time," she remembers. "I didn't want the callers to hear her cry, and at that moment I whispered to myself, 'If they could only see me now!' "

Grandma still watches Havana, who is too young to actively participate in the business but "has the most sophisticated wedding vocabulary for a child," according to her mother. Roney also credits her supportive, hardworking staff with making it possible for her to juggle the responsibilities of work and motherhood without getting totally stressed out. "My husband is part of my secret weapon, too." she admits. "He understands what's going on with the business and keeps me sane." Although she's best known for giving brides and grooms helpful, down-to-earth advice, Roney offers up some valuable words of wisdom for mompreneurs as well: "Be realistic about your expectations as a mom and an entrepreneur, and think about when and how you want your business to grow. Set your priorities and don't grow for the sake of growing—a small, manageable business can be very successful and fulfilling."

CHAPTER SIX

Master of Your Domain: Protecting Yourself in Cyberspace

 Sound Byte

"There is little regulation and protection for businesses on the Internet and I have had to learn many hard legal lessons. Because this is still a relatively new arena, I have encountered lots of problems along the way, and had no recourse or resources to turn to for assistance."

Andrea Milrad, mother of two; Deerfield Beach, Florida
Owner of Little BIG Man *(www.littlebigman.org)*

As the Mompreneurs®, one of our most valuable business possessions has been our catchy name, which we were careful to trademark and use in commerce way before we popularized the term with the publication of our first book. Yet even with trademark protection, we have found many individuals and businesses "borrowing" the word "mompreneur" for their own profit in cyberspace.

The Web is a little like a vast uncharted sea, where pirates can easily rob you of your business riches. At greatest risk is your intellectual property—the creative concepts, inventions, and products that are the essence of your business and likely to be proudly displayed on your site for all to see (and, unfortunately, sometimes steal).

As you stake your claim in cyberspace, you must vigilantly guard your intellectual property and business and personal assets. It's equally important to respect the intellectual property rights of others, and to insure the privacy of all who come to your site. As legislators rush to create new laws to protect Web business owners and consumers, there is likely to be a slew of court cases down the road related to Internet rights and privacy issues.

The legal considerations can be complex when you're doing business on the Web, but we'll help simplify them. We'll show you how to safeguard your enterprise through the use of copyrights, trademarks, insurance, and other protective measures. But remember: Things move at light speed in cyberspace, so some of what we've written may already have become obsolete in the time it took to publish this book. Therefore, we urge you to consult with your own legal counsel and check the "Click and Save" sites we've featured throughout the chapter to keep current on cutting-edge developments.

IDENTITY CRISIS

Your business name and logos are your hottest commodities. With millions of companies vying for traffic on the Web, you want yours to stand out so that clients and customers can easily find you. Your business name (and its accompanying domain name, which ideally should be the same) is your brand. It must be unique, and convey your special mission. Most important, the name must not infringe on someone else's trademark.

Just because you register a domain name doesn't mean you have the right to use it as your business name, cautions D. Jennings Meincke, an attorney in Laguna Beach, California, who specializes in patents, trademarks, and copyrights for entrepreneurs. If your domain name conflicts with a trademark, you could be forced to give it up, and you run the risk of being sued for infringement. So before registering any domain name, you should do a trademark search to make sure that someone else doesn't already own the rights to the word or phrase you want. (We'll show you how to search and register a trademark in "® Marks the Spot," page 174.)

If the name has not already been trademarked, you should strongly consider filing for a federal trademark. It's a costly step, but well worth the investment. "Trademarks are becoming more and more important for business owners to have," notes attorney Harvey S. Jacobs, an expert in

Internet law and intellectual property and managing director of the Jacobs and Associates law firm in Washington, D.C. As the Web gives your business universal exposure, a trademark provides comprehensive protection. With a federal trademark, your business and product names cannot be used by anyone else in the U.S. for a similar purpose without your permission. A trademark also gives you the power to defend your name against infringement in federal court, if necessary.

"A trademark helps you secure your place in the great dot.com gold rush," Jacobs says. "If you own the trademark to your business name, you should be able to trump any domain holder who tries to use it." With a trademark, you have access to the new dispute resolution proceedings established by ICANN (the Internet Corporation for Assigned Names and Numbers), the group that oversees all domain names. The arbitration process is designed to help you recover your rightful domain name in the event it's been registered by someone else and used in bad faith. (See "Defending Your Good Name," page 176.)

WHAT'S IN A NAME?

Pick a name that clearly defines your product, service, or audience. When searching for a name for her online coupon and resale shop, Anne Fognano of Leesburg, Virginia, considered words that would describe budget-conscious parents without offending them. "Many of the names I wanted were already taken, like 'thrifty,' 'budget,' and 'smart,' " she recalls. She thought the phrase "cheap moms" portrayed her audience, but didn't think it sounded very nice. So she got out her thesaurus, looked up synonyms for "smart," and spotted the word "clever." "I wanted moms to feel good about being moms, so Clevermoms.com was perfect!" Fognano says.

Kim Martins DeYoung of Metromom went through three names before deciding upon one that was best for her maternity-wear site. Her first name of choice was "Interlude," and she had garment labels made before checking whether that name was being used by any other company. "Big mistake," says DeYoung. It turned out that there was already a lingerie company with the same name, and DeYoung's attorney suggested that lingerie and maternity clothing could potentially conflict if the lingerie company decided to expand its product offerings. Fortunately, she hadn't yet produced too many tags, "but it was still aggravating and a waste of time and money to correct the mistake," DeYoung says. After more careful research, she decided upon "Metromom," which she says sums up her customer even better than the previous names she considered.

When Terri Bose registered the domain name for her kids' crafts site, MakingFriends.com, she was amazed that it was still available. She was even more surprised when many men commented that it sounded like a pornography site, and as a result considered changing the name to Free Kids' Crafts. But when she ran a survey on the MakingFriends site, she found that 97 percent of her audience said they liked her original name. Bose kept MakingFriends, and has since incorporated it; but she also purchased the other domain name, too, and has started a companion site called FreeKidsCrafts.com.

When you name your business, think carefully about any hidden meanings. When Robyn Zimmerman and Tracy Scudder of Paris, Texas, teamed up to become party consultants for 1800Partyshop, they thought they'd choosen a name that was "cute" and "easy to remember." So they called themselves the Paris Party Girls. They got their website up and running and were amazed to see that they had a huge wave of traffic without even advertising. "We just thought we were fabulous businesswomen," says Zimmerman. But then they noticed that despite the heavy traffic, they had no sales. In an effort to promote their business offline at a local art festival, Scudder called the organization that was hosting the fair. Using her most professional voice, she began her business pitch: "Hi, my name is Tracy and I'm with the Paris Party Girls. We specialize in 'Theme Parties in a Box,' and would like to find out about purchasing space at the art fair." An appalled voice on the other end of the phone answered: "Ma'am, this is a family event. . . . with children! What's this about jumping out of a box?" The Paris Party Girls were flabbergasted, but soon realized that their business name implied a different line of work than they'd intended it to! And it became clear why the site was generating no sales. Talk about a business with a buzz! "I don't think anyone will be forgetting us anytime soon!" says Zimmerman, laughing.

CLAIM YOUR NAME!

What do you do once you've narrowed down your choices? Follow these steps to selecting and safeguarding your business and product names.

1. **Check Domain Availability.** Go to any of the domain registration sites, such as NetworkSolutions.com, NameSecure.com, NetNames.com, or Nameboy.com, and search to see if the name you want is already registered. If it's available, you can register it now, but keep in mind that you'll need to choose something different if it turns out to be trademarked.

2. **Do a Trademark Search.** To make sure no one already owns the trademark to the name you want, do a trademark search before proceeding further. (See details in "® Marks the Spot," page 174.) If you're interested in trademarking the name, start the process.

3. **Buy In Bulk.** If you haven't done so already, register your domain name at one of the domain registration sites. Also consider purchasing any domain name that is remotely similar to yours. When she saw that Metromom.com was available on Network Solutions, Kim DeYoung grabbed it, and also registered Metrodad.com, for good measure. In addition, she registered the.org and .net versions of Metromom, and is in the process of trademarking it. Barbara Spangler of Reflections Safety Mirrors bought several near-miss domain names to insure that if people misspelled her name they would still get to the right website. In addition to Clevermoms.com, Fognano bought Clevermoms.net, and Clevermom.com. "You don't want someone else cashing in on your name and your hard work," she says. But if you have an idea for a name, don't bounce it off anyone you don't know or trust, Fognano adds. "I told a stranger at my ISP that I was planning to buy a domain name that sounded similar to Clevermoms. He must have hung up the phone and purchased it himself, because the domain name was registered within four hours of our conversation!" she says. "That site is now getting my default traffic, so people who forget our site name and make an educated

guess will end up there instead. My big mouth has landed someone else a successful site from my misdirected traffic!"

MORE LEGAL BASES TO COVER

Before you start running your home-based e-Biz, you'll also need to do the following:

■ **Decide on Your Business Structure.** Will it be a sole proprietorship, partnership, corporation, or limited liability corporation (LLC)? For more details on business structure, see "Another Safety Net: Your e-Biz Structure," page 195.

■ **File Your Name with Your Local Government Office.** If you are going to operate the business under a name different from your own, you'll need to file a fictitious name statement, also known as a DBA (for "doing business as"). This is usually done through your county clerk's office.

■ **Secure Necessary Permits and Licenses.** Business license and permit requirements depend on where you live and what you do. For example, food businesses need to comply with Board of Health regulations. Check with your local and state governments to see what licenses and permits you might need.

■ **Check Local Zoning Laws.** Just because your business is "virtual" doesn't mean you're allowed to set up shop from home. Check with your city or county government (usually someone in the planning or building inspector's office) to make sure there are no zoning laws restricting home businesses. Also check with your home owners' association or co-op board. Some neighborhoods are stricter than others. Before launching her accounting service, Datamaster, Brigitte Thompson had to pay a fee, report to a meeting, show blueprints of her home and office, and address parking concerns, potential noise disturbances, and other burdens on the neighborhood.

Lesson Learned:
File Domain Name Registration Forms Yourself!

Mistake Made: When Andrea Milrad hired a local webhosting company for Little BIG Man, her custom birth announcement and invitation business, domain name registration was included as part of the deal. So she let the company register *littlebigman.org*, without realizing that the Web host also claimed ownership of her site on the paperwork. It wasn't until some time later that Milrad discovered the error, after she had become dissatisfied with her Web host's service and had decided to go with a new company. When she went to Network Solutions to change the name of the Web host, she saw that it was listed as owner of the site. "I don't know if it was an honest mistake or done deliberately," Milrad says. "Maybe they were going to try to sell the site back to me if it took off," she speculates. But there was one thing Milrad knew for sure: "I wanted my site back!"

Legal Recourse: Milrad began calling and then writing to the original Web host, who ignored her pleas to transfer the ownership. The procedure would require the Web host to notarize a new registration form, giving control back to Milrad. Milrad informed the webhosting company that she would simplify the process by bringing a notary public to its office. After her relentless phone calls, the company finally agreed, and the change of ownership was made without any further hitches.

What She'd Do Differently: "If I ever create another domain name, I won't trust anyone else to register it for me," Milrad says. So many things could have happened as a result of the mistake. "The Web host could have decided to close us down at any time, and I wouldn't have been able to do a thing about it. Or they could have let the domain registration renewal lapse." What's the moral of Milrad's story? Retain complete control of your site—your livelihood depends on it.

Advice From an Expert: "This is one of the most common pitfalls I see," says Philadelphia attorney Mark G. McCreary of the firm Fox, Rothschild, O'Brien and Frankel, who advises Web-based entrepreneurs on intellectual property rights. When you enter into an agreement with a webhosting agent, it's very important to stipulate in writing what belongs to you, McCreary emphasizes. Make sure you document that the domain name and all the content on the site (including Web page coding) is your property, not the host's. It's safest to register your domain name yourself, he adds, so there's no confusion over who is the rightful owner of the site. "The domain name sites make registration so easy to do, and it only takes a few minutes of your time."

® MARKS THE SPOT!

It's not necessary to officially trademark your business or product name—
you have common-law trademark protection from the time you begin
using it to identify your goods or services in commerce. But federal trademark registration strengthens your rights to your name and makes it
much easier to keep other people from using it in a way that confuses your
customers. It also prevents others from suing you for infringement.

What Can Be Trademarked?

Any name, logo, symbol, or slogan used to market a product or service can
be trademarked, as long as it is "distinctive" rather than merely "descriptive." For example, "mompreneurs"® is unique and distinctive, while
"work-at-home moms" is merely descriptive. Technically, a trademark protects words or phrases used in marketing a product, while a service mark
covers those related to a service (such as marketing or consulting). But
both are commonly referred to as the "trademark," or the "mark."

Is It Available?

Make sure the word or phrase you want has not already been trademarked
by doing a free online preliminary trademark search at the United States
Patent and Trademark Office (USPTO; www.uspto.gov) or through NamePro-
tect.com (www.nameprotect.com). If this limited search indicates that the
name is clear, you'll need to do a more thorough search before filing for
your trademark. It's best to have a trademark attorney help you with this
more extensive search.

On Your Mark, Get Set . . .

Download registration forms from the USPTO site. When registering a
trademark, you should be already using the mark, or be close to using it,
in commerce. There are two types of trademark applications: "use-based"
and "intent-to-use." If you haven't yet used the word or phrase in inter-

state sales or services, file the intent-to-use application. If you've already been using the mark, you can file a use-based application.

On the registration form, you will need to indicate what class of goods or services you're going to use the trademark for. For example, if you're an online coach, you'd register your trademark under "Education." Someone who creates kids' Halloween costumes would register under "Clothing."

Since different companies can have the same trademark in noncompeting categories, it's probable that you will not own the trademark to your name for all purposes, points out Jacobs. That means your domain name might already be legally taken by another trademark owner without you having any recourse. Though it can be pricey to trademark in multiple classes, you should register for any category that is directly related to your business, so that you can give your mark the broadest protection possible in this Internet age. It's wise to consult with a trademark attorney before filing, to determine which categories will best cover your name for the future. Trademarks cost $325 per class, and can take two years or more to become official. You can begin using the TM symbol from the moment you file your registration forms. Trademarks need to be renewed between the fifth and sixth year and then every 10 years after that.

Use It or Lose It

You can't just file your trademark and assume your name is protected, warns Jacobs. "Registration doesn't give you automatic rights to a trademark," he explains. You must use the mark in interstate commerce to secure your rights to it. It's also important to be on the lookout for anyone infringing on your trademark, either online or off. If you don't make an effort to stop people from using your trademarked name or logo, you could be charged with "abandonment of your trademark," Jacobs says, and wind up forfeiting your rights to the name. Do frequent searches of your business and product names with the major search engines and have your attorney send "cease and desist" letters to anyone using your trademark without permission. Jacobs also suggests signing up with free online name-monitoring services, such as NameGuard, found on www.nameprotect.com.

Respect Others' Property

If you're using another business's trademarked name or product on your site or in marketing materials, you'd better have permission to do so. Otherwise *you're* likely to receive a "cease and desist" letter. When Terri Bose featured costumes kids can make for their Beanie Babies® on her crafts site, MakingFriends.com, she got a letter from Ty Inc. asking that she remove them.

Be especially careful that you do not use any trademarked names in your domain name or in the meta tags and keywords that lead search engines to your site. These also constitute trademark infringement.

DEFENDING YOUR GOOD NAME

Has someone already registered a domain name that's identical or confusingly similar to your trademark? You can try to get it back through ICANN's Uniform Domain Name Dispute Resolution Policy. The arbitration process takes about two months' time and approximately $1,000 to $2,500 in fees—much quicker and more cost-effective than taking someone to court. The dispute policy was implemented after Congress passed the recent Anti Cybersquatter Protection Act, designed to curb speculators from registering trademarked or famous names as domain names, and then trying to sell them back to the owner or another third party for a profit. After someone snatched the domain name juliaroberts.com and tried to sell it on e-Bay, the actress was able to win back control of her electronic address. But you don't have to be a celebrity to claim what's rightfully yours. The arbitrators are ruling in favor of trademark owners, many of whom are ordinary digital moms like you. But you must be able to prove that your domain name is being used in bad faith.

For more information and to file a complaint go to www.domain-magistrate.com.

CLICK AND SAVE: *To Protect Intellectual Property Rights*

>> *www.cybercrime.gov/ip.html* The Justice Department's guide on Intellectual Property Rights.

>> *www.icannwatch.org* Keeps you posted on new domain name developments

>> *www.inta.org* International Trademark Association

>> *www.ipnetwork.com* Helps you determine licensing deals for your name or invention

>> *www.loc.gov/copyright* United States Copyright Office

>> *www.nameprotect.com* Offers online trademark searches and application services, a referral network of trademark attorneys, and a free trademark monitoring service

>> *www.uspto.gov* United States Patent and Trademark Office

>> *www.wipo.org* World Intellectual Property Organization

DO YOU COPY?

Your business and product names aren't your only valuable intellectual property. Any original content you create and display on your website—from text descriptions to artwork to articles to graphics—is automatically protected under copyright law from the moment you create it. You can post a copyright notice on your work without officially registering for copyright. But if someone plagiarizes your material, you won't be able to defend it in litigation unless it's been formally copyrighted through the U.S. Copyright Office. "Although it can be very time-consuming, I highly recommend it," says Brigitte Thompson of Datamaster accounting services, who has registered the copyright on all of her works. Registration costs $30 per application, and you can easily download the forms from the Library of Congress (www.loc.gov/copyright).

Milrad, of Little BIG Man, copyrighted her name, logo, graphics, and designs, and is in the process of trademarking her business name. "I copyrighted every single piece of my work, since each one is unique. That way, people are legally prohibited from copying my invitations or announcements on their own computers," she says.

Unfortunately, plagiarism is rampant in cyberspace. "I worry that if I put my catalog online, people will just copy my patterns," says craftsperson Susan Neiberg Terkel, who designs decorative knobs for cabinets. So rather than showcase and sell her knobs on her site, GobsOfKnobs.com, this mom of three from Hudson, Ohio, uses her site to direct customers to the stores that sell her creations.

"I think that because the Internet puts so much information at your fingertips, people feel that what they see on the screen is theirs for the taking," says Lori Thompson of AttachmentsCatalog.com, an online gift catalog celebrating breast-feeding and natural parenting. "It's very simple for someone to cut and paste your words or download your images," the freelance photographer and mom of two from Bremerton, Washington, adds. Thompson specializes in taking pictures of babies nursing. However, she has found that breast-feeding advocacy professionals have been downloading her images from her site and incorporating them into their brochures or slide presentations without her permission. "I will usually allow nonprofit groups to use my photos if their mission is akin to mine and as long as they list my name, copyright notice, and a link to my site. But they can't take my work without asking!" she says with frustration. Thompson says she has friends who have had their entire website source codes duplicated and used by competitors to build similar sites. That's why it's important to copyright the code of your site, as well as its contents.

Anne Fognano of Clevermoms.com says that there are people who get her newsletters, edit out her affiliate codes, insert their own, and then send them out to their own members. "When you work all day putting together great deals for a weekly newsletter and then see that someone has stolen your work to profit from it, it is really heartbreaking," Fognano says.

If someone is disreputable enough to steal and then disguise your work, there's little you can do, admits Juliette Passer, an attorney in Manhasset, New York. But there are preventative measures you can take to thwart outright theft. Here are some suggestions.

Declare Your Rights

Display copyright notices for all to see on every page of your site. "They should appear frequently enough so that it becomes difficult for pirates to rob your work," advises Passer. Milrad puts her copyright notice on every single invitation and announcement she creates. "Sometimes I come across customers who don't want my copyright on their invitations, but I explain that it needs to be there, and I let them choose where I put it," she says.

Thompson puts the notice, © 1997–2001 Lori Thompson Photography, on every page of AttachmentsCatalog.com. She also lists this friendly announcement on her "About our photos" page: "It never fails. Each time I go to a conference, someone will tell me they just saw one of my pictures in a slide show during the previous session. I'm always surprised to hear this, as I don't make my images available as slides for presentations unless I have given specific permission. My cards have my copyright mark on them, but it seems that people don't understand the implications of using a copyrighted photo for personal use. It's just not OK to use anyone's copyrighted images without asking permission. And you know what? If asked, I will almost always say yes! It's easy to go to a website and download an image right into your own computer, but that doesn't make it OK. I do liberally give permission to breast-feeding advocacy sites and other information sites to use my photos, but if you have a retail sales site, I don't allow the use of my photos unless you are selling my cards! I don't mean to be grumpy, but my work is my livelihood. Please respect it and ask before you download."

Alert Copycats

Terri Bose says she's found her content duplicated all over the Web, mostly on small sites. She'll e-mail webmasters and ask them to remove it. "They usually comply," she says.

For Web writers, plagiarism is particularly problematic. Brigitte Thompson, who authored *The Home Daycare Complete Recordkeeping System* (sold at her website: www.angelfire.com/biz/datamaster), has had two people take her book and sell it as their own. The books were slightly modified, but the format, layout, and most of her actual wording was still included. "My lawyers sent formal letters hinting of copyright infringement, but I have no idea if that made an impact," Thompson says. "Anything you put on the Web could be taken by another person. And anything printed can be photocopied or retyped and printed out. I have had to come to terms with the fact that some people are so unscrupulous that no matter what I do to protect my work, they will have no qualms about using it as their own."

Diana Ennen, author of *Words From Home: How to Start and Operate a Home-Based Word Processing Business,* once had a woman e-mail her asking for her free booklet on attracting clients. "She had an extensive list of questions, which I gladly answered, since many people often contact me for help starting their business," Ennen says. This mompreneur later found out that her "e-friend" subsequently produced a manual very similar to hers and set up a directory of nationwide word processors on her website that was nearly identical to Ennen's. "I was able to resolve this with a simple but powerful e-mail," Ennen says. "I informed her that I would contact my attorney if she continued to market her manual." That was all that was needed. "I believe she thought she could get away with it. But now that my name is getting around on the Internet, I've made friends at chats and online message boards who let me know quickly when they spot someone else copying my work," says Ennen.

Stay in the Loop

Having a strong network of contacts is essential for guarding your material from copycats. We've often had mompreneurs e-mail us when they see that an individual or company is using our trademarked name to sell their own products or services. The Web is way too big to patrol on your own, and other moms will often spot infringement before you do. Anne Fognano belongs to a network of coupon sites owned by moms who watch out for each other. "We all recognize each other's style and let each other know when our work has been copied, so we can report it to our affiliate programs," she says. "Fortunately, our affiliates are very good about dumping people who steal other site owners' work."

Of course, you must keep your own eyes and ears open too. Shannon Rubio of TheSmileBox.com regularly goes to search engine sites to make sure that none of her competitors are using her information. "In fact, the other day, I went to a competitor who I have heard has three million dollars in venture capital funding," she says. "There were about three lines of text which I have no doubt came off my page! I read it and thought, I wrote that! But what can you do? It's a product description, and very hard to prove. At least I know the 'big guys' are watching me," Rubio says.

Click-Proof Your Work

There are a number of tech tools you can use to discourage people from downloading or cutting and pasting your creations. For example, Fognano programmed a script onto her site's pages that prevents viewers from clicking and saving her images and stealing her graphics. Lori Thompson uses PhotoShop to embed an invisible code into her photographs. If someone copies them, the code appears, making it difficult for the photographs to be used elsewhere.

Watch Your Step

Just as you protect your own copyright, you must make sure that the material on your site does not infringe on the copyright of others. If you didn't create it, you should *not* post it without permission from the owner of the work. When Rubio wanted to use some photographs from a specific manufacturer on TheSmileBox.com, she e-mailed the company first, asking if she could use the photos in exchange for a credit line. "They were very nice about it," Rubio says. "I always try to use common sense when deciding what to put on my site," she says. "If you wouldn't want this copied from your site, don't copy it from someone else's!"

When featuring anything that belongs to someone else, make sure you include that person's copyright and/or trademark notice. Because Cynthia Bungard runs an antifraud site that helps protect collectors of Beanie Babies, Barbies, and other toys, she frequently features those products. So she also puts the following copyright notice and disclaimer on her site,

Traderlist.com: "Ty Beanie Babies, Disney, or Mattel do not endorse or support this site in any way. Individual Beanie Baby graphics are copyrighted by Ty, Inc.®"

Barbara Spangler of Reflections Safety Mirrors feels that the best way to keep from infringing on others' copyrights is to be original. "I write all the content for my site, and then check to make sure it doesn't resemble any copy on sites featuring similar products to mine," she says.

PATENT POWER

If you've come up with a clever new invention like many of the mompreneurs in this book, you'll want to protect it with a patent to prevent others from manufacturing or marketing your idea. But the procedure is complicated and costly, warns patent attorney D. Jennings Meincke. Before you rush into patenting your invention, you should do lots of research to make sure it's a worthwhile risk. Meincke suggests several steps for assessing and protecting your great idea.

Document Your Invention

Put a description of your idea down on paper, along with any relevant drawings or sketches. Include your name, date, and the date the idea was conceived; then have a trustworthy witness sign and date it. Also keep a record of any changes you make to the invention as you develop it. This information is best kept in a notebook and stored in a safe place. For added protection, it's wise to keep another copy of the notebook in a separate location.

Keep Your Lips Sealed!

If you suspect you have a winner in the works, don't tell anyone you can't trust. Not only do you risk someone's stealing your idea, but if you disclose the invention publicly before filing a patent application, it could limit your rights. If you must talk to people about the idea (such as vendors or manufacturers), have them sign a nondisclosure agreement promising that they will keep it confidential. (An attorney should draft this.)

Do Your Homework

To be awarded a patent, your idea must be "novel and not obvious," says Meincke. It must be different from anything else already patented and have some new, unexpected, surprising, or better results than other items or processes, he explains. You'll need to do a thorough patent search with the United States Patent and Trademark Office (www.uspto.gov) to check whether similar patents have already been awarded. Though you can do the patent search yourself, be prepared for a lot of time and legwork.

Start With a Provisional Patent

A provisional patent is a preliminary patent application that buys you some time to refine your invention before plunking down big bucks on the more expensive and complex utility patent application. But a provisional patent must be followed up by a utility patent application within a year, in order to secure protection for your invention. A provisional patent provides two major benefits. Most important, it establishes a filing date for your invention. This is key because "in a patent fight, presumption is always on the side of the person who filed first," says Meincke. The provisional patent also allows you to use the "patent pending" notice on your product to notify others that you have filed for a patent and are protecting your idea. A provisional patent costs just $75 to file, as opposed to a minimum of $355 for a utility patent.

Get Legal Help

Patents are extremely complicated, and you shouldn't try to file one on your own. But you can cut your legal expenses by doing much of the preliminary work yourself and then having a patent attorney assist you with the reviewing and filing of the application. Your attorney fees can run anywhere from around $500 to $1,000 or more for a provisional patent, to several thousand dollars for a full-fledged utility patent. "The more educated a client you are, the less expensive your legal costs will be," notes Meincke. "Make sure your attorney asks specific questions about your business plan and goals so that he or she can help you do strategic intellectual property protection," he advises. "You want to work with professionals who are interested in your business and how it's going to grow."

THE TRIPLE WHAMMY

Sometimes your business idea should be covered under patent, trademark, and copyright laws, Meincke says. "For example, a website that does something new may be entitled to get a patent for its innovative business method, a trademark for the website name and logo, and a copyright for the design and content of the website."

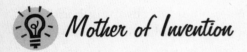 *Mother of Invention*

One hot July afternoon in 1999, April Deckert placed her five-month-old son Brady in his crib for a nap and went downstairs to fold laundry. "I heard a strange, muffled whine, but thought it was coming from an animal outside," recalls the mother of five from Arendtsville, Pennsylvania. A few minutes later, she heard the noise again, and went to check on her sleeping kids. When she walked into Brady's bedroom, she found him tangled up in his crib sheet, which had come loose from the mattress. "He was motionless, and wrapped so tightly that you couldn't even tell there was a child in the bed," Deckert says. She screamed and called her baby's name as she unrolled him from the sheet, but he was unresponsive. Then, suddenly, Brady opened his eyes. "I stood there for the longest time just crying and holding him," Deckert says, "thanking God that he was OK. After I recovered from my initial shock, my first thought was: How on earth could this have happened?"

A seamstress by trade, Deckert immediately went to work to make something to remedy this hazard. Her solution? A crib sheet anchoring device called Baby Sleep Safe™, which keeps standard crib sheets firmly in place to prevent entrapment and suffocation. It's now sold for $19.99 on her website, www.babysleepsafe.com, which launched in January 2000.

While protecting babies is her mission, Deckert says that protecting her product idea was essential, too, if she was going to save lives. "I knew I had never seen anything like it on the market, and I was sure it was something parents needed. So I didn't want to breathe a word of my idea to anybody," she says, for fear they'd steal it and come up with an inferior, less effective product. Yet, in order to bring an invention to market, it is necessary to talk about it somewhat. Here are Deckert's tips for getting a product off the ground while still safeguarding trade secrets.

SHIELD YOURSELF WITH WEB RESEARCH. The Internet allows you to do your homework anonymously as you explore whether your idea is worthwhile. Deckert's first stop on the Web was the United States Patent and Trademark Office, where she searched the database to see if there were any similar ideas already patented. "I searched under every phrase I could possibly think of that might be related to my idea, such as 'sheet anchors,' 'sheet clips,' and 'infant safety,' " she explains.

PROCEED WITH CONFIDENCE AND CAUTION. When Deckert was making the prototype for Baby Sleep Safe, she had trouble finding fastening clips that were strong enough, and had to call various manufacturers for free samples. When asked, "What do you need them for?" she simply replied, "I can't tell you that—I'm still in product development." She suggests identifying yourself as the "president" or "owner" of your company, so that you'll be taken seriously. Otherwise, you'll be perceived as an amateur and won't be able to get the supplies you need to create your great idea.

KEEP PATENT LANGUAGE VAGUE. As soon as you have a prototype, file a provisional patent to protect the idea for a year until you file your official utility patent. "You want to so broadly define your product that you end up with a halo of protection around it," making it more difficult for someone to steal and copy it, says Deckert. For example, instead of describing the specific components used for Baby Sleep Safe in her patent, Deckert used generic terms like "strap" and "attachment device." Don't let the patent process intimidate you, she adds. "There's so much you can do on your own." She saved considerable legal fees by doing much of her patent research and writing herself, and then having her attorney review what she'd written and make necessary changes.

GET FINANCIAL BACKING. A safety product invention takes big bucks to get off the ground. Deckert found invaluable financial and business support from a Pennyslvania organization called Ben Franklin Technology Partners (www.benfranklin.org), which was recommended by her patent attorney. After presenting her business plan to its board of directors, she was awarded $63,000 in start-up funds. The money will help cover the cost of safety testing so that she can establish her product as one that meets stringent manufacturing and performance standards. (Not only is this essential for a baby product, but it's key for finding affordable product liability insurance. Product liability insurance is required when you're manufacturing any product that will be touched, used, or consumed. For more information on liability insurance, see "What Insurance Do You Need?" later in this chapter, page 199).

BUILD A TRUSTWORTHY TEAM. Surround yourself with professionals who share your vision and can offer optimistic but realistic advice. Deckert's close-knit team includes her accountant, patent attorney (whom she found by searching the list of registered patent agents on the USPTO site), and business attorney (who handles the incorporation process and division of shares). She also values her Pennsylvania-based manufacturer, whom she found by going online to the Thomas Register (www.thomasregister.com) and looking under "Sewn Goods" and "Sewing Contractors."All of her team members agreed to work without payment until the product became profitable. "I've been blessed with advisors who believe in my cause and have been so sharing with their advice. Hopefully, together we can help save families from tragedy," Deckert says.

MORE INVENTIVE STRATEGIES

Sell on Mommy-Owned Sites

Innovative mompreneurs are doing more than just creating imaginative products. They're launching e-commerce sites for mothers of invention, which can be great showcases for your ideas. For example, at Inventive Parent.com, New Hampshire mom Sharon Mullen sells juvenile products that have been created and patented by parents. Judi Cohen of Martinez, Georgia, invites manufacturing moms and dads to submit their parenting products to her e-commerce site, WeBehave.com.

Look Into Licensing

Think about venues that best suit your product and mission. When Judi Cohen first started manufacturing 'Lastic Laces, squiggly elastic shoelaces that don't need to be tied, she emphasized how they were "a blessing" to the physically challenged. Thanks to her niche marketing, 'Lastic Laces were licensed by the 1996 Atlanta Paralympics, and have been approved for licensing by the Special Olympics.

Broaden Your Scope

Find offbeat ways to position your product. Though she started out selling invitations and birth announcements to parents, Andrea Milrad of Little BIG Man is now branching out into corporate markets, which are far more lucrative. "I can do five thousand corporate invitations in the same time it takes to do forty birth announcements," she says. But she's extra-careful to protect her trade secrets. "I'm always a little hesitant about pitching my ideas to companies' creative services departments," Milrad says. "I feel like if I reveal too much, they can take my designs and use their own equipment and resources to develop something similar. It's a tough position: Do I hold back and risk losing the business? It's something I continuously struggle with."

SECURITY SYSTEMS

While trademarks, copyrights, and patents help protect your creations, they won't tamper-proof your website. It's important to utilize as many protective measures as possible on your site to make it "less hackable" and to insure the privacy of your customers and clients, urges attorney Juliette Passer. She suggests you take the following precautions.

Use The Tools

Safeguard your site with technology. Use firewall software programs (such as Norton Internet Security) to prevent outsiders from breaking into your computer system and hijacking your data. Antivirus software that you update regularly is also a must. And don't forget to implement backup systems in the event your computer crashes. All of these are high-tech ways to avert disaster and the liability issues that can accompany them.

"You must also be a gatekeeper for your site," Passer emphasizes. "It's your responsibility to regularly check the links that appear on your website to make sure that the content is suitable to your mission and not offensive or harmful to your audience." If you don't have the time for this, hire a tech-savvy teen to handle it for you, she suggests. Also consider purchasing insurance (see "Insuring Peace of Mind," page 197) to cover equipment, loss of service, and professional or product liability.

Curb Credit Card Fraud

Many consumers still get anxious about using their credit cards online. "Yet customers want the security of knowing that you accept credit cards," notes Ann Allen of WearableMamas. To protect your customers and yourself from credit card theft, use a secure server featuring SSL (secure sockets layer). List your mailing address and phone number prominently on your site so customers can verify orders. And be sure to post information on how you safeguard customers' credit card information.

Lesson Learned: Guard Your High-Tech Ideas

If you've come up with a unique way to conduct business on the Web, apply for a patent quickly, recommends Diana West, creator of Mothers' Online Thrift Shop *(www.motshop. com),* an e-commerce site for the resale of new and gently used mother and baby goods. "When properly protected, your innovative business methods can be a gold mine," says the Gaithersburg, Maryland, mother of three.

This high-tech mama should know. Her site was the first to utilize a business method called the Virtual Consignment technology and business model, which she claims to have invented and is in the process of patenting. A variation on the auction format, the technology enables online consumers to buy and sell directly from each other. But shortly after her site launched, another site began using the same technology to sell books, toys, and games. Before she knew it, she was forced to fight for her intellectual property rights. Here's how her bright idea became the center of a dot.com dispute.

From Sleepless Night to Innovative Concept. The idea for Mothers' Online Thrift Shop came to West in the middle of the night as she soothed her teething baby. "As I rocked Ben, I began thinking about the significant level of business for resale products I was seeing at online sites like eBay and Mother's Nature," she says. From her own auction experiences, West knew that the prices were often inflated and unaffordable for parents on a budget. "It's much cheaper to buy at a thrift shop, yet many moms don't have consignment stores in their neighborhood," she says. She dreamed of a Virtual Consignment store, where moms could buy and sell used baby clothes and equipment.

A Brand-New Baby Is Born. With the help of her tech-savvy husband, Brad, West created *Motshop.com* and funded it with personal resources. But a few months after the site launched, West discovered that a larger and very well-funded Internet start-up company was using identical technology on its website.

Patents Take Time. Unfortunately, the other company also claims to have invented the technology, and has filed for a patent. It could take three to four years before West finds out whether she is awarded hers. But she's confident that she'll eventually be recognized as the sole owner of the technology, and can then begin to license it to other companies. In the meantime she's comforted by the fact that even home-based moms can brainstorm big-business ideas. It took the other company millions of dollars and a huge staff to come up with this technology, she says. "What makes us feel really good is that Brad and I implemented the same technology on a shoestring budget, on nights and weekends, while always putting our family's needs first."

Lesson Learned: Guard Your High-Tech Ideas, continued

Advice from an Expert. The inventor who first conceives the business method is considered the rightful owner of the technology, says Mark Joy, a patent attorney with the Chicago-based firm of Leydig, Voit and Mayer. That's why it's extremely important to keep detailed notes on the development of your invention. "As soon as you conceive an idea, put it in writing and have it signed by a trustworthy witness," he urges. There's a record number of applications for "cyber-patents" being filed now, he says, because up until recently, business methods, computer software, and other tech tools were not considered patentable. But since these applications won't show up on a U.S. patent search until the patents are officially issued (which could take two years or more), an inventor has no way of knowing whether another company is developing something similar. However, you might get a hint of whether a patent has been filed for in the U.S. by checking international patents called PCTs, Joy says. Foreign patents are processed more quickly than those in the U.S., and American inventors will often apply for their U.S. and international patents simultaneously, he explains. Besides doing a traditional patent search through the USPTO, Joy recommends you check the Delphion Intellectual Property Network *(www.delphion.com)*, which has sources for checking PCTs.

Paula Polman of Mossberry Hollow Natural Care Products uses a secure payment processing service which looks after the management, approval, and collection of credit card funds from sales on her site. (For advice on finding a secure server, see Chapter 5.) "I post their URLs on my site so my customers can see who I am using and what their credentials are," she explains. "It's a nice service for someone in a small business, and it minimizes the risk of fraud. They do a better job at security than I could, and it's one less banking headache for me to manage," Polman says. Lori Thompson of AttachmentsCatalog.com has a regular merchant account with a brick-and-mortar bank, and processes all credit card transactions on a terminal separate from her computer, using an address verification system provided by her bank.

But even with a secure server and a credit card merchant, you can still be vulnerable to credit card theft. "We have to do a lot of work to make sure that the sales are legitimate, which is much harder online when there is no credit card signature," says Shannon Rubio of TheSmileBox.com. While consumers are not held liable for purchases over $50 made with a stolen card, online merchants are generally expected to absorb fraudulent charges. That's why Rubio always checks the name, e-mail, address, and phone number on all orders to make sure they match. "If I have any doubts, I call the person to be sure that they're aware an order is being placed in their name. So far, we've had only one bad order," she says.

Sometimes you have to trust your instincts, agrees Kim Martins DeYoung of Metromom.com. She thought it was strange when she heard her business phone ringing in the wee hours at 3 A.M. It turned out to be a hang-up call, but the next morning she had an order of over $700 of maternity clothes from Louisiana. Yet the billing address was in Texas. What's more, the unusually large order included nothing in black (the color most popular with pregnant women). "My intuition told me something was wrong," DeYoung says. When she tried to process the credit card, it wouldn't go through. Wanting to give her buyer the benefit of the doubt, DeYoung called, but still didn't have a good feeling about the transaction. So she contacted her Merchant Service Account, which was willing to process the order anyway. "I asked who would be liable for the cost of this merchandise if the credit card turned out to be stolen," she says. The answer? "I would have been responsible. And I just can't afford that."

Credit card companies are coming up with protective solutions for consumers, which could ultimately benefit business owners as well. Fairly recently, American Express unveiled its "Private Payments" service, which gives its customers single-use disposable credit card numbers for Web shopping. And Visa is testing payer authentication technology that will enable customers to sign sales receipts electronically.

Request Payment Upfront

What if your site doesn't take credit cards? Brigitte Thompson doesn't have a secure server, so she only accepts checks. And she's had several bounce over the years, even though her book costs only $22.50. "Now I verify all funds before I ship orders," she says.

Protect Privacy

"Your website is very much like a contract with the public," says Passer. You must not only be careful of what you put on it, but you must reassure your visitors that their privacy will not be compromised. Terms of Agreement and Privacy Policies state your responsibilities to your consumers and must be clearly visible on the site for all to read. And if your site is geared to kids, be aware of the Children's Online Privacy Protection Act, which requires you to get parental consent before collecting personal information from kids under 13.

Polman makes it very clear upfront how she handles complaints or problems with any of the natural care products she sells. She emphasizes that products are shipped only after payment has cleared. And every page of her site has a link to her privacy policy so customers don't have to search for it. "Privacy policies protect you and your customers by stating what you intend to do with any client information you collect," she states. "Without a privacy policy you cannot inspire confidence or provide a satisfactory level of customer service."

According to Passer, "There are two tricks to privacy policies." First, never promise anything you'll regret later. Second, state your current procedures but explain that the privacy policy could be updated without notice. Anne Fognano wrote the privacy policy for her coupon and resale site with help from recommendations on the Better Business Bureau website. "Basically, our privacy policy promises that no personal information will be released on any member unless they buy or sell an item on our boards," Fognano says. "We need to be able to notify buyers and sellers when their transactions go through," she explains, "or they'd never know whether their item was bought or sold."

Barbara Spangler's privacy policy reads: "You may rest assured that any information you provide will be held in confidence and not sold." Spangler says, "I try to be honest with people and say what's necessary in the simplest way I can." She had her attorney approve her draft before she officially posted it.

Provide Freedom of Choice

You must give visitors the ability to decide whether or not they want to be on mailing lists, Passer says. Invite them to sign up for your newsletters or other marketing materials through opt-in clauses. But also make it very easy for people to unsubscribe when they wish. Polman's customers can remove themselves from her newsletter by typing the word "Remove" in the subject line of the e-mail. "Our free coupon newsletter is a hundred percent opt-in," says Fognano. Shoppers do not receive e-mails unless they specifically choose to do so, and they can unsubscribe at any time.

Do not send unsolicited bulk e-mail to clients or customers, or sell your mailing lists to any third party. "You never want to be labeled a spammer!" warns Rubio. And besides, an antispam law now prohibits the sending of unsolicited e-mail and gives online consumers legal recourse when their privacy has been violated.

"Although it's a great way to get repeat business, I do not send out mass e-mails of any sort," says Brigitte Thompson, who offers a free e-mail newsletter with tax tips. "They only get mail from me if they sign up for it on my website," she says.

Use Disclaimers Where Necessary

Disclaimers help clarify the limitations of your service or products, and protect you in the event of a lawsuit. They are particularly essential if your site features services or products related to kids, health, safety, cosmetics, sports, or any other area where liability could be high. But mompreneurs in all fields find them helpful. Fognano has a legal disclaimer on her site indicating that Clevermoms.com is only a vehicle for surfers to find coupons, and that all transactions are between the merchant and the customer. Because Brigitte Thompson's book, *The Home Daycare Complete Recordkeeping System,* is based on federal tax law, she alerts readers that her information could be invalid if the laws change after publication.

But use disclaimers sparingly, urges Passer. "Too many can make you look disreputable." It's best to consult with an attorney when writing disclaimers. "They need to be worded in a way that makes it clear that the consumer is using the product or service at his or her own risk," Passer says.

Don't be afraid to be "bold and honest about your products," says Spangler of Reflections Safety Mirrors. She posts this disclaimer on her site: "Notice: This product may not fit all rear view mirror mounting brackets or columns." She then features a drop-down menu listing the types of cars the mirror *will* fit on. "Remember that you cannot control what happens to your product once it leaves your hands," she adds. "Do not allow any room for prosecution." Spangler's product also carries the following warnings: "Use of this product may not be legal in all jurisdictions. Check your state/local laws for legal restrictions. Please use caution in the use of this product. Please drive carefully."

Put Agreements in Writing

Use contracts and letters of agreement to confirm deals with clients, customers, consultants, and other businesspeople. For example, Judi Cohen of WeBehave.com has written agreements with the vendors on her e-commerce site giving her permission to feature their parenting products.

Make sure that contracts clearly spell out each party's rights and responsibilities. Even though Rubio runs TheSmileBox.com with her mom, who's an attorney, "we messed up early on," she says. When hiring a local agency to do website design and marketing, they signed a contract that was much too vague. "We ended up having to sue the company, and swore that we would never again sign another contract without all the details covered," Rubio says.

When negotiating with Web developers, try to get as much ownership over your site as possible by specifically allocating what is yours and what is the developer's, advises Passer. Even if your site utilizes very sophisticated tools that are only available from that Web developer, you should still try to negotiate some exclusivity to keep the developer from duplicating the layout and other features of your site for your competitors, she says. Passer also suggests you always ask for a "royalty-free, worldwide, perpetual license." This way a developer can't come back after your site takes off and claim that you owe money.

"You can create a lot of paper (and paper-free!) trails to help cover your legal bases," according to Passer. For example, if you and a client discussed the details of a project over lunch, follow up with a friendly e-mail note afterward, confirming your conversation and agreement. Most e-mail programs allow you to activate an automatic receipt function, so you have proof your mail was delivered; and many will even indicate whether the e-mail has been read. Though e-mail contracts are becoming widely used now, it's always a good idea to back up the e-mailed version with a hard copy containing your signature, Passer says. "Even if you're striving for a paper-free office, you should at least keep a file with just the signature pages of contracts. The rest of the document can be stored electronically."

ANOTHER SAFETY NET: Your Business Structure

You can give your e-Biz added protection by the way you structure it when starting up. "When you're doing business on the Internet, you have more contact with people, so there's more chance for liability issues to occur," says Richard Oster, an attorney with Business Filings Incorporated (www.bizfilings.com). There are many ways to structure your business, and some provide more protection against lawsuits than others. The form your business takes also has important tax implications.

Sole proprietorship is the quickest and cheapest way to get started, and is a common choice for mompreneurs running low-risk, service-based enterprises on their own. You and your business are considered one legal entity, and your income and losses are reported on your federal income tax return (Form 1040, Schedule C). However, you will personally be responsible for all business debt and liability. If you should get sued by a client or customer or incur business-related debt, creditors can come after all your personal assets, including your home, car, bank accounts, and investments.

A *partnership* is a nonincorporated business with one or more owners who share in the funding, running, and profits of the venture. Similarly to sole proprietorship, you and your partners report business income and losses on your individual tax returns. A partnership allows you to team up to share talents, resources, and responsibility. However, if your co-owner gets into business-related legal or financial trouble, you must accept blame, too, and your personal assets will be at risk.

Deborah Elias of Stephens City, Virginia, partnered with her husband to run Elias Consulting, and her biggest challenge has been learning about the legalities and accounting requirements. "If I could do things over, I would talk with experts before I started the business," she says. "There was no time or money for that because the idea came up quickly. But then it quickly became successful, and I have been playing catch-up ever since. I think maybe we should have incorporated right away, because we have had to pay high personal taxes for the last two years."

A *Limited Liability Corporation* (LLC) is a relatively new legal business entity that is particularly popular with mompreneurs who have invented products. But service-based e-Businesses specializing in professional advice can also benefit. After filing a DBA ("doing business as") certificate for her accounting services business, Brigitte Thompson went one step further and made Datamaster a one-person LLC, something that's permitted in most states. "This still lets me file a Schedule C at tax time, but allows me some limited liability similar to that of a corporation, which is wonderful!" Thompson says. "In the event of a lawsuit, my assets are separate from the business." Along with liability protection, the LLC also offers you the tax advantages of a sole proprietorship or partnership. The profits and losses of the LLC are reported on your individual tax returns. LLCs are less complicated to set up than a corporation—and you can even file the form online with your secretary of state's office.

The main benefit of a *corporation* is that it is considered a separate legal entity from its owner. You get liability protection, and, as an employee of the corporation, you receive a steady salary, from which taxes are regularly withheld. "The primary reason I incorporated was for that extra bit of protection that the corporate structure offers for my family's personal assets," says Liane Hetherington-Ward, an environmental policy consultant and mom of one from Lockport, Illinois, who owns LH Ward, Inc.

Since shareholders receive stock, a corporation also makes it easier for you to attract investors to the business when you're ready to grow. However, it is costly and time-consuming to incorporate, and you relinquish some control over your venture, since your shareholders have a say in how the company is run. There are different types of corporations, including C-corporations, S-corporations and Personal Service Corporations (PSCs), each with its own advantages and disadvantages. Your attorney and accountant can offer advice on which is best for you.

SHOULD YOU INCORPORATE?

To determine the best structure for your business, consider the field you're in and your risk for personal liability. Ask yourself the following questions, suggests Jan Zobel, author of *Minding Her Own Business, 3rd Edition: The Self-Employed Woman's Guide to Taxes and Recordkeeping* (Adams Media Corporation, 2000):

- Are you in a type of business in which lawsuits are common?

- Are you going into business with other people?

- Do you feel that you won't be taken seriously as a sole proprietor, and that you could get more business if you were incorporated?

- Do you have large child care or medical expenses that could be covered by an employee benefit program if you were incorporated?

- Do you anticipate several years of losses before you start making a profit in your business?

Zobel says it's important to sit down with an attorney, accountant, or tax practitioner to discuss your particular liability and tax concerns. Remember, you can always start off with a simple structure, like sole proprietorship or partnership, and then incorporate later. You can get help incorporating or forming an LLC at www.bizfilings.com.

INSURING PEACE OF MIND

To supplement the security systems we've mentioned throughout this chapter, it's wise to consider getting insurance coverage for your equipment and/or products and services.

The Web introduces a "whole new world of insurance issues," says David Golden, director of commercial lines for the National Association of Independent Insurers in Des Plaines, Illinois. "With traditional brick-and-mortar businesses, common risks were related to property damage, bodily injury, or other concrete liability issues. But with cyber-risks, the damage may not be physical or tangible. Yet it can still have devastating effects on your business," Golden says. For example, if your server goes down and you run an e-commerce site, you could lose thousands of dollars in sales. What if a hacker decides to spam your clients and customers? Or suppose you feature a seemingly reputable link on your home page that turns out to lead to a pornographic site? Your business and reputation could be crippled with a single click of the mouse.

A number of business owner policies (BOPs) now offer a limited amount of Internet coverage for problems like denial of service, hacker attacks, system failures, data theft or loss, and privacy issues, Golden says. But insurance is often too expensive for a mompreneur on a start-up budget. "I do not know how to affordably protect our venture from liability," says scientific writer Elias, who runs a consulting firm with her husband, John, an aircraft inspector. "We both do our work for other companies, and I worry about John's liability, since he inspects jets," she says. "I think that if someone is going to sue, they will go after everything you have." That's why the couple recently started paperwork to incorporate their company. They will soon officially be an S-corp with some protection from liability. As for other insurance, they are looking into increasing their home owner's coverage to make sure it includes their computers. Since they're both self-employed, they are also investigating long-term disability insurance, but find it cost-prohibitive, so far.

Because the Internet is still an emerging industry, insurance plans can be quite costly, and not all cover the cyber-risks most important to e-Business owners. But Golden predicts that in the relatively near future these services will become more affordable and readily available to owners of small and home businesses. (Incorporating or forming a Limited Liability Corporation is another way to protect your business assets; see "Should You Incorporate?" page 197.)

WHAT INSURANCE DO YOU NEED?

Insurance requirements depend on the type of activities you conduct on the Net. Golden suggests figuring out where you require the most protection and then buying the amount and type of insurance you can afford. (Your attorney or financial advisor can help you assess your biggest areas of risk.) You can always build onto your plan later as your enterprise becomes profitable.

Remember, every mompreneur and her business is unique. Review the various options and then contact an insurance agent who's savvy in home business and Internet issues to put together an insurance plan that's right for you.

Here are some things to consider when you're doing business on the Net:

PROPERTY AND GENERAL LIABILITY INSURANCE

Is your business equipment covered in the event of theft, fire, or some other disaster? A typical home owner's policy provides only up to $2,500 or less of coverage for business equipment, according to the Insurance Information Institute. That's not much when you consider the cost of your computer system and other high-tech tools, and your financial loss if you're forced to shut down your business temporarily.

Business-related injuries are a big concern too. Suppose that while delivering a business package, the UPS driver trips over the baseball bat your Little Leaguer left on the walkway. While your home owner's policy may cover injuries to guests incurred on your property, it probably doesn't include delivery people, clients, customers, or employees.

Some extra property and liability insurance can protect you from service interruptions and lawsuits filed by injured or dissatisfied associates. And it doesn't always have to cost a fortune. Here are suggestions from the Insurance Information Institute on how you can increase your coverage to protect your business.

1. Beef Up Your Home Owner's or Renter's Insurance.

You can add endorsements or riders to your existing policy for a nominal fee to extend the coverage of your equipment and protect it when it's out of your home (essential if you're constantly toting your laptop around). Consider purchasing replacement cost insurance for computer equipment, rather than an actual cash value policy, which only covers the depreciated cost.

Some home owner insurance policies offer riders for limited business liability, covering injury to customers or clients in your home. But to qualify, your business will have to generate less than $5,000 in income, so this may be an option only while you're in the start-up stage. And the rider won't offer coverage for product or professional liability. (For more complete coverage for these areas, see "Check Out Business Owners' Package Policies," below; "Purchase Product Liability Insurance," page 201; and "Don't Forget Professional Liability Insurance," page 201.)

2. Buy an In-Home Business Policy.

These relatively new miniplans are designed especially for home-based businesses and offer more extensive coverage for equipment and business liability than a typical home owner's insurance plan. For a minimum of about $200 per year you can insure your business property (computers and other equipment, software, product inventory, data, and important files) for $10,000 or more. If your business is unable to operate because of damage to your house, an in-home business policy will cover lost income and ongoing expenses for up to a year. You can also purchase additional general liability coverage as part of this plan for protection from personal injury lawsuits and certain other business liability lawsuits.

3 Check Out Business Owners' Package Policies (BOPs).

Though they can cost $500 a year or more, these all-in-one plans offer more complete property and liability protection. Many of the newer policies cover not only basic business equipment and property, but offer protection in the event of data theft, system crashes, and loss or denial of Internet service. In addition, most plans extend the liability coverage

Attention Service Businesses:
Don't Forget Professional Liability Insurance!

Known more commonly as malpractice insurance, this is especially important if you're in the business of offering advice, whether online or off. It covers you in the event that someone sues for damages after following your instructions. Personal coaches, Web designers, computer consultants, investment counselors, and nutritionists are among the many Web professionals buying these protective but pricey policies. "I recommend that consultants look into obtaining professional errors and omissions insurance," says environmental consultant Hetherington-Ward. "It's generally available for a percent of your gross income, and the percentage goes down as your gross increases. The cost usually goes down as your business matures and claims aren't forthcoming," she explains.

beyond physical injury, covering advertising damages, slander, libel, and product failure.

4. Purchase Product Liability Insurance.

If you manufacture anything that's consumed, touched, or used, product liability is essential. Most business owner policies (see above) cover product liability, but if yours doesn't, you may have to purchase a separate policy.

Judi Cohen carries about $2 million worth of product liability insurance to cover the parenting and children's products she sells on WeBehave.com. Because Paula Polman, of the Canadian-based Mossberry Hollow Natural Care Products, accepts both U.S. and Canadian currency, she needs Canadian general business and inventory coverage, general liability for Canada, and general liability for the U.S. "Many Canadian insurance companies won't touch you if you sell anything to the U.S., even if it is a small percentage," she says. She's searched for the cheapest premiums she can find, but so far her total premiums would be close to $1,700 a year. "For someone of my size, that's a fair chunk of change," she says.

WORKERS' COMPENSATION

If you have employees, most states will require you to purchase workers' compensation insurance to take care of injuries or illness suffered on the job. If your business is incorporated, you can cover both your employees and yourself with a workers' compensation policy.

CLICK AND SAVE: *Report Scams Here*

>> *www.abuse.net* For reporting unsolicited e-mail

>> *www.bbb.org* Better Business Bureau

>> *www.fraud.org* National Fraud Information Center

>> *www.ftc.gov* Federal Trade Commission's Consumer Response Center

>> *www.ifccfbi.gov* Internet Fraud Complaint Center

>> *www.traderlist.com* A mom-owned fraud mediation site for collectors of toys

When Should You Call . . . ?

AN ACCOUNTANT

Assistance with business
plan and financial projections

Structuring the business

Setting up record-keeping
systems

Computing estimated taxes

Evaluating whether you qualify
for the home office deduction

AN ATTORNEY

Forming a partnership, LLC,
or corporation

Changing your business structure

Liability protection

Registering trademarks and patents

Protecting intellectual property

When Should You Call . . . ?, continued

AN ACCOUNTANT	AN ATTORNEY
Preparing your tax returns (at least for the first year in business)	Drafting or reviewing privacy policies and legal disclaimers on your site
Setting up retirement plans	Trademark or patent infringement
Hiring employees	Drafting contracts or nondisclosure agreements

Finding a Net-Savvy Insurance Agent

"Shop around," urges David Golden of the National Association of Independent Insurers. "It's important that your insurance agent not only understand the type of business you're in, but is knowledgeable about the Web, its protective tools, and the insurance coverage that's available to address Internet risks and liabilities."
Here's how to find the right agent for you and your e-Biz.

★ **Talk With "Real" Voices.** Don't try to find an insurance agent via e-mail. "It's important to build a relationship with potential agents," says Golden, and that's best done in person or by phone. Ask lots of questions and make sure the broker is asking you about your business, too.

★ **Network With Other Mompreneurs.** Before purchasing product liability insurance for her Reflections Safety Mirrors, Barbara Spangler visited online women's home business forums and asked fellow inventors for recommendations. She then found the best deal by calling local insurance carriers in her area.

★ **Follow up Frequently.** Once you have selected an insurance agent, check in every few months to make sure that your policy is properly updated to give you the coverage you need in the fast-changing world of the Web.

★ **Try These Sites:** The following links can refer you to insurance companies: the Insurance Industry Internet Network *(www.iiin.com)*; Insurance Information Institute *(www.iii.org)*; National Association of Independent Insurers *(www.naii.org)*; and Working Today *(www.workingtoday.org)*, an organization for independent contractors which offers access to group rates for health and dental benefits and prepaid legal assistance for a nominal membership fee.

Lesson Learned: Scammers Are Smart Cookies!

In 1999, single mom Terri Vincent was searching the Internet for home-based franchises and moneymaking opportunities to supplement her virtual assistant business. When she got an e-mail about buying into an Internet mall, she thought it might be a great way to reach a market far beyond her small hometown of Cody, Wyoming. Still, she proceeded with caution. She had several conversations with the company spokespeople, and even had her dad, a business advisor, talk with them about the details of the arrangement. "They had a good concept and seemed reputable," Vincent says.

Here's the Deal: The owners of the Internet mall would team Vincent up with approximately 20 other people from all over the world to run one of the online stores in the mall. The store would sell products manufactured by a particular name-brand company that the Internet mall would select from its participating sponsors. (Each store in the Internet mall would feature a different company's products.) To buy into the store, Vincent and her partners would be required to purchase a minimum of three units per person, at $6,000 apiece. In return, the company would host the store on its Internet mall site, provide Vincent and her team with extensive sales and marketing training, and hook them up with a big-name manufacturer who would ship product directly to the customers (a process known as drop-shipping). The owners of the Internet mall also pledged a multimillion-dollar ad campaign and IPO by the end of 1999. Profits from sales on the site would belong to Vincent and her partners. "We were especially impressed by the amount of training offered and the idea that the manufacturer would drop-ship merchandise from its own warehouses," Vincent says. That way, the partners wouldn't have to invest in any inventory, warehouse space, or shipping costs.

Count Us In: Vincent plunked down $18,000 for her shares in the store, and started corresponding and chatting online with her international partners—which included people from Australia, Peru, Canada, and Hawaii. In total, they invested about $300,000 in the Internet mall. They were thrilled to hear they'd be selling a well-known brand of toys, and were eager to begin their training and get their store up and running.

What Went Wrong: Though the training was extensive and very helpful, the partners hit a glitch when it came time to work with the toy manufacturer. The toy company seemed to know nothing about the arrangement to be featured in the Internet mall. What's worse, says Vincent, "They told us they couldn't drop-ship products." When she and her team complained to the Internet mall company, it was suggested that they invest more money in a fulfillment house which could ship the toys for them. "We weren't interested in that

Lesson Learned: Scammers Are Smart Coo

and fought all year with them," says Vincent. The matter is no
ners are hoping to recoup at least some of their investment.

"We had some very savvy people on our team," includir
sive experience in merchandising, accounting, and law, Vin
people can get fooled."

Every Cloud Has a Silver Lining: Luckily, the ordeal has not
partners discovered that they worked well together and ha
launch their own Internet boutique, *estore2000.com*. It featur
by manufacturers who will agree to drop-ship the items direc
met her partners face-to-face for the first time at a trade show in L
lined up manufacturers and shared strategies for their new venture. Th
scammed once, but it won't happen again. "We learned so much about
from this experience, we are going to make it work to our advantage," Vincen

Advice From an Expert: "Before you invest any money in a business opportunity,
thorough background check on the company and the principals involved," stresses Ho
Cherico of the Better Business Bureau. Use Web search engines to extensively research
the company and its owners; ask the BBB for a reliability report on the company; and contact the secretary of state's office where the company is headquartered to find out how
long it has been in business. You should also have an attorney with experience in business
opportunities thoroughly review the prospectus. "You can't judge a business opportunity
by how sophisticated it looks or sounds," Cherico warns. "Anyone can put up a slick website and claim to have brand-name partners." In fact that is often the sign of a scam.
Beware of high-pressure pitches urging you to decide now so you can get in on the
"ground floor" of a deal. "When you hear claims like that, walk away," Cherico says.

CLICK AND SAVE: *Accounting, Tax, and Legal Resources*

>> *www.findlaw.com*

>> *www.icaccounting.com*

>> *www.IRS.gov*

>> *www.lawvantage.com*

>> *www.Nolo.com*

;mbiz.com

v.taxprophet.com

ww.1040.com

RECORD-KEEPING 101

record-keeping is essential if you want to maximize your deduc-
while keeping the IRS happy," says Jan Zobel, author of *Minding*
Own Business, 3rd Edition. Establish easy ways to keep track of the
ney coming in and out of your business, she suggests. But for many
ompreneurs, record-keeping is a daunting task. "The most difficult
thing about running my site has been keeping track of my earnings, and
learning how to pay taxes!" says Anne Fognano. "With a site like mine, I
have over two hundred different companies paying me. Each company has
their own policy and method for payment, so keeping that straight is
quite a chore!" Here's how she and other dot.com mompreneurs have sim-
plified the process.

- **Keep A Diary**

  "I record every check in a ledger as it arrives and I don't deposit
  anything until I've done that," Fognano says. Judi Cohen, checks
  each order on WeBehave.com to see if it has come through an affiliate,
  and then pays each affiliate when due.

- **Get Support from Software**

  Use an accounting software program that is compatible with
  your accountant, advises Deborah Elias. And "make sure it has a
  telephone support line, online Q and As, and a hard-copy how-to
  manual," adds Hetherington-Ward. Many of the mompreneurs we
  interviewed recommend Quick Books. DeYoung downloads her
  Quick Books files monthly and sends them to her accountant to
  review.

▪ Be a Pack Rat

Save all the receipts you incur while doing business. Barbara Spangler keeps one file labeled "Receipts" for everything she has purchased for the month. When she gets her bank statement, she schedules a day to balance her account and go through her file of receipts, and compiles a list. "This always makes my accountant smile," she says. "And everyone loves a happy accountant."

TAX TIME Q & A

We asked tax expert Zobel to answer some commonly asked questions.

Can You Take the Home Office Deduction?

"The IRS home office rules have been greatly liberalized since 1999," she says. A deductible home office no longer has to be your primary place of business. It can be where you do administrative work for the business, as long as you have no other fixed location where you spend substantial time on these tasks. But the home office must be used regularly and exclusively for business. It doesn't have to be a separate room, but it should be a clearly defined space. For example, if your computer is in middle of the family room for everyone to use, you cannot take the home office deduction. Even if you have a separate office set aside, you cannot claim it as a home office if your computer is shared with the kids. In addition, you cannot deduct home office expenses if your business is unprofitable that year. (And business losses are common in the first year of a start-up.) But you *can* carry any unused expenses over until the next year's return and deduct them then.

Who Needs An Employer ID Number?

"All business entities other than sole proprietorships must have an Employer Identification Number (EIN)," also known as a Federal Employer Identification Number (FEIN) or tax ID number, says Zobel. (Sole proprietors use their social security numbers when filing taxes. But if you're a sole proprietor with employees or with a Keogh retirement plan, you will need an EIN, too.) You can get it by applying to the IRS on Form SS-4.

Is Child Care Deductible?

You can deduct child care expenses needed to enable you to work if the care is for a dependent under age 13 or a dependent of any age who is unable to care for herself or himself. You can also deduct home care expenses for a disabled spouse or parent. But you and the dependent or disabled person must live in the same home.

 *Web Celeb*

Jane Applegate
CEO and Executive Producer of *SBTV.com (www.sbtv.com)*
Pelham, New York
Mom of 2

"The pioneers are always the ones with the arrows in their backs," jokes Jane Applegate, who is breaking through the frontiers of cyberspace with the grit and determination demonstrated by the early pioneer women during America's westward expansion. In May 2000, she launched SBTV.com—the only site to produce television-quality small business content on the Internet. Although Applegate concedes that there are hundreds of small business sites on the Web, "We're focusing on bringing small business to lots of people in a new and exciting light." Streaming video and audio make it possible to watch and/or listen to informational and entertaining segments 24/7 on several channels targeted to the varied interests of entrepreneurs. There's very little text and no affiliates or banner ads; instead, sponsors' messages "stream" around the shows—a business model so unique at the time, it was a tough sell at first. But now SBTV.com counts Aetna, CNNfn, MasterCard, and IBM among its sponsors.

Pioneering is nothing new for Applegate. When she began to write a column for the *Los Angeles Times* in 1988, she was one of the first female investigative reporters on staff. During her stint at the newspaper, she conducted many an interview and often wrote copy from her garage office while she watched her young son, Evan, running around in the backyard with his friends. Her "Succeeding in Small Business®" column went on to be syndicated, and by 2000, Jane Applegate was America's number one small business journalist, reaching 10 million people a week in print and with her Web-based newsletter of the same name. She has also authored three books and been the featured small business expert on CNNfn and Bloomberg Television.

It was the short life span of business TV shows that convinced her of the need for SBTV.com. "I was frustrated as a TV segment producer, doing a show that aired only once or twice," she says. Applegate's goal has always been to help as many people as possible—especially women—start and run viable small businesses. "Now I'm thinking about syndicating what we do on the Web back to TV!"

As a small business expert, Applegate knew that registering and trademarking both her Web presence, SBTV.com, and her company name, SBTV (Small Business Television), immediately after she conceived the idea was a priority. The legal process went smoothly; in fact, she couldn't believe the name wasn't taken already! She emphasizes the importance of protecting your business by clearing all the names or brands you may want to use—both online and off. She also strongly suggests that e-Biz owners protect themselves on the Internet by doing what SBTV.com does—place disclaimers along with any advice or opinions you post on your web-site. "At the end of articles and tips, we state that the content is 'for information purposes only' and is 'not legally binding.' That way, you won't be held responsible," says Applegate.

Reversing the trek of the original pioneers, the Applegate family went east in 1996, relocating to Pelham, New York. The Applegate Group news service continued operations there, with Jane as president and hus-band, Joe, as managing editor.

SBTV was set up four years later as a separate C-corporation and has 10 employees. Daughter Jeanne, a college student, and son Evan, now a teenager, have helped out from time to time, but their mom doesn't think they'll follow in her entrepreneurial footsteps. "They want cushy corporate jobs," Applegate claims with a chuckle. "They don't ever want to work this hard!"

Jane Applegate's hard work is far from over. She is in the process of expanding SBTV.com into a global network, with a bureau in London and segments being produced in other parts of the United Kingdom and Greece. Start-up funding was provided by profits from the Applegate Group and angel investors, but she's looking to expand through venture capital and outside funding. "It's very expensive to produce video and streamline it every day," she says. "That's our challenge as pioneers . . . to get sponsors and funding and stay ahead of the game."

CHAPTER SEVEN

Hot Links: Networking and Marketing on the Net

Sound Byte

"The Internet is not a 'field of dreams'; 'if you build it, they will come' does not apply here. Imagine yourself standing on the side of the road selling apples in apple country. There are vendors on both sides of the highway for hundreds of miles. People are driving through with the intention of buying apples, but you have to come up with a reason for them to stop at your apple stand."

Renee Hogan, mother of two; Marion, North Carolina
Owner of Renee Barry & Company gifts *(www.reneebarry.com)*

One of the first things we learned as mompreneurs is this: A strong network of contacts and support gives you a big head start in selling your products and services. Networking lays the groundwork for marketing a home business. And what's true in the "real" work-from-home world is just as true in the virtual world.

We're longtime advocates of face-to-face interaction as the best way to reach out, combat isolation, and make crucial contacts. But we can't deny the power of the Internet as a remarkably effective networking tool. Where else can you connect with millions of others who share your interests and can offer almost instant support? Although we still enjoy meeting mompreneurs and professional associates in person (or at least hearing a voice behind a screen name!), our e-friends and colleagues have greatly enriched our lives—and our business. The community and camaraderie you find online can speed you onto the ramp of the cyber-highway to success!

The Internet puts a whole new spin on marketing your business, too. Networking cements the foundation, making it simpler and cheaper to perform a multitude of marketing tasks on the Web. Once you learn the rules of the road, you can test-market concepts in virtual communities, get referrals and leads, easily pinpoint target audiences, create and place promotional materials, and advertise your products or services—all online. While a lot of tried-and-true strategies still work, cyber-marketing some-times needs a slightly different approach. Building your website is just the first leg of the trip—now we'll show you how to make this "billboard" that is your e-Biz visible to the whole world.

ELECTRONIC BONDING

Way back in the dark ages of the 1990s, most Internet users logged on in search of information. In their cyber-travels, they met up with people who shared their interests and together they formed the first virtual networking groups. The original online forums, Internet newsgroups, and discussion groups revolved around the quest for information. Ellen first ventured into cyberspace via CompuServe's Work-From-Home Forum, where she traded stories and gripes with other mompreneurs. She's still in touch with some of these e-friends, and has even met two of them in person!

Gathering information is still a very important motivation for logging on. But what today's users have discovered is that the support and kinship they find along the way is just as vital—and sometimes even more valu-able. "The real power of the Internet is its ability to build community," states Cheryl Demas, founder of WAHM.com, a site for work-at-home moms. With a few clicks of your mouse, you can join communities of like-minded souls in chat rooms, message boards, discussion groups, and other interactive areas on the Net. And the members of these communi-ties often turn out to be the cheerleaders, mentors, clients, customers, or just plain friends you rely on every day to help you achieve your personal and professional best. "It's amazing to me how, in such a high-tech medium, the Internet can truly spark relationships, helpfulness, and feelings of goodwill toward others," says Mia Cronan, founder of Main Street Mom, a support site for stay-at-home mothers.

A WEB OF SUPPORT

Whether it's a colicky newborn who is up all night screaming his head off or a preschooler who insists on wearing her Minnie Mouse pajamas *every day,* moms have always turned to other moms for solace and solutions. Twenty-first century moms are finding the personal and professional support they need right at their fingertips! With a mouse and a keyboard, we can join countless online communities and instantly communicate 24/7 with millions of moms about the things we care about most. And the anonymity of the Internet puts the shy person and the outgoing one on equal footing. Here's where mompreneurs told us they go when they are looking for advice, crave company, or have the urge to e-network:

SITE: Bizy Moms (www.bizymoms.com)
BOOKMARK IT: This website is an electronic venue for author and columnist Liz Folger (*The Stay-at-Home Mom's Guide to Making Money*). "If working for yourself is your goal, don't let anyone or anything stand in your way" is her motto, and she and other contributors point the way through an in-depth look at a variety of home business ideas and information. Visitors can find articles, first-person experiences, scam alerts, advice, chats, and subscriptions to a free e-mail newsletter.

SITE: ClubMom (www.clubmom.com)
BOOKMARK IT: Many areas of interest to mothers are covered here, from food to sibling rivalry, but if you're looking for work-from-home content, click on "Movers and Shakers." There you'll find such choices as Mothers@Work, Entrepreneurs, Stay-at-Home Moms, and Work-at-Home Moms—all with lively discussion boards. A newer feature is an Entrepreneur Moms Directory. Viewers are greeted with the words "If you're a mom, you're a member," and editor-in-chief Nicola Godfrey and TV host Meredith Vieiria are among the cofounders *and* mothers who make it happen.

SITE: Entrepreneurial Parent (www.en-parent.com)

BOOKMARK IT: Daily discussion groups, online career counseling, and a newsletter keep parents up to snuff on the ins and outs of working from home. Information about legitimate and rewarding work-at-home options is provided by Lisa Roberts, author of *How to Raise a Family & a Career Under One Roof,* and support is offered from other parents with home-based businesses.

SITE: Hip Mama (www.hipmama.com)

BOOKMARK IT: When she became a mother at age 19, Ariel Gore couldn't find much parenting advice or support that related to her lifestyle. As a college project, she created *Hip Mama* magazine—a print vehicle for single, urban moms like herself. The 'zine "expanded into an online community in 1996 to meet the needs of a more alternative group of parents," says Gore, and the site for progressive moms now offers interactive features and a "Mamashop."

SITE: Home-Based Working Moms (www.hbwm.com)

BOOKMARK IT: Founder Lesley Spencer, herself a work-from-home mom, has combined expert content and great networking opportunities into a super site for mompreneurs. Timely articles, job listings, member-to-member advice, and more are available free; for a small yearly membership fee you also receive a monthly print newsletter, notice of publicity/media opportunities, an online membership directory, and other perks.

SITE: iVillage—Work Channel (www.ivillage.com/work)

BOOKMARK IT: Connect with moms in many types of home businesses through the message boards and chat rooms on this megasite. There are areas for virtual assistants, craftswomen, errand runners, event planners, medical billers, and telecommuters, as well as more general-interest work-from-home sections. You can ask us specific questions plus meet other home-based working moms on the Mompreneurs® board and chats we host there.

SITE: Main Street Mom (www.mainstreetmom.com)

BOOKMARK IT: Mompreneur Mia Cronan launched this advocacy site for stay-at-home moms as an e-zine for "modern mothers with traditional values." The content helps moms make the transition from the workforce to the home, offering articles on everything from managing the family budget, to helping kids learn, to work-at-home ideas and strategies. Online forums provide the networking and support needed "to keep new moms' sanity in check!"

SITE: Moms Help Moms (www.momshelpmoms.com)

BOOKMARK IT: In her quest for better work/family balance, Misty Weaver-Ostinato gathered lots of useful information and decided to "put it all in one place to make moms' lives a little easier." The result is this website—a comprehensive collection of resources for starting and running a home business, choosing child care, evaluating school choices, and promoting childhood safety. Chats, message boards, and contests encourage interaction.

SITE: Moms Network (www.momsnetwork.com)

BOOKMARK IT: This site is dedicated to offering the tools, resources, and networking that work-at-home moms need to achieve balance in their lives. Easy navigation from the home page leads you to "Job Search," "Biz Directory," and "Biz Opps" listings, and interactive features promote the belief that "moms learn and grow most from each other and the relationships we build both personally and professionally." Lots of freebies here, including websites.

SITE: Moms Online (www.momsonline.com)

BOOKMARK IT: One of AOL's original virtual communities, Moms Online has built up a large, loyal, and caring group of fans. It's now operated by Oxygen Media, but has retained its whimsical navigational icons and down-home approach to motherhood, including good coverage of work/family issues in its "Ma'Zine," chats, and boards.

SITE: Mother's Home Business Network (www.HomeWorkingMom.com)
BOOKMARK IT: HomeWorkingMom.com is the electronic extension of Mother's Home Business Network—a large national organization that has been offering inspiration and support to work-at-home moms since 1984. Online services include a free monthly newsletter, a job finder, an entrepreneurial moms directory, success steps, and information about telecommuting and home-based businesses.

SITE: National Association of At-Home Mothers (www.AtHomeMothers.com)
BOOKMARK IT: Offline, this advocacy organization provides information and help for mothers who opt to stay at home. Online, the site contains article reprints from *At-Home Mother* magazine, free tips, work-from-home advice, a bookstore, and Web resources. All validate the importance of at-home motherhood.

SITE: The NOBOSS ParentPreneur Club (www.parentpreneurclub.com)
BOOKMARK IT: Here's a spot where busy parents with home-based businesses can find articles, tips, sources, and tools for working at home. Affiliated with the National Organization of Business Opportunity Seekers (NOBOSS), the site has a large database of low-cost biz opportunities as well. Moms (and dads!) can join the online "club" for free, and receive newsletters and the site's e-book of the month.

SITE: 20ish Parents (www.20ishparents.com)
BOOKMARK IT: Articles, chats, discussion boards, and mothering advice by and for parents in their 20s fill this site. Amy Schamburek, a 20-something mother of four, believed that this demographic was being overlooked on the Web, so she started her e-Biz to fill the niche. "I have a passion for reaching out to other moms in my situation," she says. Schamburek's personal touch and relevant topics nurture a close-knit community of Gen X parents.

SITE: WAHM.com (www.wahm.com)
BOOKMARK IT: Billed as "The Online Magazine for Work at Home Moms," this site offers meaty content, humorous cartoons (drawn by founder and

mompreneur Cheryl Demas), supportive bulletin boards and chats, and lots of articles and links to turn your work-from-home dream into a reality. On-site maketing tools such as Web rings, site popularity lists, and directories can help build your business. The community spirit here is strong, and the resources helpful and inspirational.

BRANCHING OUT

Mom-to-mom virtual communities are a supportive and rewarding place to begin your networking efforts and make valuable contacts—perhaps even extending them into the "real world" as Debra Haas did. An educational policy consultant in Austin, Texas, Haas became involved in hbwm.com, also based in Austin. Through this national cyber-network, she connected with several other local mompreneurs, and they decided to get together on a regular basis—outside their homes. They now meet for monthly lunches, discussing everything from child care to marketing tips to fee negotiations. All love the face-to-face interaction and exchange of ideas.

Groups for work-at-home moms are only one of the many networking opportunities that can give you and your business a boost. Professional organizations for women, small business/entrepreneur support services, business and store owners clubs, and your county Chamber of Commerce are some of the other options—both online and off. Dana Victoria Sophia, a mompreneur who provides website development and concierge services from her home in Westchester, New York, became active in digital-women.com, a community of businesswomen on the Web. Through her involvement on the site, she rounded up other women living in New York City's suburbs, and eventually spun off the Cyburban Chapter, which she directs. (Sophia also came up with the catchy name!) Though its members' roots are in cyberspace, they get together in person, too—networking and marketing home business ideas.

To explore other networking possibilities, search the Web for professional organizations and trade associations that are aimed at your particular business. A few examples are the National Association of Professional

Networking Netiquette

Whether you're a newbie or an Internet pioneer, you'll be a better cyber-communicator if you practice good manners.

* **Lurk before you leap.** If you're a newcomer to a discussion list, newsgroup, or message board, it's OK—and often smarter—to lurk for about two weeks before you "speak up." Lurking isn't as sinister as it sounds—it simply means reading the posts without responding. You'll be a more effective communicator once you get to know the "personality" of the group and the thread of conversation. It's a little more difficult to lurk at online chats because your screen name automatically shows up in the chat room. Simply explain that you're trying to learn the ropes by observing, and chatters will usually respect your wishes.

* **Beware of spam.** Blatant solicitations (aka spam) are unwelcome in chat rooms, message boards, and discussion groups unless the policy states otherwise. That doesn't mean you can't share information about your business as part of the normal conversational thread. It *does* mean that you shouldn't be selling your products or services or advertising your URL in one of these online forums if it's not permitted. Also resist buying targeted e-mail lists from online hawkers—the recipients usually have *not* opted in to receive unsolicited messages, and any e-mail you send their way will be considered spam. (See Chapter 6 for more tips on e-mail protocol.)

* **Be polite.** Insulting or putting down a poster or chatter is just plain bad manners. On the Internet, this is called flaming, and it's frowned upon. If someone is offensibly flaunting her business or pushing her opinions on you, report it to the leader or host of the chat or board—don't try to handle it yourself.

* **Reciprocate.** If an e-buddy gives you a lead, referral, great marketing idea, or any other kind of help, return the favor. It can only help nurture the relationship and foster future support.

Organizers, V-A Alliance (for virtual assistants), Juvenile Products Association (for inventors and retailers of children's products), Public Relations Society of America, and National Association for the Specialty Food Trade. Some of the search engines provide industry directories to help you pinpoint the right group for you. Do some investigating and find out if there's a "live" local chapter of the group near your home. These chapters

The Mighty Mompreneur Network

Andrea Mudd of *www.getamom.com,* a job placement e-source for professional mothers, was formulating a business plan to submit to investors when she ran into a familiar catch 22:—"You need management to get money and money to get management." To find intelligent, technologically adept candidates, this Englewood, Colorado, mother of two tapped the Internet, posting messages on several sites. "On iVillage's Mompreneurs® board I found Kathy to help me with financials; Tami, my marketing director; and Laurie, a human resources pro who was trying to line up a more flexible work arrangement in anticipation of having kids," says Mudd. "Through *networkingmoms.com,* I connected with Julie, Sherry, and Carol—all technical and financial experts—and on *guru.com* I met Crystal, a recruiting professional. My team now stretches east to west, from New Hampshire, New Jersey, and Florida, to California, Colorado, and Washington State, making it possible to have a company with a nationwide presence."

The seven women on the team compose *getamom.com's* "advisory board," and will move into permanent positions as the site grows. In the meantime, their credentials make the business attractive to investors, and their expertise is invaluable to Mudd.

Even if you're not trying to impress investors, developing cyber-partnerships can be beneficial to your business. For Joanne Marsili, who runs a full-service marketing firm from her Pennsylvania home, networking with other moms has enabled her to establish a "virtual office base" and enhance her productivity. "I have built relationships with women who have complementary skills, so my weaknesses (like graphic design!) don't hold me back from accepting a project. And I always have someone to bounce ideas off."

often hold regular meetings, networking lunches or dinners, workshops, conferences, and other events that can give you a chance to connect with and learn from others in the same field.

And be sure to take regular breaks from your computer and venture outside—you never know when or where a networking opportunity may present itself! Mompreneurs have gotten leads and referrals on the playground, on the sidelines of their kids' soccer and softball games, during workouts at the gym, and while volunteering for school, community, or religious committees. Ellen found out about one of the moms we featured in this book while she was getting a haircut! It pays to bring your business cards along wherever you go—a neighbor, local store owner, or babysitter may be your next client or customer.

CLICK AND SAVE: *Favorite Places for Businesswomen*

>> *www.digital-women.com* Noted experts and women entrepreneurs share information, advice, and resources on starting and marketing an online business on this easy-to-navigate site. You'll also find an abundance of great networking opportunities and website-building tools here.

>> *www.herplanet.com* In this virtual world designed by and for women, you can connect with others and find resources for the family, businesses, Web design, free banner ads, and more. Each woman-run site in the network is overseen by mompreneur Dottie Gruhler to keep it "family-friendly."

>> *www.siliconsalley.com* This content-rich, cutting-edge e-zine is dedicated to promoting visibility to those women who are building and innovating the Web. Live radio interviews and lively writing make this a fun, educational site to visit.

>> *www.webgrrls.com* Techno-savvy women can connect with programmers, business owners, webmistresses, dot.com leaders and other women involved in the high-tech world, plus learn the latest about industry trends and career opportunities. Part of the Cybergrrl! Network.

>> *www.womensforum.com* Supporting and growing a partnership of entrepreneurial women's websites is what this portal is all about. Resources, community spirirt, and lots of support help women take their e-Businesses to the next level.

>> *www.womeninc.com* Articles, expert advice, sources for financing and other business needs, and a business exchange network add up to a smart Web destination for women starting or running a small business.

Mother of Invention

Before she became a mom, Jeanette Benway worked as a specialist in clinical laboratory computing. She always had a talent for sewing, but never thought she could earn a living from her avocation. Parenthood sparked a moneymaking idea, and now this mother of three operates a crafty business out of her home office in Mount Kisco, New York, where she manufactures, markets, and distributes Cozy Rosie®—a unique cuddly blanket that fits over a baby's stroller. Some imaginative networking and promotion tactics have gained Benway a dedicated following.

THE INSPIRATION: On a cool spring day, Benway was out walking with her youngest child, Elizabeth, in the stroller. Elizabeth was cold and complaining, so mother and daughter decided to cut their walk short and head home. On the way, Benway hatched her bright idea, and put it into action almost immediately. "That afternoon, I designed and sewed a polar fleece blanket that wouldn't fall off the stroller or get tangled in the wheels," she remembers. "It worked beautifully, and people began to notice and comment about our blanket whenever Elizabeth and I walked around the neighborhood." Benway soon realized that her blanket could become a business—it solved a parenting problem and filled a niche in the juvenile products market.

THE START-UP: In May 1997, Benway applied for a patent and began looking for a contract sewing company to manufacture her product. "Finding a manufacturer was not easy," Benway recalls. "Most companies were looking for a much higher volume than I was prepared to offer." She searched the Web, found some good matches, sent out materials to a few manufacturers, and got back samples and prices. "The contractor I finally chose made a beautiful sample at a reasonable cost," says Benway. By March 1998, she was marketing the blanket to children's mail order catalogs and retailers and had developed her website, www.cozyrosie.com. At first, the site provided prospective customers with lots of photos and information about the blanket, but with no way to order it. Then, in June 1999, Benway added a secure order form and opened her e-store for business. "I wanted to give my customers as many easy ways to buy Cozy Rosie® as possible," she says.

GETTING THE WORD OUT: Doing your own publicity can be time-consuming, but the effort paid off for Benway. She wrote her own press release, using advice she found online at www.PublicityHound.com, and sent it out to the parenting magazines and other media outlets. As a result, product information about the blanket appeared in such publications as *American Baby, Twins,* and many local magazines and newspapers. Benway's biggest coup—Cozy Rosie® was selected as a *New York* magazine "Best Bet," and an article about the business was printed in the *New York Times.*

THE CURE FOR ISOLATION BLUES: "My biggest challenge was finding the support and feedback I used to get from my coworkers at the office," says Benway. Although she discovered many women's business organizations, they seemed to be geared toward service businesses rather than product-based ventures. So Benway created her own support group of small manufacturers. "We meet once a month to share ideas and learn from each other," she says.

THE REWARDS: Benway's kids are her best marketers! Whenever they see parents with strollers, they're on the lookout for "problem blankets" and are eager to hand out Mom's cards to solve the problem. Their admiration for her business has boosted Benway's confidence and drive. "I believe in my product and know that my customer base is growing," she says. "I feel that one day Cozy Rosie® will be viewed as a 'must-have' baby product."

MAKING THE MOST OF YOUR WEBSITE

Establishing a Web presence is an important first step, and an informational site is the most affordable way to get on the Internet. But as your business grows, so can your website. "Having a website is the bare minimum these days . . . it's like a listing in the white pages. And an e-commerce site is like a huge yellow pages ad at a fraction of the cost," notes a mompreneur who answered our survey. But once those cyber-explorers see your "ad," how do you get them to come back for a return visit? That's the problem that plagues many e-Businesses. We think moms hold the secret to generating more traffic without spending a fortune.

CRUISING FOR CUSTOMERS AND CLIENTS

Moms are especially adept at forging relationships and networks of support—in both the virtual world and the real one. This skill can lead to lucrative marketing opportunities. "There are so many ads and so much junk mail out there on the Internet that many people are leery about checking out sites referred by strangers," feels Lani Parker, a Daly City, California, mompreneur who runs E-Comm Central, a private franchise designed for the Internet. "I've worked through this challenge by building online relationships and developing rapport first, so the other person is more likely to trust me and listen." Lesley Spencer, founder of Home-Based Working Moms, has seen again and again how profitable a cyber-networking group is for her members. "Get known in an online community, offer your advice and input, and watch your business grow," she says.

There are several ways to start developing a customer and client base by "word of mouth" before you even put together a more formal marketing plan. Terri Gray, owner of SavvySites.net, a website development company, says, "Networking on sites and in newsgroups where your target market may also be participating is one of the best ways to increase your exposure. Not only will you benefit from other people's experience, you will start generating leads and referrals from competitors."

Many mompreneurs are frequent participants in chats, message boards, and other website forums (see pages 212 to 220 for networking how-tos). Internet newsgroups and discussion lists tend to be a little more specialized. Operated by UseNet, news groups cover almost every business interest—from antiques to zodiacs!—forming a large collection of discussion groups involving millions of people around the globe. Members post articles under particular topics and others respond, creating an evolving cyber-conversation. Although you can't advertise in newsgroups, you can offer advice or tips in your area of expertise. And when you identify yourself, it's usually fine to subtly mention your business or add your digital signature (known as your "sig file"; see page 231).

Discussion lists or *listservs* are e-mail versions of newsgroups or message boards. You subscribe to a list and every time you want to join in a discussion, you post your comment or response and it is e-mailed to everyone on the list. If the members of this list are your target audience and you attach your digital signature, word of your business is constantly spreading to potential clients and customers.

CLICK-AND-SAVE: *Newsgroups & Lists Search*

>> *www.forumone.com*

>> *www.groups.google.com* (formerly *deja.com*)

>> *www.groups.yahoo.com* (formerly *egroups.com*)

>> *www.Liszt.com*

>> *www.Lsoft.com/lists/listref.html*

>> *www.talkbiz.com*

>> *www.usenet.com*

CREATING YOUR OWN COMMUNITY

A dynamic online community can play a big role in getting visitors to return again and again to your website. Cheryl Demas, founder of WAHM.com, attributes some of her success to the fact that "visitors form relationships and associate their friendships with my site." How can you establish the kind of community that will generate good feelings *and* great traffic?

Start with the design

Make sure your site's home page clearly displays navigation buttons to take visitors to pages where they can get a personal glimpse into your business. Every site should have at least these three areas:

■ ABOUT US to describe your e-Biz and offer bios of who is running it

■ FAQs (Frequently Asked Questions) to answer common questions customers and clients may raise

■ CONTACT US to post your company's snail mail address, phone number, and e-mail addresses for customer service and other functions

A sense of community begins with feelings of familiarity and trust.

Concentrate on content

Provide up-to-date information relevant to your business and your audience. You may decide to write a changing weekly article related to your area of expertise, whether it be gardening, nutrition, child safety, or marketing. You can also offer a weekly quiz to viewers, and post the answers a week later to entice them to make a return visit. Another idea is to hold a trivia contest on your site, announcing the winners by name and digital photo. Surveys, polls, and questions-of-the-week are more ways to initiate responses that you can then convert into site content.

Include interactive tools

Message boards, newsletters, and chat rooms create "stickiness"—a quality that encourages visitors to interact, stay a while, and come back for more. Some Web businesses give their sites a clubby atmosphere by asking viewers to join as "members"; a password then gains them entry to special interactive areas. When visitors can stop by and ask questions, share advice, offer their opinions, brainstorm ideas, and talk about important issues in a comfortable forum, they'll want to stick around. A high comfort level, in turn, builds loyalty and trust—two valuable assets when it comes time to purchase products and services.

Convert Community Spirit Into Cash

"The grassroots coalition of mompreneurs in North America is more powerful than all the men in suits on Wall Street could ever imagine," states Diana West, founder of Mothers' Online Thrift Shop *(www.motshop.com).* "These moms are above seeing each other competitively, so they work together cooperatively for mutual success."

Mompreneur Darcy Miller harnessed this incredible spirit of helpfulness into an Internet venture with major marketing clout. She started Little Did I Know *(www.littledid iknow.com)* as an online shop and directory of unique keepsakes and gifts for babies, children, and mothers—all handmade or distributed by MOMs (Moms on a Mission: to stay at home with their children!). As a result, Miller says, "The LDIK moms have formed a strong community of friends that allows all of us to learn, mentor, share ideas, and motivate and encourage each other in a safe haven."

Capitalizing on this supportive community, Miller launched a co-op marketing plan. "Together we do what would be almost impossible to do alone—advertising, marketing, publicity, and more advertising, marketing, and publicity," she says. LDIK members, whom now number over 140 mothers, have been able to take out ads in parenting magazines and participate in trade shows by pitching in and dividing the expense. A $1,000, 1-inch ad in *Parents* or *Parenting* magazine suddenly becomes very reasonable at less than $10 a month per participant; a trade show booth shared by four or five moms under the LDIK name can be an affordable and profitable experience for all.

Co-op marketing can create terrific media opportunities as well. "With all of the moms involved in LDIK, someone somewhere always knows someone else who is Oprah Winfrey's best friend," Miller says, laughing. "And instead of one person spreading the word and 'planting the seeds,' we have over a hundred. I've always said, 'A hundred mouths are louder than one!' "

E-MARKETING ON A SHOESTRING

"Failing to plan is planning to fail," warns Patti Londre, president of the Londre Company, a Los Angeles firm that specializes in public relations and bootstrap marketing. That doesn't mean you should hire a pricey consultant, formulate a lengthy marketing plan, and spend tens of thousands of dollars promoting and advertising your business. New mompreneurs rarely have that kind of money anyhow, and sinking too much dough into a dot.com venture is actually what has sunk many well-known start-ups! So who needs a huge budget?

What you *do* need to do is plan out your strategy and goals. Through informational websites and your support network, listen to those who have traveled through cyberspace before you—certain e-marketing techniques are universally effective. In addition, keep your mind open to "out-of-the-box" ideas that may be a perfect fit for your unique venture. Last of all, make sure you're driving the "right" prospects to your site. "For the small business owner, high website traffic is not as important as *focused* website traffic," Londre says. "A million hits may sound great, but a hundred hits AND a hundred sales is the goal."

Believe it or not, some of the best online marketing techniques are pretty inexpensive, available for barter, or even FREE! The drawback is that they may take time to implement. But according to writer and editor Tina Gasperson, it's well worth it. "I marketed myself like crazy in the beginning . . . spending more time on that than on my actual work," she remembers. This Tampa-based mother of five still devotes time every morning to her online marketing efforts, visiting the job boards that post project work for writers and sending messages to the writers' mailing list she has joined. "It's always fun to see how many hits I get on my website after I post a message that includes my URL," she says.

Lori Thompson agrees that constant hard work makes for a busy, productive site. To promote her breast-feeding and natural parenting advocacy and shopping site, her plan of action includes monthly specials, contests, e-mail announcements to opt-in customers, and an electronic newsletter. "You also have to join banner exchanges, link with like-minded sites, and barter advertising," she says.

The mompreneurs we surveyed agree that "do-it-yourself" is the thriftiest and safest online marketing strategy. Warns Judi Cohen, "Beware of Internet solicitors who push you to join their marketing programs. Most of them are people with lots of buzzwords and big egos who won't be around for long."

See how you can put your own plan into action without spending a bundle.

TOP TEN MARKETING MOVES . . . AND HOW TO PULL THEM OFF

1. Get Noticed

There are at least a billion Web pages out there, so how can you make your business stand out—and be picked up by the search engines?

Keywords: Most of the big search engines scour Web pages for coded key-words or meta tags that concisely describe a business and state its mission. Take extra care in crafting these tools and placing them close to the top of all your pages—they help determine how high your site shows up in the rankings. (See Chapter 5 for how-tos.) But keep in mind that each search engine may have different rules for deciding how businesses are listed in relation to their keywords. What's more, the rules can change, so it's important to stay current. Make sure your choices are relevant, too— the search engines are getting more vigilant and may be "turned off" to your site if you use an inappropriate keyword ("Bargain" to describe upscale jewelry, for example).

Search Engine Submissions: "Manually submit your site to the major search engines," advises Terri Gray of SavvySites.net. Automatic submission pro-grams don't always give you the best placement, she warns. To submit, go to the search engine's home page, look for a link that says "Add URL," "Suggest a Site," or "Submit Your Site," and paste on your URL. (Site submission is sometimes buried in the "About Us" page.) This can be a tedious and frustrating task—you may get ranked in the top ten one week and be on the bottom of the heap the next!—but it's an essential one. Some of the major search engines include Yahoo!, Go.To, Excite, Webcrawler, Google, LookSmart, Infoseek, and Lycos.

It's smart to set aside some time each week for site submission. Machele Towle, a party planner who runs Select-A-Celebration, spends every Sunday evening on the activity. To supplement your efforts, you may want to try a service that registers sites. While some can be pricey, ISPs and a few of the domain registration services (register.com, for exam-ple) offer low-cost packages (getsubmitted.com is another option).

Directories: Hundreds of online directories offer free or low-cost business listings. Check out electronic yellow pages (www.yellow-pg.com), city directories (www.citysurf.com), directories specific to your industry or business (www.bizweb.com), and guides (www.about.com).

Classified Ads: Write up a short (200 words or fewer) all-text ad for your business and you can post it for free or a small fee at specified sites, including http://classifieds.yahoo.com and www.classifieds2000.com, as well as on the big commercial services like AOL and MSN. Check out online malls and both electronic and traditional newsletters for cheap space as well.

2. Cross-Promote

Developing alliances in cyberspace is a win-win marketing move—if you make the right matches.

Link Exchanges: Search for sites that target the same market as yours (but are not direct competitors) or complement your product or service. For example, a children's clothing e-Biz is a logical fit with a parenting information site. Find the e-mail address in the "Contact Us" or "Info@" areas, and send a friendly request to trade website links. Most sites are happy to comply! Or list your site with a reciprocal link directory, such as www.reciprocalink.com. "Search engines are ranking higher based on 'link popularity,' so the more sites you can link to, the better," notes Gray. A few words of caution: Avoid placing reciprocal links on your home page—you don't want visitors surfing off your site before they get a chance to explore it.

Banner Ads: The big companies may pay thousands of dollars for their ads to run across selected websites, but many small e-Biz owners swap banners for free. There are several online link exchange services that offer this barter arrangement—MSN's LinkExchange is the oldest (www.linkexchange.com); www.BannerSwap.com is another popular one. You can't count on every click-through to immediately become a new client or customer, but you can count on banner ads to help build awareness about your business. For best results, arrange to swap ads with sites that relate to your products or services.

Affiliates: Offering an affiliate program can also boost traffic, suggests Georganne Fiumara, founder of HomeWorkingMom.com. You can either go through one of the established affiliate managers like www.Commission Junction.com or www.reporting.net, or purchase special software to set one up yourself. "The way it works is you offer a 'per click' bounty or percentage of sales to sites that use your banner ads and send traffic your way," she explains.

Some mompreneurs sign up for affiliate programs to place on their sites—a move that won't increase traffic but can boost income. When Shelley Taylor first launched www.singleparentcentral.com, she put up banners from several online companies, including amazon.com—one of the best-known and highest-paying affiliate programs. Every time a visitor clicks on a banner placed on her site, Taylor gets paid a percentage. Some programs pay for referrals even if no sale is made. "I shopped around for the best affiliate programs and the ones that matched the interests of my target audience," says Taylor, "and some of the ones I chose generated quite a nice income."

Anne Fognano belongs to over 200 affiliate programs and runs a successful one of her own, allowing her to make money from both ends. "I've teamed up with partners ranging from small mom-run businesses to large companies," she says, and her business has steadily grown.

To find out how to become an affiliate or get a banner ad, go to the site you're interested in and click on "Join Affiliates" or "Join Associates." The information might also be in the "About Us" section of the website.

Web Rings: Another way to create free reciprocal linking is by forming your own Web ring. These are designed to link together business owners with related products or interests so visitors can easily browse similar sites. You click on the designated link on the bottom of each member's page and can access everyone in the ring. The goal is to drive traffic to all the sites, which is exactly what happened for a group of craftswomen who formed a Web ring using a free iVillage home page. One craftswoman started the ring and runs it; others may join if their wares meet the group's standards. The downside is that a viewer may quickly click off one site if another in the ring catches her eye.

Group Sites: Service businesses can also link together, setting up a marketing and referral website like Debra Haas and an "amazing group" of entrepreneurial women did. The educational policy consultant joined with other professionals she had met through networking groups and grad school and launched WizerWorks.com—a polished website that "works smarter" by marketing all their businesses and linking to all their sites. "On the home page of the site, a visitor goes through the 'front door' and is led down hallways to explore all the individual skill sets of the participants," Haas explains. "It has a very professional, unified look—no one would ever guess we're home-based!"

3. Use E-mail Effectively

Spread the word about your business through electronic mail—it's the cheapest and fastest way to reach the most people.

Digital Signature or "Sig File": Compose a tag line to attach to the end of all your e-mail messages, articles, and other written materials that go out over the Internet. This four-to-six-line "addendum" should contain your name, company name, a one-line phrase describing your product or service, phone number, and Web address/URL. Fax number, e-mail address, and snail-mail address are optional. Here's an example of a typical sig file:

Lesley Spencer, MS; Founder & Director
Home-Based Working Moms (HBWM)
"The association that helps bring working moms closer to their children"
www.HBWM.com

Custom Mailing List: Develop a database from your e-mail contacts and website visitors and convert it into a subscriber-based list of potential customers or clients. "Send to a prequalified list of people that have an interest in your business and have communicated with you in the past," recommends Donald Bass, an Internet marketing consultant. DO NOT add anyone to the list without first providing them with the choice to "opt in"—and the opportunity to remove themselves from the list at any time. (See Chapter 6 for legalities and how-tos.) Cindy Woods, owner of Watermark Creations, a custom stationery business (www.watermark.invitations.com), put a feature on her website called "eFriends." "Visitors sign up here and I can easily e-mail the entire list with specials or new products," she says. A "guest book" area on your site is another way to collect names for a subscriber list.

Once you have your list, use it to e-mail out discount offers, a tip of the day, a newsletter that offers a good mix of trends, tips, and special promotions, and even articles of interest from other Internet sources—always attaching your sig file! Keep in touch, but don't overdo it—people get turned off by too many e-mails.

4. Communicate

The Internet is the ultimate mass medium—take advantage of its reach.

Share Content. All those great articles and tips you've written for your own website or newsletter can be shared with sites and e-zines that have similar interests. Arrange with other Web biz owners to swap content on a regular basis, making sure they include your sig file and a link to your site every time. (Keep the "big boys" in mind, too, such as InternetDay.) You can also barter original content to specific sites in exchange for their services or free publicity. Tina Gasperson writes short pieces for a city resources/business site in her hometown of Tampa in exchange for a link to her website, www.gasperson.com.

Online Hosting: Volunteer to host a chat, moderate a message board, or lead a discussion group on another site, targeting those that focus on moms, women, small businesses, or your particular market. The online forums on AOL, CompuServe, and other large carriers are particularly hospitable. "AOL is always looking for lunch chat hosts in the small biz area," says Terri Gray.

Electronic Press Releases: As soon as you launch your website, write up a short press release to announce it. But don't stop there—continue to write releases as you expand your product line or services, take your business in a new direction, can tie into a timely news topic or holiday, or have helpful tips to offer. E-mail your releases to the general Internet e-zines and newsletters and those in your specialty (check online directories), as well as publicity distribution sites (such as (www.prweb.com) and online press rooms. While you're at it, print out some snail-mail releases to send to your local newspaper, the technology magazines (*Internet Life, Family PC*, etc.), and the technology editors at mass magazines like *Newsweek* and *People*. It's just a little extra postage! (See "The Power of Publicity," page 240.)

Minnesota mompreneur Corrie Pokrzywa of www.babyeshop.com got very good exposure after submitting releases to the news websites, especially DigitalWork.com. "Our first press release reached every news agency in our state, and we were even picked up by Bloomberg," she boasts. For help on creating releases, check out www.press-release-writing.com. And if you want to see where on the Net your news appears, Alta Vista offers a personal "clipping service," reports Debbie Williams of www.organized times.com. Simply type in your URL or business name, and the search engine results show you all the links to and mentions of your site. Once you've collected a few clips, consider creating a "press room" on your website to showcase the most flattering ones.

5. Offer Great Customer Service

Existing customers and clients can be your biggest source of leads and referrals, so keep them happy!

A Little TLC: Provide perks that encourage repeat visits, such as money-back guarantees, frequent-shopper discounts, a "personal catalog" of past purchases, and an online "suggestion box." "I go directly to the source and ask my customers for feedback on ways to improve my site and the convenience of shopping at my store," says BZ Riger-Hull, owner of www.charlottesgardens.com, an online shop offering gourmet foods and botanical bath and beauty products. She also acts as a "personal shopper," walking visitors through the Web store (by phone) to help them make selections. "Customer service is very important to me, and I am pleased when my customers tell me how thrilled they are with their shopping experience," Riger-Hull reports.

Personal E-mails: Auto-responders may lighten your workload, but they don't create close relationships. Go the extra mile and send personal e-mails when an existing or potential client or customer contacts you through your website, places an order, or requests information.

Visitor Rewards: Show your appreciation by reciprocating. Mia Cronan e-mails a free recipe to each new subscriber of her e-zine. When Web developer Terri Gray needs to buy a gift, she shops the sites of past and current clients first, and places her orders with them.

"Live" Interaction: Post your phone number on every one of your Web pages so viewers know there's a real person out there in cyberspace. And don't hesitate to pick up the phone yourself when a customer or client needs a little handholding. Sharon Mullen, who sells juvenile products from www.InventiveParent.com, remembers, "I recently had a problem with an order and phoned my customer. She was so thrilled to hear a real voice!"

6. Provide a Personal Touch

High-tech doesn't have to mean low touch! Mompreneurs are learning to pamper clients and customers in small ways to counteract the anonymity of the Net.

▪ Diane Long, owner of D's Stitcheree, a custom embroidery and design business, sends customers samples of her work before she starts a job. "It's hard to trust someone you can't see, so I try to go the extra step to please my customers and make them feel like they're dealing with a friend."

■ Nancy Hayes, a virtual assistant from Arnold, Missouri, offers clients unique handmade thank-you cards along with her secretarial services. "I grow flowers in my backyard as a hobby, and I incorporate the flower seeds into the cards," says the owner of Accurate Office Services. Hayes's idea has become so popular, she now markets the cards—and packages of seeds and dried herbs—on the side.

■ Vicki Mote Bodwell, founder of warmbiscuit.com, a children's bedding and furnishings business, sends out fabric swatches via snail mail so customers can get a feel for her products before ordering.

■ Gina Bruce, partner in a virtual advertising agency, gathers magazine and newspaper clips of product mentions and sends them to clients, along with handwritten thank-you notes.

■ Writer Tina Gasperson splurges on beautiful holiday cards for her clients. We do the same, frequently hand-delivering seasonal "goody bags" to local clients (sometimes with our children in tow!).

7. Give away Freebies

Free products and services can help put your business in a positive light—but don't go overboard and break the bank.

Contests: Sherri Ingram Breetzke of The Creativity Zone runs a monthly contest for her subscriber list, and gives away gift certificates winners can redeem at her website. Mompreneurs offering services can do the same. On a tight budget? Contest prizes can cost you nothing—a blurb or short article on your website about the winner is attention-grabbing and *free*!

Samples: "If you're selling a product, give away something with every order, recommends Amy Schlicht, owner of MyPerfectCandle.com in Milwaukee. "Internet customers are always looking for deals." Schlicht sends out a free votive candle with every online purchase—an inexpensive token of appreciation.

Pro Bono Work: Donating products or services generates great word of mouth about your business—especially if you write up a brief press release to get the word out. "I offered my services for free to one client," says Kristie Tamsevicius, a Web designer and e-book publisher (www. kcustom.com). "From there it spread like wildfire. Before I knew it, my business was building itself!" To give potential customers hands-on experience with her product, Laurie Moore of PartyInABoxOnline.com contributed party kits to nonprofit groups for fund-raising purposes.

8. Establish Your "Brand"

Give your marketing materials a unified graphic look—and you'll be giving your business a polished, professional image.

Essential Elements: Online, a well-designed website is key to your success (See Chapter 5). Offline, your business cards, letterhead, envelopes, mailing labels, and other "paper" promotionals should all tie together and relate to your website. You can either create these materials on your computer using downloaded graphics or desktop publishing software, or hire a designer to give you the look you want. *Be sure* to include your URL on every piece. And use those business cards liberally, attaching them to everything you send out or give away, including flyers, brochures, catalogs, customer orders, gifts, and personal correspondence.

Brand Identity: A logo that integrates your company name and website address with eye-catching graphics provides instant recognition for your business. One easy and cost-effective way to get a logo designed is through the LogoLab site (www.logolab.com)—an e-Business that works interactively with small business clients. Once you have your logo, it can go on all the marketing materials we mentioned above, as well as any promotional items (stickers, pens, mouse pads, and the like). Mompreneurs use their logos creatively, displaying them on everything from license plate frames to car window decals, bookmarks, coffee mugs, and postcards.

Shameless Promotion: Build name recognition by sponsoring a community Little League team, a booth at a local crafts fair, or a fund-raising run or walk-a-thon. Have T-shirts, caps, balloons, and/or water bottles made up with your logo prominently printed on them. And don't forget your branded "giveaways" when you exhibit at trade shows and small business expos. WAHMfest (www.wahmfest.org), founded by mompreneur Marybeth Henry and now being held regionally around the country, is a friendly initiation into the world of trade shows.

9. Position yourself as an expert

Get known online as an expert in your field, and you and your e-Biz will be in great demand.

Columns: Sell a noncompetitive website on the idea of your writing a weekly or monthly column in your area of expertise. Once you gain an audience, consider syndicating the column to other outlets.

Virtual Conferences: Gather a panel of mompreneurs to present an online workshop or conference on a broadly appealing topic, such as website design or electronic marketing. Propose holding the conference at a scheduled time in a chat room on one of the work-at-home moms' or women's business sites.

Public Speaking: Leave the comfort of your computer chair and offer to speak at a real-time meeting, conference, or seminar. Conquer stage fright by beginning with a "nonthreatening" group, such as the Junior League or PTA. Then you may work your way up to your local continuing education program, Chamber of Commerce, or chapter of a professional or small business organization. Shannon Entin, founder of www.fitnesslink.com, forced herself to accept speaking engagements as an essential part of promoting her business. Her best move—attending meetings of the local Toastmasters Club to gain confidence and learn presentation tips.

Awards Competitions: Almost every field of business has an annual awards competition. Check the professional association in your line of business, and see when and how to enter. If you win, be sure to write that press release!

10. Make the Most of Word-of-Mouth Advertising

Word of mouth is "viral"—it has the ability to spread to every portal in cyberspace. "It's the best customer referral on the Web," says Jodi Turek, cofounder of womensforum.com, a support network for businesswomen, "much more so than a full-page newspaper ad." Positive buzz is one of the oldest, most powerful, and *cheapest* advertising tools you can use, online or off. So keep spreading the word! Tell everyone you know about your business: family, friends, neighbors, former colleagues, your kids' teachers— you name it.

When satisfied customers and clients praise your products or services, get it in writing. Debra Haas (www.haaspolicy.com) suggests using their comments as testimonials on your website and in other promotional materials, with their consent, of course. "On my site, I put the testimonials under the heading 'Here's what clients are saying about Haas Policy Consulting,' then add a link to the client's website," says Haas. "It's been very effective."

CLICK AND SAVE: *Marketing Tips*

>> *www.clickz.com*

>> *www.gmarketing.com*

>> *www.ideamarketers.com*

>> *www.marketing1to1.com*

>> *www.press-release-writing.com*

>> *www.promoteyourself.com*

>> *www.targeting.com*

A Face in the Virtual Crowd

At last count, Azriela Jaffe's name had popped up 79,000 times in a standard Web search—figures that would thrill any mompreneur! How did this mother of three from Yardley, Pennsylvania, get such enviable exposure? She focused on what she did best—writing content—and didn't waste her energy and money on programming her website, conducting e-commerce, or advertising.

Carve Out a Niche: Jaffe specializes in writing about small businesses and relationships, and not only produces her own Internet newsletters (including *The Best Ideas in Business, Create Your Own Luck,* and *Entrepreneurial Couples Success Letter*), but has become a sought-after contributor to many e-zines, e-mail newsletters, and websites. Her syndicated columns are featured on *entrepreneurmag.com, infoUSA.com, fortunesb.com,* and *isquare.com.* Jaffe's very basic website, Anchored Dreams *(www.isquare.com/crlink. htm),* simply displays information on her books (with links to *amazon.com)* and syndicated columns, and offers quizzes, tips, and other resources for entrepreneurial couples.

Make a Name for Yourself: "Developing a niche takes a long time," says Jaffe, who began her first online newsletter in 1996. "But once I established credibility as an expert in my field, business began to flow to me." Although she doesn't sell any products on the Web, Jaffe has built a "brand" based on her expertise. She's been able to capitalize on her brand offline, too—as a book author, syndicated newspaper columnist, and speaker.

Market-Smart: Sponsorships and bartering have kept Jaffe's marketing expenses low. Business Filings, Inc. and Web Cards, Inc. each sponsor one of her e-newsletters; she barters for online and offline services with other business professionals; and she pays very little to get two newsletters out to her list. Jaffe's sig file, attached to every piece of writing she does online, identifies the many hats she wears as a mompreneur.

Best Byte: "Become an expert in a very defined niche, then get yourself interviewed by the media—particularly online sources—as often as possible," says Jaffe. "Over time, the Internet will fill up with transcripts containing interviews about you. When a researcher keys in your subject matter, there you are—showing up a zillion times on their search engines."

THE POWER OF PUBLICITY

Print reporters and television producers are hungry for "new media" news, and you may be able to get their attention with some timely, topical public relations. Start small, sending out a note and press release to your local TV and radio stations, newspapers, and regional magazines. Once you have some tapes or clips, you can put together a more impressive-looking press packet and go for the national guys. On a per-project basis, you may find it worthwhile to hire a professional publicist to announce and support "big" news items, such as a site redesign or a product line expansion.

Mary Tenety and Lori Tesla Schmid, cofounders of The Female Athlete (www.thefemaleathlete.com), targeted the right media at the right time, and became high scorers in the dot.com competition. It began when they issued their first print catalog in 1997—the result of their participating in many conversations on the sidelines of their daughters' games (soccer, basketball, or softball, depending on the season), scouring the market for sporting equipment designed for girls, and test-marketing the merchandise at local tournaments. "We built up a mailing list and got a lot of positive feedback from our grassroots marketing efforts," says Tenety, who is based on Long Island, New York. "Most importantly, we were able to interact with our customers—Gen Y female athletes and their parents, grandparents, and coaches."

The pair of soccer moms generated plenty of good local buzz, but their Christmas catalog was going national and they needed to reach a wider audience. "The two of us couldn't do much nationally on our own," says Tenety, "so we hired a one-shot publicist to get the word out." With its fresh slant, The Female Athlete story was picked up by over 100 newspapers around the country, and orders poured in. Another media blitz accompanied the website launch in 1998, and the Tenety-Schmid team amassed more clips. The unique mission of The Female Athlete "to provide apparel, gear, and accessories that are not only functional but also inspirational and motivational"—shines through in both its product line and its supportive online community for girls. It makes a great story, and by the end of 2000, it was being told in many large-circulation magazines and newspapers, including *People, Redbook, Working Mother, USA Today,* and the *New York Times.* Publicity builds publicity!

 ## Web Celeb

Nancy Evans

Cofounder and Editor-in-Chief, *iVillage.com:* The Women's Network
(www.ivillage.com)
New York City
Mom of 1

The first time Nancy Evans logged on to the Internet in the early 1990s, she stumbled into an AOL chat room, didn't know what to do, and cautiously tiptoed out the moment someone mentioned her screen name. That's when she decided to make it her mission to humanize cyberspace. The result is iVillage.com—the Web's premier portal for women, boasting millions of visitors a month.

When Evans and her partner, Candice Carpenter, cofounded iVillage in 1995, only 9 percent of Net users were women. "It wasn't a 'slam dunk,' " she recalls. "But as soon as I became familiar with the Internet myself, I realized it could be the ultimate 'home appliance' for women, helping us balance our work and family lives." Armed with her personal list of Web-related pet peeves, she set out to create a friendly, feminine "home" in cyberspace that women could call their own. Evans made sure the content and commands were written in plain English and that the color palette was warm and inviting. "Magazine colors didn't work," says the former print editor for such publications as *Family Life, Glamour,* and *Harper's Weekly.* "I also stayed away from whizzy-bang things and never used technology before its time," she adds, realizing that many women were probably a bit technophobic back in those days.

With the launch of the network's flagship channel, Parent Soup, in 1996, Evans was on her way to accomplishing her mission. AOL contributed to the funding, and she contributed to the channel's comfortable look and feel. "I thought it was very important to be greeted by a host in every chat room and message board, just like at a party," says Evans. "That made everyone feel welcome and part of the community." By talking to each other in these online forums, visitors to Parent Soup soon developed a strong camaraderie and sense of community. And that community is what came to set iVillage apart and drive its growth.

As the network grew, the partners added content channels that covered the issues women care about most—relationships, health, work, money, and dieting, among others. Each is a branded community providing interactive services, peer support, and online access to experts. "The site is designed with doors of entry to each channel—these became community doors, and women congregate inside much like they do at the playground," Evans says. What eventually happened was that the visitors coming to iVillage began to help the site evolve. "Women started bringing in ideas and seeding the content, creating a new medium that could no longer be compartmentalized like magazine departments."

Evans has seen firsthand how the personal connections women make online can lead the way to great marketing opportunities. A customized approach works best—finding mompreneurs or sites that are a good fit with yours and suggesting an exchange of links, either by e-mail or snail mail. Forming partnerships can certainly power up your business, as it did for Evans and Carpenter's. Each brought her own skill sets to the table— Evans her editorial talents, and Carpenter her corporate management experience by way of Time-Warner and American Express. "I can't imagine starting a business like this without having a person to strategize with and bounce ideas off," Evans says. "There are days when you're very tired, and if one partner is down, the other can be bullish and rearing to go."

How did Evans manage to balance the demands of motherhood with those of an Internet start-up? For one thing, she worked on the concept in the basement of her house, and her daughter, Samantha, was involved from the beginning. "When we were looking over the first design for Parent Soup, Samantha was at the meeting. We wanted the design to reflect the spirit of childhood, but she thought it was too childish, so we revamped it," Evans remembers. "You wind up with a different type of child when you're a mompreneur . . . a much more capable person who is aware of her ability to make things happen and feels more control over her life." Samantha is filled with entrepreneurial enthusiasm, according to her mother, and wants to start a business when she grows up. "She thinks it's eminently doable."

As cofounder of a large, successful Internet company, Evans is in a good position to look ahead and tell us what she thinks will be the hottest e-Businesses for the near future. Her vote goes to service businesses. "Professional counseling, legal assistance, and other fee-based services will make a bigger impact on the Web," she says, "along with lifelong learning courses and personal services that cater to time-crunched women." She certainly guessed right the first time!

CHAPTER EIGHT

Survive & Thrive:
Staying Strong in a Dot.Com World

 **Sound Byte**

"Never make the mistake of assuming that because you are a work-at-home mom, that you are a small player in your industry. Empower yourself by visualizing that you're a significant player who will have inevitable success."

Diana West, mother of two; Gaithersburg, Maryland
Founder of Mothers' Online Thrift Shop (*www.motshop.com*)

Where will you and your business be five years from now? If someone had asked us that question five years ago, we would have been hard-pressed to give the right answer. We had just finished up our first book, *Mompreneurs®: A Mother's Practical Step-by-Step Guide to Work-at-Home Success,* and were awaiting its publication. We knew we were on to a big trend—everywhere we turned, we came across more and more moms who were choosing the flexibility and freedom of the work-from-home lifestyle. But little did we know that we were on the cusp of a major mompreneur movement!

As soon as our book was published, the word "mompreneur®" was popping up everywhere. As we were finishing up the book you are now reading, we realized that the mompreneur movement had actually caught up with the word. The amazing growth of the Internet, coupled with the recent "baby boomlet," has brought many more moms (and dads) home to work. Wireless Net connections, easy-access broadband, and almost weekly advances in technology can only fuel this entrepreneurial trend. The future certainly looks bright for small or home-based businesses on the Web!

Our most recent survey revealed an electronic migration of mompreneurs into new and exciting fields. Most of our respondents had started their e-Businesses or established an online presence in the last couple of years. Many are making more money than they had made in previous jobs, and a few of the more established e-mompreneurs were close to or above the $100,000-a-year salary mark!

What will it take for your business to survive and thrive well into the 21st century? You may be surprised to find out that some of the strategies for achieving long-term success are the very things that mompreneurs do best . . . like nurturing relationships and forging alliances . . . forming networks of support and active communities . . . focusing on personalization and service . . . spotting trends and defining a niche . . . multitasking for maximum efficiency.

But let's not forget those mothering skills! Your ability to set priorities and achieve balance in your life will help prevent burnout and boost your staying power. Patience and perseverance—the two most universal mommy traits!—will pay off in a big way, too. One of the top tips for avoiding dot.com disaster is to grow your business slowly and steadily. Internet pioneer Aliza Sherman, founder of Cybergrrl and Webgrrls and author of *Cybergrrl @ Work: Tips and Inspiration for the Professional You,* stresses that the key to creating a successful e-Biz is to build in stages. "Build slowly, adapt and change based on feedback, and constantly evaluate and reevaluate your product or service as you go along," she advises. "And don't spend a ton of money upfront without proving your concept."

MAKING IT ON THE NET

Isn't it necessary to attract venture capitalists and wealthy investors to become a successful online entrepreneur? How about a huge advertising campaign, lots of media exposure, and a pricey, cutting-edge website?

While these tactics have catapulted a handful of Internet start-ups into overnight sensations, they've also contributed to the downfall of too many others—especially after the dot.com meltdown of 2000, when investors became more cautious and IPOs lost their luster. It's now clear that "slow and steady" is a smarter way to go, so we've mapped out a less risky route on the cyber-highway to success—with the help of a group of Web experts and trend watchers to guide us around the bumps!

Julian Lange, a professor of entrepreneurship at Babson College in Massachusetts, is optimistic about the future of doing business on the Web. "Both entrepreneurship and the Internet are experiencing a revolution," he says, adding that opportunities will continue to open up online over the next few years. But he cautions, "Just because you're working in a different medium, the rules of business are not suspended. You still have to be businesslike in assessing opportunities and clever in marketing your business."

Stephen M. Smith, adjunct professor at Johns Hopkins University and CEO of Intellispark, Inc., an e-commerce consulting firm, agrees. "Many of the rules of the 'old economy' are just as relevant to the newer electronic marketplace," he says. "Building a small business on the Internet is a lot like building any other small business. Start with sufficient, but not excessive capital to pay expenses for three months or so while ramping up the business, set achievable goals for revenue and growth, and keep an eye on cash flow." Smith recommends these strategies to keep your business going strong:

Don't Overreach

Many would-be entrepreneurs have been lured to the Internet by promises of million-dollar returns. The reality is that there are comparatively few million-dollar businesses out there, but plenty of ways to build profitable businesses. Being realistic about what you can expect to achieve and about the funding you'll need will help you develop a stable business.

Focus on a Market, Not a Product

Products may come and go as you develop your business. Provided you are serving the changing needs of your market, you'll find a way to flourish.

Find Something You're Passionate About

Building a successful business takes a tremendous effort. If you don't have passion for serving the needs of your target market, the effort will overshadow the reward.

Passion is something that Jodi Turek, cofounder and president of womensforum.com, is certainly not lacking. Dedicated to helping women achieve business success, she created a grassroots partnership of independent entrepreneurial websites in 1996 and gradually expanded it into a powerful and prosperous support network for businesswomen. Many sites are now competing with hers for the the attention of women entrepreneurs, just as you're sure to find e-Businesses similar to yours vying for *your* target market. To meet this challenge, Turek advises, "Don't focus on who is doing more, doing better, or getting all the industry buzz. Instead, stay focused on your goals, differentiate yourself and your company, and talk up your differences."

"Talking up" your business requires a marketing plan with a strong communications component to build awareness. "What the brick-and-mortar companies did for branding their names through advertising in the past, click-and-mortar and e-Business companies are doing through public relations today," says Kristin Gabriel, a partner in e-com communications. She suggests developing a plan early on to create key messages about your product or service that will give your cyber-business "a face and personality." These messages should articulate who you are, why your business differs from the competition, and how you fill a niche in the marketplace. Differentiation is key, feels Lange of Babson College. You must "get above the noise level" in the Web marketplace, he says.

If your e-Business doesn't already have an offline presence, down the road you may want to think about expanding it into other channels to increase your sales or generate more income. An e-tailer may try a print catalog, for example, and an e-zine a paperback book. A website offering unusual jewelry may consider selling at crafts fairs, and an online tutor "live" classes. According to James L. McQuivey, a research director with Forrester Research, "An Internet company may reach part of the population, but it will never have the same kind of long-term relationships and sales volume as a company that has mastered many sales channels." The possibilities are endless—and we know that mompreneurs will be there!

DATA BANK: *What Is Your Secret to Success?*

Stick to it 30%

Be passionate about your business 16%

Network 16%

Evaluate and evolve the business 13%

Provide customer service 9%

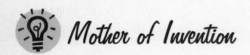 ## *Mother of Invention*

Michelle Mix had always used the computer to create designs for her home-based stitchery business, Mixed Thredz, Inc., which contracted with local customers, such as sporting goods stores, to embroider team hats, T-shirts, and other garments. But it wasn't until 1999 that the St. Michael, Minnesota, mom moved her business onto the Internet—with a product that utilized her embroidery machines and skills to accomplish a very different goal.

THE INSPIRATION: A news story about a car accident involving a nanny and the child she was caring for motivated this mom to combine her two loves—sewing and children—into the More About Me™ Emergency Information Kit. Mix recalls the incident: "The pair was transported to the hospital, where it was discovered that the nanny had no children of her

Growth Chart

As your business grows, you're bound to experience challenges and setbacks. Learn how these mompreneurs handled their "growing pains."

Mompreneur: Clarissa Chestnut *(www.candlesbyclarissa.com)*
Growing Pain: Launching a website. "I started my business with the full intention of doing Internet-only sales," says this Florida mom of two, "but I couldn't find the right person to design my site."
Cyber-Cure: To get her product out there, Chestnut started making her candles, scented body lotions, and bath gels in her garage and selling them offline. "I did home parties, sold person-to-person, and marketed my products wholesale before my website was up," she says.

Mompreneur: Ginger Jungling *(www.blissbaskets.com)*
Growing Pain: Expanding to the Web. Jungling's boss—owner of the Pure Bliss and Something Different gift basket shops in Anoka, Minnesota, didn't want to lose her able assistant when she became pregnant. "I wanted to be home with my baby, but still wished to use my creative talents," Jungling says.
Cyber-Cure: The two decided to take the stores online, launching a website that allowed Jungling to work from home, direct her creative energy into making beautiful gift baskets, and generate income. "I love that I can still be professional with clients even though it's three in the afternoon, I haven't taken a hot shower, and my son is singing 'da, da, da' while he bangs on my keyboard with his chubby, saliva-drenched fingers," says Jungling with a laugh.

Mompreneur: Penny Tallent *(www.fromtheheartsoap.com)*
Growing Pain: Getting a merchant account. "Most credit card companies charge outrageous prices to establish a merchant account, but not having one was the biggest mistake I made," says Tallent.
Cyber-Cure: This soapmaker talked with other small business people and found an issuer that offered reasonable rates. "Don't take the first company that solicits you," she warns. "It's likely to be the most expensive one." Tallent's sales have increased monthly since she's been accepting credit card payment.

Mompreneur: Shelley Sampson *(www.herwebbiz.com)*
Growing Pain: Building a client base electronically. "The traditional client meeting doesn't take place because you are negotiating via telephone and e-mail," says Sampson, whose site provides resources and tools for women entrepreneurs.

Growth Chart, continued

Cyber-Cure: Constant communication is the way Sampson has overcome this problem. "I make sure everything is 'down on paper' before I start a project so both sides know how we are to progress," she says. "Then I follow up with daily e-mail updates."

Mompreneur: Brenda Kofford *(www.saldage.com)*
Growing Pain: Developing trust over the Internet. Psychotherapist Kofford set up a website to reach women who do not have access to individual counseling. "My concern is that those who seek mental health counseling through the Internet are wishing for a quick resolution and do not take the time to insure that they are receiving services from a licensed therapist," she says.
Cyber-Cure: "E-mail counseling may be an avenue by which women can implement positive changes in their lives," says Kofford, but she realizes she has to be patient—it's going to take time to win people over to the idea of cyber-therapy.

Mompreneur: Debra M. Cohen *(www.homeownersreferral.com)*
Growing Pain: You can't do it all yourself! Running a service that links home owners with prescreened home improvement contractors takes a lot of time and energy. "I never dreamed the response to this type of service would be so tremendous," says this mom of two, who has also written a business manual that she markets to other entrepreneurs.
Cyber-Cure: Cohen delegates her least-favorite tasks to others. "I'm not a 'computer person' by nature," she says, "so I've chosen to outsource those responsibilities and focus on the day-to-day operation of my business."

Mompreneur: Laurie Wing *(www.cribbumper.com)*
Growing Pain: If you want it done right, do it yourself! When Wing invented the Next Stage Crib Bumper, a thinner crib bumper for older babies, she planned to sell the idea—not the product. "It became very time-consuming working with companies who would then market my product," she says.
Cyber-Cure: Wing patented the crib bumper and set up a website to sell it herself. "Don't sit back and wait for results," advises this mompreneur. "Make them happen."

own, and no one could find out the name of the little boy who had accompanied her." The story did have a happy ending—after about four hours, the child was reunited with his parents—but Mix felt in her heart that the next unidentified child might not be so lucky. "As a parent, I knew there had to be a way to give children safe identification," she says.

THE START-UP: The mother of two set to work designing a fabric panel that she embroidered with the words "More About Me Emergency Information Kit." It serves as the cover of a small pouch; inside is a plastic-protected ID card on which a person's name, address, phone number, and medical history can be written. The original kits are designed to attach with Velcro fasteners to a car seat belt; a newer version can be worn on a skirt or pants belt—a response to requests by senior citizens.

STEPS TO SUCCESS: Almost immediately, Mix trademarked the name and applied for a patent, then went to register her domain name. "I wanted to expand onto the Internet, because I needed the fastest, most effective method to reach as many people as I could in a short period of time," she says. Unfortunately, moreaboutme.com was already reserved. Instead of contesting its use, Mix went with emoreaboutme.com.

The kits caught on quickly. Parents who found the website e-mailed the URL to friends, generating lots of word-of-mouth traffic. Several parenting sites have included information about the product in their electronic newsletters, and Mix frequently speaks at community organizations and child care events about safety awareness. She's developed a press package that contains the story of her business, car seat safety statistics, and a sample kit, and has gotten good local and national media coverage as a result. "My best marketers have turned out to be the police and fire departments," Mix says. "They've spread the word near and far."

THE BALANCING ACT: All the production, packaging, and shipping of the kits takes place in her basement "workshop," allowing Mix to be there for her two children. Employees (some of whom are stay-at-home moms) piece together the kits' panels, topstitch, and add the Velcro, and the kids help out with other tasks and are always included in the business successes. When things get hectic, Mix's extended family and friends lend a hand, too. "It does require balance and it takes some time to find it, but once you figure it out, it's awesome," she says.

SURVIVE AND THRIVE: Mix has proven that you can have a successful e-Biz based on just one reasonably priced product. Although she's still doing custom embroidery work, she says, "The website is now the single most important aspect of my business." *And* the most rewarding. In the back of her mind, this mompreneur knew that one day she was going to get that phone call reporting that her kit had helped save a life. "After only six months in business, I was called by the friend of a man who was wearing the kit on his belt when he had a heart attack," Mix says. "When the EMTs arrived, they were able to instantly read his medical history, find out about his heart condition, and contact his doctor while in transit to the hospital. The patient immediately received lifesaving treatment specific to his condition." It's emotional moments like these that fire up this mom's continuing passion for her business.

REAL SURVIVAL STRATEGIES FOR VIRTUAL BUSINESSES

The most successful e-Businesses share a number of common survival strategies. Consider these as you climb the cyber-ladder of success.

Survival Strategy #1: Watch the Trends

Every "next best thing" that comes along is not going to make a profitable business, but some long-term trends certainly can. Take mompreneur Mary Lou Andre, for example. She started an offline fashion consulting company called Organization By Design (OBD) back in the "dressier" days of 1992, but now spends much of her time helping corporations establish casual dress code policies. In the early years of her business, she worked one-on-one with individuals, teaching effective wardrobe management and image-building skills. By 1995, Andre was presenting retail seminars and corporate workshops to Fortune 500 companies and publishing a popular, subscription-based fashion newsletter, *Dressing Well.* "By pouring my heart and soul into very low-cost/no-cost marketing activities and granting hundreds of interviews to the media, I built credibility for my company," she says.

Andre's ability to adapt to the trends and roll with the punches kept OBD going strong as fashion styles—and her lifestyle—changed. "I broke my leg in 1997, which forced me to slow down, hire a fashion consultant to work with our individual clients, and explore opportunities on the Web," she recalls. Soon, Dressingwell.com was launched and OBD was elevated into the national spotlight. Andre began publishing an online version of *Dressing Well,* selling her branded wardrobe-organization product, and connecting with clients around the country (and the world!)—all from her website. When she gave birth to twin boys in 1999, she says, "Everything fell into place, thanks largely to the Web. Large national accounts started e-mailing me about business casual consulting (a lasting trend!) and other professional image development projects. I was on the computer constantly and getting more done more effectively." The Internet helps her keep up with the times while watching her twin boys grow up.

Be hip to what's hot, but don't shorten the life span of your business by being *too* trendy. When Texan Shannon Rubio was searching for a business idea, she wanted something with broad appeal (other than books and CDs) that was not limited by seasonality, geography, or age. She hit upon the Smile Box, a cross between a gift basket and a care package, all wrapped up in a smiley-face box Rubio designed herself. "My website has a wide selection of ready-made Smile Boxes to go, but we also offer a 'Create A Box' page where customers can choose the contents and add their personal touch," says Rubio. TheSmileBox.com has just the right blend of "trendy" and "timeless"!

Survival Strategy #2: Think Out of the Box

You may believe that every possible niche on the Net has been filled by now, but there's always a new angle or a new way to position your product or service. For seven years, Kim Michaux ran a popular semiannual consignment sale featuring past-season children's clothing from specialty shops and manufacturers. None of the stores wanted the unsold merchandise back, so it sat in the basement of Michaux's Virginia home. "I was trying to figure out a way to sell the clothes when it occurred to me that these children's boutiques didn't have an outlet—they were too small for the big discounters," says this mom of three. So Michaux created One of a Kind Kid (oneofakindkid.com), an online "outlet" and the only place to find specialty store brands at 40 percent to 60 percent off all the time. "Our customers love the prices and quality," she says, adding "Word has spread and stores are now contacting us!"

Draftswoman Dawn Vaughan was designing house plans for building contractors and private clients from her home office in the garage when she decided to put up a website. Her goal was to attract business when the local work slowed down during the off-season. From www.vhdesign.com, she now designs custom homes for clients all over the country . . . and even overseas! "I create a password-protected Web page for each client on which I upload 3-D views and floor plans so they can see the progress of their home at their convenience." Technology and a bit of visionary thinking turned the impossible into the possible for this mom of three.

Survival Strategy #3: Narrow Your Niche

Specialization can give you a competitive edge as the number of businesses on the Web continues to multiply. Dayle Hayes runs "Nutrition for the Future" from her home in Billings, Montana. Although there are many dietitians around the country doing what she does—counseling patients via e-mail and writing nutrition pieces for e-zines and health websites—she has positioned herself as a leader in the world of e-nutrition. "I am a regular speaker on Internet-related topics at meetings of the American Dietetic Assocation, major food companies, and trade associations," she says. Hayes has developed a specialty educating dietitians and food executives about electronic communication. By doing so, she has placed herself on equal footing with consultants who live in New York City, Chicago, and Washington, D.C. "I just have a lot less stress, because I live in the 'Last Best Place,' " she says with a laugh.

Patricia Aycock Mertz loves collecting sterling silver and crystal beads and semiprecious stones from around the world. She learned how to make beaded jewelry in a class at her local fabric store, but the bead-stringing took some practice and concentration. "I'm not a very patient person," Aycock Mertz admits. "At the end of the class, when the instructor showed us how to make earrings, I picked it up quickly." That, coupled with a lifelong love of this particular type of jewelry, convinced the designer to feature just earrings on her website, www.aycockmertzltd.com.

After one pair was selected as part of QVC's "Quest for the Best Tour" and Aycock Mertz was profiled in *Victoria* magazine, the website became a popular destination for people looking for unique, handcrafted earrings.

Survival Strategy #4: Expand Your Brand

If you've established a branded product or service offline, use the Web to extend the brand online. Kim Samuelson had worked in her father's northern Minnesota restaurant, RBJ's, since she was 12 years old, and when he died prematurely of cancer, she took over the business at the young age of 19. The restaurant continued to gain in reputation, and when Samuelson decided to branch out, it was logical to expand on the RBJ's name. She and her husband, a farmer in the agricultural industry, began growing rhubarb, and this tireless entrepreneur started making batches of rhubarb/strawberry spreadable fruit from her mother's recipe. The jamlike product was a local hit, and the line soon expanded to include other flavors. "After the first round of sales, we realized the need to reach the masses, and took RBJ's Spreadable Fruit online in 1998," Samuelson says.

Fruit syrups, sauces, and greeting cards with an edible chocolate twist were soon being sold under the RBJ's label from www.spreadablefruit.com, along with the site's namesake product. "The business started as a family business and remains that today," says this mompreneur. "I needed something that was flexible enough so I could still have time to parent my three daughters and be a wife to my husband." Harvest time brings the whole family, assorted neighbors, and employees of the restaurant to the Samuelson orchards to pick chokeberries, rhubarb, plums, and apples for the product line. RBJ's Spreadable Fruit has grown from a very small business to a national company, and is getting bigger every day. But Samuelson warns, "The Internet is simply a tool; it is not the end-all and will not drive your business. Each woman-owned business still depends on that woman to drive her own business."

Survival of the Fittest

Shannon Entin put herself on the cyber-map way back in the dark ages of the mid-1990s. An experienced group exercise instructor and dedicated fitness buff, she wanted to share her knowledge with as many folks as possible. "I saw the tremendous potential to help people by publishing credible, timely fitness and health information online," she remembers. "I really thought the Internet was going to be huge. Turns out I was right!" When she went on the Web to see what was available in the fitness arena, she came up practically empty-handed. Entin immediately nailed her niche and created FitnessLink *(www.fitnesslink.com).*

Steps to Success: With a computer, modem, and lots of enthusiasm, she launched her website in 1995. It started out as a small, informational e-zine offering news, tips, and recommendations—some written by Entin herself and others culled from reliable Internet sources. "I just love having all that information at my fingertips and spreading what I feel is worthwhile to other people," she says. "It gives me a great sense of power. And that's what I hope FitnessLink brings to viewers—a sense of power over their own health and fitness and the ability to implement a healthy lifestyle."

Entin worked long hours, slept little, and scrimped and saved to grow her e-Biz. Husband Paul, a public relations specialist, developed a media kit and press releases. As a result, stories appeared in the *Wall Street Journal,* the *Los Angeles Times,* and *Shape* magazine. Traffic increased and advertisers became interested. Four years after the site's launch, the Lambertville, New Jersey, mom was ready to take FitnessLink to the next level, and applied for a small business loan.

Stay Competitive: Entin grew her site by maintaining the high quality of the content and staying true to her original mission. "I didn't try to branch out into areas that weren't related to mine," she says. "I think a lot of businesses fail because they try too hard to be everything to everybody." Instead, she narrowed her niche to target dedicated exercisers and competitive athletes after online surveys revealed that these were her most frequent and loyal visitors. To keep her edge and a little balance in her life, Entin now hires professional writers to contribute some of the content. "FitnessLink remains a leader in the industry by giving our readers what they want and providing credible information," says this mompreneur.

Boost the Brand: In the fall of 2000, FitnessLink was acquired by iBoost Technology, Inc. The parent company takes care of many of the day-to-day tasks of running the business—tasks Entin was all too happy to give up! Now she can devote more of her time to conceptualizing ideas, writing, assigning, and editing stories, leading offline workshops,

Survival of the Fittest, continued

and speaking at public events. And iBoost will give FitnessLink the marketing "boost" it needs to continue as a prime Internet destination. "We'll be growing by leaps and bounds in the next three to five years," Entin predicts. "As part of the huge iBoost network, our content will be syndicated all over the Web, and we now have a full-time sales staff to sell advertising."

Survive and Thrive: "Keeping a healthy, balanced outlook is essential to long-term survival," says Entin. "Seeing how happy, confident, and stable my son is each day is my reward." She remembers one particularly trying day when the house was in a shambles, two days of work was backed up on her desk, and she had a terrible cold. "My son, Logan, ran into my home office and announced, 'Hi there,' for the first time ever. I was so happy it was me who heard those words, and not a day care provider, that I forgot all about the day's challenges."

Survival Strategy #5: Team Up for Success

Forming partnerships and alliances—online and off—has helped many a mompreneur grow her business. Web tools have eased the way to cross-promoting and co-op marketing (see Chapter 7), and several moms are making the most of these tools to propel their businesses to the next level.

Michelle Donahue-Arpas of GeniusBabies.com and Dawn Lloyd of Baby University.com, "met" on the Internet, supported each other's businesses via e-mail, and cross-marketed their websites before they established a more proactive virtual partnership. Along with other small e-commerce companies owned by moms, they formed MyBabyShops.com. "We decided that if we didn't join together and help one another, we wouldn't survive," says Donahue-Arpas, who is the marketing expert of the online mall, while Lloyd is the webmaster. Every cent contributed by the mompreneurs is put into an advertising budget so that MyBabyShops.com can get its message out far and wide. "Extra-personal service is our big thing," Donahue-Arpas boasts, whose GeniusBabies.com sells developmental and educational toys, videos, and music. Surprisingly, all but one of the mompreneurs are in direct competition with each other—Lloyd is the only one who doesn't offer baby merchandise; she runs a pregnancy/parenting resource and community site. Even so, all the e-Bizzes in the online mall have bene-fited.

As far-fetched as it may sound, don't overlook teaming up as a player with a bigger dot.com company. Some are now interested in bringing small entrepreneurs online in an effort to beef up revenues. If you sell gar-dening supplies, for example, by joining forces with amazon.com's zShops, every time a visitor clicks on a gardening book, a link would appear to your website. This type of arrangement should gain in popularity as e-commerce expands.

Survival Strategy #6: Embrace the Power of the Internet

Michelle Storrusten, a virtual assistant who owns galfridayenterprises.com, couldn't have said it better: "Be willing to change and grow with the new technology. Don't wait for someone else to get there first." Former high-tech industry employee Debbie Swanson realized that the Internet was growing and changing rapidly, so when she saw the potential for a busi-ness that would help websites build and sustain online communities, she jumped on it. Soon after her daughter was born in 1999, she launched iPopulate.com—a niche e-Biz that specializes in "community relationship management." "Technology now provides countless opportunities to con-nect people in useful and innovative ways," says Swanson, whose mission is to humanize the Internet by developing meaningful relationships among members of online communities. These vibrant communities, in turn, can spur website traffic and e-commerce. Swanson's ultimate goal is to build "a corporation without walls" that will be managed and operated by a home-based network of employees.

Survival Strategy #7: Service With a Capital P

Personal service is proving to be a rewarding way to keep a competitive edge and counteract the impersonality of the Internet. Mompreneurs' direct, hands-on approach allows them to personalize their sites with increasing success—much to the delight of their clients and customers.

Jodie Freeman, who sells imaginatively packaged baby gifts online, handwrites charming cards to accompany each order. "I keep a record of previous messages in my database so a shopper doesn't have to think up something original each time she sends a present for a shower or a newborn," she says. Recently, Freeman added a pop-up window to her site, www.sendababygift.com, asking shoppers if they would like to purchase something special for a big brother or big sister to send along with the baby gift.

Personalization is poised to become more of a marketing force, as competition intensifies and technology improves. At the time we were finishing up this book, innovative websites had added virtual shopping advisors (electronic images of human clerks!), Instant Messaging and hosted chats to answer questions *immediately,* and toll-free access for real-time phone conversations. But this is just the tip of the personalization iceberg, as e-shoppers continue to expect and demand the same quality service they get from upscale brick-and-mortar stores.

Technology will also advance the concept of customization—the watchword of 21st-century e-marketing, according to the Connecticut-based Peppers & Rogers Group, originators of "1 to 1 marketing." Large sites like American Airlines and Amazon were among the first to customize Web pages to target individual visitors, and other e-Businesses are following suit as the technology matures.

Survival Strategy #8: Explore New Markets

Most mompreneurs on the Web target their products or services directly to consumers—known in e-talk as B2C. And you can develop a lucrative business by sticking with that market. But it also pays to look into the B2B (business to business) and B2G (business to government) marketplaces. Even if your end user is still the consumer, you may find it more practical and attractive to market your product or service through an established e-commerce distribution channel, feels Stephen M. Smith of Johns Hopkins University.

When Susan Neiberg Terkel of Hudson, Ohio, started Gobs of Knobs, a small company selling the hand-painted wooden knobs she designed and patented, she used her website as a referral source only. "I had decided to market directly to decorative hardware stores and kitchen designers through their sales reps, and these distributors don't want you competing for the same customer in an area," says Terkel. So the first version of www. gobsofknobs.com simply provided information for obtaining a print catalog, contacting the company, and getting connected with a local distributor.

Once the business got going, Terkel revamped the website to showcase her imaginative knobs in use on kitchen cabinets, dresser drawers, and bathroom vanities. Her target market is still interior decorators, designers, and retailers; consumers can't order products directly from the website, but they can e-mail Terkel for shopping sources, a print catalog, or advice. "E-mail allows me to be more personal with my customers. I can offer them custom painting and make decorating suggestions," says the mom of three. "Close contact is important to my business, because my knobs are pricey and appeal to the customer who wants to do something very special."

Survival Strategy #9: Go Global

Of the 295 million people worldwide who surfed the Net via a home computer in 2000, the top five nations represented were the United States (about 137 million), Japan (26.3 million), the United Kingdom (19.4 million), Germany (15.5 million), and Canada (13.1 million), according to a Nielsen/Net Ratings survey. That same year, Forrester Research reported that global Internet trade will hit $6.8 trillion in 2004, comprised of both B2B and B2C sales.

There's no doubt that going global can increase your market exponentially. Thanks to the worldwide nature of the Web, Sharon Roe, a Seattle native and mother of two who was transplanted to Scotland, earns twice as much as she did working full-time for a local marketing agency. Her home-based media relations business counts oil and technology companies and golf courses among its clients. "At any one time, I may have press releases in the pipeline for review in Nigeria, Seattle, England, Singapore, Brazil, Norway, and Newfoundland," says Roe. Communication is all done through e-mail and telephone.

However, the international scope of the Internet can be a double-edged sword—it can boost your customer and client base to an interesting and profitable level or it may literally smother you with tons of work! Judicious marketing and the ability to say no will help you find a happy medium. In addition, keep in mind that you may experience currency and credit card snafus, shipping and language problems, and legal kinks when you do business across the borders (see Chapter 6).

Survival Strategy #10: Keep Learning

Certain fields demand that you brush up on the latest technology, developments, and information or you'll be left behind in the cyber-dust. Web businesses are especially vulnerable. "This is a field that is constantly changing, and in order to stay competitive, you have to learn new skills," says Web developer Jean Lentz, who takes classes to keep current. Adds Charlene Wilhelmson, a Web designer/Internet technician from British Columbia, Canada, "When you work in information technology, you are always upgrading, researching, learning. I didn't know the brain could hold that much!" she jokes.

Mompreneurs in other specialties have gone back to school (both online and off) to gather knowledge and expertise that would add value to their businesses. Soon after Andrea Moyer of Clinton, Maryland, set up www.amets.net/essentials to market essential oils and accessories, she enrolled in a course to become an aromatherapist and learn more about the products she was selling. Not only did Moyer pick up relevant information and research to enhance the content of her website, she was able to pass on a very important lesson. "One of my study materials was tasting the different essential oils, and when the 'anise' came around, instead of putting a small drop on my finger, I ingested it!" she remembers. "Turns out that when overdosed, anise can have a narcotic effect, and even that small drop is a large quantity when it comes to essential oils." Luckily, Moyer ended up with nothing more than a slight buzz, but she certainly learned to be more cautious—and to tell others to do the same.

Slick Site for City Kids

New York City mom Susan Maloney had worked in the fashion and publishing businesses before her daughter was born in 1996. Like new moms everywhere, she was always searching for useful parenting and child-rearing information, and often surfed the Internet to find it. "What I quickly discovered was there wasn't any local information online," she remembers. "Everything was very general and national—such as 'How do I comfort a colicky baby?'—and the sites were all designed in cutesy pink and blue."

Narrowing the Niche: As a parent raising a child in a metropolitan area, Maloney had particular needs that weren't being addressed on the Web. She wanted answers to questions such as "Where are the 'Mommy and Me' classes in my neighborhood?" and "How can I find the best local doctors?" and "How do I travel safely with an infant on public transportation?" To answer these questions and others, and provide city parents with a forum of their own, she began creating *urbanbaby.com.* "I felt that raising a child really starts in the community, and local information is what parents need most."

Designing the Website: The flagship site, *newyork.urbanbaby.com,* was launched in August 1999. To reflect the personality and attitude of city parents, Maloney commissioned renowned artist Ruben Toledo to illustrate the images. The result is a sophisticated but fun look that ties together all the site's components—content, community, and the urbanbaby e-store. To keep the site fresh and up-to-date—very important priorities for a resource guide—Maloney had to rethink the way she worked. "When I first created urbanbaby, I approached it in the same way I had with fashion and publishing, thinking that once a design was done, we could never change. But when I realized that a website is an evolution—that it evolves as your business does and in response to your audience—it was liberating."

Steps to Success: In January 2000, sites in Boston, Los Angeles, and the San Francisco Bay Area joined the New York site. Recent additions include Austin, Chicago, and Seattle, with more to follow, as well as plans for a bilingual Miami site and a London urbanbaby. Influential investors, family, and friends helped fund the growth. With their pleasing mix of content, community, and commerce, all the urbanbabies offer "one-stop shopping" for expectant and new parents through the toddler years. Each has resources, original content, an interactive community of parents, and baby shops unique to that specific city. Maloney and her staff choose the clothing, toys, and accessories sold on the site, tapping local boutiques and small mom-and-pop stores for some of the items and providing a percentage of their online sales to these vendors.

Slick Site for City Kids, continued

Working on the Internet has been a very exciting and creative experience for this mompreneur. "I've learned so much about starting and running a business, it's as if I've gone through an accelerated MBA program," she says. Her secret to long-term success: "Believe in your business model and keep abreast of what's going on—it's an ever-changing climate."

The Balancing Act: As an equal partner in *urbanbaby.com,* Maloney's husband, John, handles the new business and strategic development side of the e-Biz. Although this means the couple is "living and breathing" their work 24/7, it also means they can cover for each other, so that at least one parent can participate in activities with their daughter while the other minds the business. "As a parent and a businesswoman, I think it's important that my daughter sees me running a business . . . that women can do these things," Maloney says. At the same time, the husband-and-wife team makes a big effort not to talk about work during family time, focusing instead on being urban parents!

Survive and Thrive: Maloney has extended the urbanbaby name to birth announcements, stationery, and other products that are sold on the website, and would like to expand the brand further in the future. Also on the drawing board are the addition of Portland (Oregon), Denver, Washington, D.C., Atlanta, and other American cities, and possibly such international spots as Paris, Milan, and Montreal. As her own daughter grows up and Maloney's online audience begins to parent older kids, urbanbaby will grow along with them. This creative mom is already thinking of expanding the city sites to service school-age children.

Survival Strategy #11: Work Smart

It's always a struggle to keep your business and family needs in balance, and taking on more projects or orders than you can handle is a sure way to upset that balance. "Delegating" is how many mompreneurs right the balance, and even when they don't have much money to spare, they've discovered thrifty ways to outsource work. At the Wisconsin headquarters of Tutor House, Louise Larson Janke enlists Internet-savvy local high school students as interns for her software business—she gets extra pairs of "smart" hands, and they get course credit or a small paycheck. "It's very important to realize you can't do it all yourself," says Dana Calhoun, who runs Baskets-U-Nique.com, a gift basket business, and Best Wishes of

Greater Dayton, a community greeting service for her hometown. "Concentrate on what you do best and barter out or exchange payment for the other services." She approaches small start-ups and other work-at-home moms for help in printing postcards, Web design, and ad copy.

"Plan ahead" is Brenda Carey's advice for dealing with this dilemma. The Massachusetts mom started an online store for specialty spices and rubs made by her husband, the chef at Boston's Linwood Grill & BBQ. "It's easy enough to get everything going, but then you have to recognize the possibility that it may get too big for your current 'from-home' plan," says Carey, whose baby daughter "takes all my business meetings with the accountant, lawyer, and others!" But the mompreneur is thinking far ahead, when sales volume may require hiring extra help to speed up delivery and "stay on top of it all." There's no shame at all in paying others to help you run your business.

Survival Strategy #12: Grow at Your Own Pace

Sometimes it's best to contain your growth and target a manageable market. "My biggest challenge is dealing with my rapidly expanding customer base," says Lara Pullen, owner of Environmental Health Consulting in Chicago. To help solve this problem, Pullen raised her rates, subcontracted out some of her work, and spent less time networking for more jobs, focusing instead on her steady clients.

Web designer Jenn Thomas realizes that her e-Biz, Aurora Developments (www.aurdev.com), is in an oversaturated and very competitive field. She overcame this by accepting that she'd never be one the huge players. "I focus on my own community, building a network of clientele from local businesses and individuals who like the idea of having a small, *local* company at the helm handling their hosting and design," says Thomas.

Losing sight of your priorities is another reason you may want to occasionally put on the brakes. "As my business continues to grow steadily, I see now that the slow times not only give me a chance to reflect and improve my business practices, they provide a chance to regroup and take advantage of being here for my kids and family," says Kathy Lindberg, owner of giftbasketgallery.com.

Survival Strategy #13: Set Flexible Goals

Formulate your vision into a simple business plan. Sue Neiditch Schwartz, founder of YarnXpress, uses her business plan as a guide, reviewing it every few months as goals are met or change. Schwartz started out by selling her novelty yarns at discount prices directly to consumers, and is now using her website to attract vendors as well, so she can enter the lucrative B2B market. "Stay open to change without compromising your principles and you'll find a way to achieve your goals," suggests Jodi Turek, cofounder and president of womensforum.com.

Survival Strategy #14: Have a Heart

Sure you want to make money with your business, but you can actually attract customers and clients by giving something back to your community or your audience. Diana West of www.motshop.com, an online thrift shop, feels that "as you grow, it's important to earmark some of your profits for charitable contributions or donate time or money to a cause you believe in—and publicize your efforts on your website. This works into the whole concept of making your site 'sticky,' and it doesn't have to involve money," she says. West suggests mentoring other businesswomen or providing resources to your virtual community.

California mom of two Joelle Burnette started fieryencounters.com as a subsidiary to J. Burnette Productions—a home business that offers website development, graphic design, writing, and publishing. But the website is her third "baby," and she directs lots of her energy to raising funds for burn victims all over the world through its educational and entertaining content. A highlight is an online "photo album" of good-looking firefighters (male and female)! "For every firefighter I place on the site, I donate twenty-five dollars out of my own pocket in their name to a burn-survivor charity of their choice," says Burnette. She soon expects the website to generate a steady enough income to be self-supporting, but in the meantime, this mompreneur is gaining a following.

Hannah Brazee Gregory has patiently developed her niche—providing creative, affordable public relations and advertising support to nonprofit organizations—building a low-overhead business that pleases her personally and professionally. Although she started out doing work for any client who came her way, Gregory made a big effort to market to nonprofits, both through her website, hannahcreative.com, and by donating services and lowering her rates to attract the type of clients "who needed me most. My big break came when I was chosen to promote the nonprofit development center at a local college," says the Kansas City, Missouri, mom. "It really legitimized my specialty."

Survival Strategy #15: Never Give Up!

Every mompreneur needs a generous helping of the three Ps—patience, persistence, and perseverance—to take her business to the top. "An Internet business takes time to succeed," says Dottie Gruhler, president and CEO of HerPlanet.com, a woman's online network. "I've seen women with a good thing go down because they lacked patience." "Patience is key," echoes Heidi Piccoli of www.MoneyMakingMommy.com. "Most people don't see instant results."

Commercial artist Terri Bose worked from home as a graphic designer for 12 years when the Internet opened up an opportunity for her to earn money in "a more enjoyable way"—an online crafts site for kids. "For almost three years, I consumed huge amounts of time and energy running both businesses," Bose says, "but it was worth it! I now have enough income from MakingFriends.com and was recently able to quit my 'day job.' "

Persistence and perseverance can also pay huge dividends. "I realize all the times I kept on going even though I wanted to quit . . . the times I persevered although I was told by so many that I was crazy to think a single mom could make it as a business owner," remembers Donna Snow, who now owns Anything Business, a company that provides small business coaching and support services. "The neighbors who assumed I sat here all day and ate bonbons and watched soaps will soon realize that I've fulfilled a dream that has been a long time in coming."

Mompreneurs on the move can overcome many obstacles by solidifying their support network. "Surround yourself with people who support you and remember to thank them when success comes your way," suggests Mary McCarthy, founder of Comfybummy.com, a Web-based natural baby products shop.

As for parting words, Laura Strathman Hulka sums it up best: "Be willing to open yourself up to others who want to learn and who want to teach," says the proprietor of the online used book store, Twice Told Tales (www.abebooks.com/home/TWICETOLDBOOKS). "Unless we are willing to share what we learn with one another, there will be no personal or business growth. The 'little guys' particularly need to support one another against the bigger, better-financed companies online, to find their niches and fill them well. We are learning not only for ourselves, but for our children, who can hopefully benefit from our business successes in the future, and then move the Internet into the next generation—with our experiences to use as stepping-stones."

Web Celeb

Laurie McCartney
Founder and CEO of estyle Inc., home of *babystyle.com,* and *kidstyle.com*
  (www.estyle.com)
Los Angeles
Mom of 2

Laurie McCartney knows just what her shoppers want, because she is her company's target customer. McCartney came up with the concept for babystyle.com, her flagship site, in 1998 when pregnant with first baby, Jack. While trying to outfit her maternity wardrobe and the baby's nursery all at once, she discovered that she had to go to several stores before finding everything she needed. It was tiring, and McCartney learned that "pregnant women don't like dragging around in stores!" She set out to simplify the experience with a fun and friendly site that offers women one-stop solutions. "We aim to be a mother's personal shopper, finding the very best selection of pregnancy and baby products all under one roof," she says. Besides giving women the opportunity to click-and-buy chic clothing and furnishings in an intimate boutique setting, babystyle.com is a mom's best friend. It dishes up fashion tips from resident celebrity mom Cindy Crawford, offers figure-flattering advice from a fashion consultant, and features a gift registry and a unique Baby Namer, which lets you create a customized list of baby names for family and friends to vote on. "We hope to provide a little sanctuary in a mom's busy day," McCartney says.

McCartney was eight months pregnant as she waddled around Silicon Valley pitching her idea to investors. But her pregnancy worked to her advantage. With her blooming belly, it was quite obvious that she knew what she was talking about. Jack was born in October 1999, and McCartney's first round of funding came through a month later. She and six employees crammed into her small house, along with her newborn, a baby-sitter, and the family's golden retriever, Otis.

Nurturing a baby and a start-up take very similar skills, and you must stay calm amid chaos, McCartney says. She remembers the day a new employee reported to work for the first time in a designer suit. "My sitter hadn't arrived yet, so I asked her to hold Jack for a minute while I took a conference call. Jack promptly spit up all over her beautiful outfit!" McCartney and staff quickly learned to "go with the flow."

Those words of wisdom are especially important now that the dot.com frenzy has died down and investors are more cautious about funding Internet ventures. "Continuously look for ways to revolutionize and make your business fresh, but at the same time be true to your original vision. And never lose sight of your customer," stresses McCartney. "Our business plan has always been built on cultivating a lifestyle brand and reaching out to our consumers in all phases of motherhood," she says. Customers can reach estyle 24/7, any way they wish, whether through e-mail, phone, or live chats. And customer service representatives are moms themselves, who understand if a mother must hang up because the baby is crying.

McCartney aims to cement a long-term relationship with her customers in many different ways, both online and off. She has extended her brand through a quarterly print catalog as well as through another site called kidstyle.com, for parents of children ages 2 to 10. It's just one of several sites the company plans to roll out to shepherd moms through the key shopping stages in their lives. Additionally, estyle is developing partnerships to sell its product through traditional brick-and-mortar retailers. "Everything we do is based on customer need," McCartney says. "I think the dot.com craziness has actually been good for us, because it has helped our business model stand out as something sustainable." Investors seem to agree, and this confident mom has so far been successful raising the capital needed to grow her multichannel venture, which now has a staff of 200 and is headquartered in a sleek office building in downtown L.A.

McCartney's family is expanding, too. Daughter Alexandra was born in June 2000, just two months after the launch of kidstyle.com. How does this busy mom juggle it all? She surrounds herself with people who complement her skill set. "Don't try to do everything yourself, because then it's very difficult to grow quickly," she warns. Be aware of the tech trends, but don't get too far ahead of your customer, she adds. "We try to create sites that are well designed, easy to use, and accessible for the average consumer. There are a lot of technology tools that we don't incorporate just yet because it doesn't make sense for the majority of consumers, and could very well alienate them."

And while you must always keep your eye on your customer, being there for your children is of utmost importance. Jack and Alexandra spend time at Mommy's office, and Jack "tests" toys which are then featured in a special "Jack Recommends" section on the site. (Alexandra will soon have her own corner on the site too.) McCartney rises early so she has time for breakfast and a morning walk with the kids before heading to work. Lunchtimes are often reserved for Mommy and Me classes, and weekends are for kids only. "My ultimate goal is to be close to my children and to be a role model that they can look up to and learn from," she says. Having kids was the inspiration for her business and will be the driving force that helps keep it balanced. "It's all about setting priorities," McCartney says. "Set a clear vision for your organization and your family, and follow through. And always persevere."

Here's a guide to the resources that we and other mompreneurs find most helpful.

Associations & Work-From-Home Sites

American Association of Home-based Businesses (www.aahbb.org)

Association for Interactive Media (www.interactivehq.org); 888-337-0008

At-Home Works (www.at-homeworks.com)

Bizy Moms (www.bizymoms.com)

Catalyst (www.catalystwomen.org): Research and advisory organization to advance women in business; 212-514-7600

Digital-Women.com (www.digitalwomen.com)

Entrepreneurial Parent (www.en-parent.com)

HerHomeOffice.com (www.herhomeoffice.com)

Home-Based Working Moms (www.hbwm.com)

HomeBizJunction.com (www.homebizjunction.com)

HIPP: Home Income Producing Parents (www.hipparents.org)

Home Office Association of America (www.hoaa.com)

Home Office Life.com (www.homeofficelife.com)

International Council of Online Professionals (www.i-cop.org)

Main Street Mom (www.mainstreetmom.com)

Moms Help Moms (www.momshelpmoms.com)

Moms Network Exchange (www.momsnetwork.com)

MOO: Mother Owned and Operated (www.m-oo.com)

Mother's Home Business Network (www.homeworkingmom.com)

National Association of At-Home Mothers (www.athomemothers.com)

National Foundation for Women Business Owners (www.nfwbo.org); 202-638-3060

ParentPreneur Club (www.parentpreneurclub.com)

Paul and Sarah Edwards Working From Home (www.paulandsarah.com)

Success-Solution (www.success-solution.com): Work-at-home moms' resources

WAHM.com (www.wahm.com): Work-at-home moms' site

Women Inc. (www.womeninc.org); 800-930-3993

World Wide Web Artists' Consortium (www.wwwac.org)

BOOKS (GENERAL BUSINESS)

Create Your Own Luck: 8 Principles of Attracting Good Fortune in Life, Love and Work by Azriela Jaffe (Adams Media Corporation, 2000)

Her Venture.com by Priscilla Y. Huff (Prima, 2000)

Let's Go Into Business Together by Azriela Jaffe (Career Press, 2001)

Making Money With your Computer at Home by Paul and Sarah Edwards (Putnam Publishing Group, 1997)

Minding Her Own Business, 3rd Edition: The Self-Employed Woman's Guide to Taxes and Recordkeeping by Jan Zobel (Adams Media Corporation, 2000)

The Complete Idiot's Guide to Starting an Online Business by Frank Fiore (Que, 2000)

The Neatest Little Guide to Making Money Online by Jason Kelly (Plume, 2000)

The Unofficial Guide to Starting a Business Online by Jason R. Rich (IDG Books Worldwide, Inc., 2000)

The Virtual Office Survival Handbook by Alice Bredin (John Wiley & Sons, 1996)

BOOKS (WORK-FROM-HOME PARENTS)

How to Raise a Family and a Career Under One Roof by Lisa M. Roberts (Book-haven, Press, 1997)

Mompreneurs®: A Mother's Practical Step-by-Step Guide to Work-at-Home Success by Ellen H. Parlapiano and Patricia Cobe (Perigee, 1996)

101 Best Home-Based Businesses for Women, Revised 2nd Edition by Priscilla Y. Huff (Prima Publishing, 1998)

The Home Office Solution: How to Balance Your Professional and Personal Lives While Working at Home by Alice Bredin and Kirsten M. Lagatree (John Wiley & Sons, 1998)

The Stay-at-Home Mom's Guide to Making Money by Liz Folger (Prima Publishing, 1997)

The Work-at-Home Balancing Act: The Professional Resource for Managing Yourself, Your Work and Your Family at Home by Sandy Anderson (Avon Books, 1998)

The Work-at-Home Mom's Guide to Home Business: Stay at Home and Make Money With WAHM.com by Cheryl Demas (Hazen Publishing, 2000)

Working at Home While the Kids Are There Too by Loriann Hoff Oberlin (Career Press, 1997)

Work-At-Home Books.com (www.workathomebooks.com): Selection of home-based business books

BUSINESS PLANS

Business Plan Shareware (www.planware.org)

Business Plan Templates (www.lowe.org)

JIAN—Business Plan Software (www.jian.com)

SBA Business Plan Tutorials (www.sbaonline.sba.gov)

BUSINESS START-UP AND SUPPORT

All Business.com (www.allbusiness.com)

All Small Biz.com (www.allsmallbiz.com)

American Express Small Business Services (www.americanexpress.com)

American Women's Economic Development Corporation; 917-368-6100

Association of Small Business Development Centers (www.asbdc-us.org)

bCentral.com (www.bcentral.com)

BizStarters.com (www.bizstarters.com)

Bizzed: Small Business Resource (www.bizzed.com)

Biz Office: Small and Home-Based Business Links (www.bizoffice.com)

Business.com (www.business.com): Business-to-business resource (B2B)

Business Filings Inc. Incorporation Service (www.bizfilings.com)

Digital Work (www.digitalwork.com)

DotCom.com (www.dotcom.com)

Entrepreneur Magazine's Entrepreneur.com (www.entrepreneur.com)

EntreWorld: Resources for Entrepreneurs From the Kauffman Center for Entrepreneurial Leadership (www.entreworld.org)

Idea Café (www.ideacafe.com)

Inc.com (www.inc.com)

Online Women's Business Center (www.onlinewbc.org)

Onvia.com (www.onvia.com)

Service Corps of Retired Executives (SCORE) (www.score.org): Small business counseling

Small Business Administration (www.sba.gov)

Small Business Now: Small Office/Home Office Success (www.smallbusiness-now.com)

SmallBizSearch.com (www.smallbizsearch.com): Entrepreneur magazine's search engine for small business owners and entrepreneurs

SmartAge.com (www.smartage.com)

The Entrepreneurial Edge From the Edward Lowe Foundation (www.lowe.org)

Working Solo (www.workingsolo.com)

Working Woman.com (www.workingwoman.com)

CAREERS

Auction Sales

How to Sell on eBay by Annette Graf (www.annetteonline.com)

Auction Watch.com: Auction sales tracking and management (www.auction watch.com)

Coaching

Coach, Inc. (www.coachinc.com): Corporate training and coaching

Coach U. (www.coachu.com); 800-482-6224

InterCoach, Inc. (www.intercoach.com)

The International Coach Federation (www.coachfederation.org); 888-423-3131

Wellcoaches.com (www.wellcoaches.com); 781-431-9538

Computer Consulting

Independent Computer Consultants Association (www.icca.org)

iVillage Computing Business Boards and Chats (www.ivillage.com/work)

Concierge/Errand Running Services

iVillage Errand Running Boards and Chats (www.ivillage.com/work)

Triangle Concierge International (www.triangleconcierge.com)

Crafts

American Craft Malls: The Professional Crafter (www.procrafter.com)

Crafter.com (www.crafter.com)

CraftNetVillage.com (www.craftnetvillage.com)

Hobby Industry Association (www.hobby.org); 201-794-1133

i-Craft (www.i-craft.com)

iVillage Crafters Corner Boards and Chats (www.ivillage.com/work)

Direct Sales

iVillage Direct Marketing Boards and Chats (www.ivillage.com/work)

The Direct Selling Association (www.dsa.org); 202-347-8866

e-Books

Adobe Acrobat Reader (www.adobe.com): pdf format software for publishing e-Books

Book Locker (www.booklocker.com): Source for self-published electronic and print books

WritersWeekly.com (www.writersweekly.com)

WritingSchool.com (www.writingschool.com)

e-Tailing

Electronic Retailing Association (www.electronicretailing.org)

eMarketer (www.emarketer.com)

E-Tailers Digest (www.gapent.com)

Sell It on the Web (www.sellitontheweb.com)

Shop.org (www.shop.org); 301-650-2321: Partnership of the National Retail Federation and e-Tailers

Event Planning

Association of Bridal Consultants (www.bridalassn.com); 860-355-0464

International Special Events Society (www.ises.com)

iVillage Event Planning Boards and Chats (www.ivillage.com/work)

Meeting Planners International (www.iami.org/ismp.html); 320-763-4919

See U There (www.seeuthere.com): Online event planning resource and promotion service

e-Zine Publishing

e-Zine University (www.ezineuniversity.com)

Gift Baskets

Gift Basket Exchange and Gift Basket Resource Center (www.autumnwinds.com)

Gift Basket Review Magazine (www.festivities-pub.com); 800-729-6338. News and product sources

iVillage Gift Basket Boards and Chats (www.iVillage.com/work)

Home Health Care

The National Association for Home Health Care (www.nahc.org); 202-547-7424

Medical Billing

America Online Business Know-How Forum: Medical Billing Board (AOL keyword: BKH)

iVillage Medical Billers Boards and Chats (www.ivillage.com/work)

National Association of Medical Billers (www.billersnetwork.com)

National Electronic Billers Association (www.nebazone.com)

Medical Transcription

American Association for Medical Transcription (www.aamt.org)

America Online Business Know-How Forum: Medical Transcription Board (AOL keyword: BKH)

MT Daily: Medical Transcription Center (http://mtdaily.com)

Medword Medical Transcription: Books, information, and home study courses (www.medword.com)

Online Research/Competitive Intelligence

Association of Independent Information Professionals (www.aiip.org); 414-766-0421

Professional Organizers

National Association of Professional Organizers (www.napo.net); 512-206-0151

Organizing Your Home Office for Success: Expert Strategies that Can Work for You by Lisa Kanarek (Blakely Press, 1998)

Technology

Society for Technical Communication (www.stc.org)

U.S. Small Business Administration Technology Resources Network (http://tech-net.sba.gov)

Women in Technology International (www.witi.com/index-c.shtml)

Travel Agents

American Society of Travel Agents (www.astanet.com); 800-275-2782

Institute of Certified Travel Agents (www.icta.com); 800-542-4282

Tutoring

Tutor2000 (www.tutor2000.com)

iVillage Tutoring Boards and Chats (www.ivillage.com/work)

Virtual Assistants

AssistU.com: Virtual Assistant Training (www.assistu.com)

Global Association of Virtual Assistants (www.gava.org)

International Virtual Assistants (www.ivaa.org); 877-440-2750

iVillage Virtual Office Services Boards and Chats (www.ivillage.com/work)

Staff Centrix Employment Service (www.staffcentrix.com)

Virtual Assistants 4 Hire (www.va4hire.com)

Web Design & Development

Association of Internet Professionals (www.webmaster.org)

HTML Writers Guild (www.hwg.org)

International Association of Web Masters and Designers (www.iawmd.com); 561-533-9008. Sponsors of the Golden Web Awards (www.goldenwebawards.com)

WebDeveloper.com (www.webdeveloper.com)

Website Tips for Designers (www.websitetips.com/designer/index.html)

COMPUTER/TECH SUPPORT

ePeople (www.epeople.com)

Expertcity (www.expertcity.com)

iVillage Click! Computing Channel (www.ivillage.com/click)

Midnight Mac Online (www.midnightmac.com): For owners of Macintosh computers

PC Support (www.pcsupport.com)

COPYRIGHTS/TRADEMARKS

International Trademark Association (www.inta.org); 212-768-9887

Thomson & Thomson Trademark and Copyright Search Services (www.thomson-thomson.com)

U.S. Copyright Office/The Library of Congress (www.loc.gov/copyright); 202-707-9100

U.S. Patent and Trademark Office (www.uspto.gov); 800-786-9199

DADS

At-Home Dad Newsletter (www.athomedad.com); 800-314-DADS

Slowlane.com: The Online Resource for Stay-at-Home Dads (http://slowlane.com)

DIRECTORIES

e-Book Directory (www.ebookdirectory.com)

Go To Small Business Directory (www.goto.com)

Internet Database (www.internetdatabase.com)

Liszt.com (www.liszt.com): Compilation of Web mailing lists

Newsannounce.com (www.newsannounce.com): Search engine directory

Newusers.com (www.newusers.com): Search engine directory

Open Directory Project (www.dmoz.com): Guide to the Web put together by individual "Net-citizens"

Small Business Community (www.smallbizcommunity.com): Free directory of businesses

Tile-Net (www.tile.net): Internet reference for lists, groups, vendors, FTP sites, and more

DISCUSSION GROUPS

Deja News (www.groups.google.com): Newsgroups on a variety of topics

eGroups (www.groups.yahoo.com): Formerly onelist.com; a great place to find list-servs (specialized news groups in your field)

Forum One Communications Group (www.forumone.com): Thousands of Web discussion forums

Talk Biz (www.talkbiz.com): Small business discussions

DOMAIN NAMES

All Domains.com (www.alldomains.com): 800-561-5131. Information about international domains

American Association of Domain Names (www.domains.com): Registration site

BuyDomains.com (www.buydomains.com)

eNom.com (www.enom.com)

GreatDomains.com (www.greatdomains.com); 800-478-8763. Marketplace for buying and selling domain names

ICANN WATCH: (www.icannwatch.org) New domain name developments

Nameback.com (www.nameback.com)

Nameboy.com (www.nameboy.com)

NameSecure.com (www.namesecure.com)

NetNames.com (www.netnames.com)

NetworkSolutions.com (www.networksolutions.com): Leading source for name registration

Register.com (www.register.com)

EDUCATION/TRAINING FOR CAREER AND TECH SKILLS

DigitalThink (www.digitalthink.com)

EduPoint (www.edupoint.com)

Federal Training Network (www.fedlearn.com)

Free Skills: Online Training (www.freeskills.com)

Hungry Minds: Online Learning Marketplace (www.hungryminds.com)

Jones International University (www.jonesinternational.edu)

KaplanCollege.com (www.kaplancollege.com)

Learn2.com (www.learn2.com)

MindEdge (www.mindedge.com)

New Horizons Computer Learning Centers (www.newhorizons.com)

Peterson's Distance Learning (www.lifelonglearning.com)

Smart Planet (www.smartplanet.com)

Thinq (www.thinq.com)

Women's Online Institute "Fast Track Entrepreneurial Series" (www.womens-onlineinstitute.com)

ENTREPRENEUR AWARDS

Ernst & Young Entrepreneur of the Year (www.ey.com/global/gec.nsf/international); 800-755-AWARD

Mompreneur of the Month Award (www.ivillage.com/work)

Webby Awards (www.webbyawards.com): Annual awards sponsored by the International Academy of Digital Arts and Sciences

Victoria Magazine Entrepeneur Awards (http://victoria.women.com)

Working Woman Magazine Entrepreneurial Excellence Awards (www.working-woman.com)

e-ZINES & e-NEWSLETTERS

Access Internet Magazine (www.accessmagazine.com): Profiles enterpreneurs

Best Ideas in Business (www.bizfilings.com): Offers inspirational small business stories and tips

Bizine (www.bizine.com): Covers off- and online marketing strategies

Business @ Home (www.gohome.com)

Black Enterprise Online (www.blackenterprise.com)

Clickz Network (www.clickz.com): Provides marketing information and advice

e-Commerce Times (www.ecommercetimes.com)

Entrepreneur's Home Office Magazine (www.entrepreneur.com)

Entrepreneurial Couples Success Letter (www.isquare.com/az4.htm): Free online newsletter for business owners and spouses

Idea Marketers (www.ideamarketers.com): Info about doing business on the Web and free articles to use on your site

Modern Mommy (www.modernmommy.com): A print and electronic newsletter

Momscape (www.momscape.com): An e-zine devoted to nurturing busy mothers

PR-Savvy Female Entrepreneur (www.womensnews-subscribe@onelist.com)

Netguide (www.netguide.com): Web directory and articles

WAHMPRENEUR (www.wahmpreneur.com): The newsmagazine for women who work where they live

Yahoo! Internet Life (http://web1.zdnet.com/yil)

FINANCING INFORMATION AND SOURCES

ACCION International (www.accion.org): Seed money for disadvantaged women and minorities; 617-492-4930

Amber Foundation Grant Competition (www.womensnet.net/amber)

AngelMoney: Seed capital and start-up investors (www.angelmoney.com)

Association for Enterprise Opportunity: List of microloan programs (www.micro-enterpriseworks.org)

Bank of America Small Business Investment Company (www.BankofAmerica.com/community): Loans and equity investments for minority- and women-owned businesses

Ben Franklin Technology Partners (www.benfranklin.org): Assists new companies in Pennsylvania; 717-234-1748

Count-Me-In (www.count-me-in.org): Business loans and scholarships for qualifying women

Fleet Boston Women Entrepreneurs' Connection (www.fleet.com): Loans for women-owned businesses in the Northeast; 800-CALL-FLEET

Fool Mart (www.fool.com): Financial news and tools for running an e-Business

Forum for Women Entrepreneurs e-Scholarship Award (www.few.org)

Passions and Dreams Funding, Inc. (www.passionsndreams.org): Loans for women who don't qualify for SBA funding; 310-273-1019

SBA's Microloan Program (www.sbaonline.sba.gov/financing/microparticipants)

Seraph Capital Forum (www.seraphcapital.com): Angel network for businesswomen in the Pacific Northwest

The U.S. Small Business Administration: LowDoc Program for Securing Loans; SBA Express Revolving Lines of Credit; and Women's Loan Pre-Qualification Program (www.sba.gov)

Venture Capital Resource Library (www.vfinance.com)

Viridian Capital Partners (www.viridian-capital.com): Woman-run venture capital firm specializing in start-ups in technology and healthcare fields

Wells Fargo Bank Women's Loan Program (www.wellsfargo.com): Offers loans from $5,000 to $100,000 nationally.

WomenAngel (www.womenangels.net): Funding sources for businesswomen in the Mid-Atlantic U.S.; 202-342-1627

Women First Capital Fund (www.womenfirstcapital.com): Angel funding for businesswomen in the Northeast; 207-828-1277

Women's Financial Network (www.wfn.com)

Women's Growth Capital Fund (www.womensgrowthcapital.com): Invests in businesses in early or expansion phases; 202-342-1431

INSURANCE

Membership organizations offering group medical and dental plans.

National Association for the Self-Employed (www.nase.com); 800-232-6273

Small Business Service Bureau (www.sbsb.com); 800-343-0939

Support Services Alliance (www.ssainfo.com): 800-836-4SSA

Working Today (www.workingtoday.org): 212-366-6066

INTELLECTUAL PROPERTY PROTECTION

ICANN's Uniform Domain Name Dispute Resolution Policy (www.domain-magistrate.com)

Name Protect.com (www.nameprotect.com): Trademark research, protection, and monitoring services

U.S. Copyright Office (www.loc.gov/copyright); 202-707-9100

U.S. Department of Justice Computer Crime and Intellectual Property Section (www.cybercrime.gov/ip.html)

U.S. Patent and Trademark Office (www.uspto.gov); 800-786-9199

World Intellectual Property Organization (www.wipo.org)

INVENTOR RESOURCES

About.com Inventor's Foum (http://inventors.about.com)

Bringing Your Product to Market by Don Debelak (John Wiley & Sons, 1997)

Delphion Intellectual Property Network (www.delphion.com): Information on international patents/PCTs

Innovation Assessment Center at Washington State University's Small Business Development Center (www.sbdc.wsu.edu); 509-358-7765

Internet Invention Store (www.inventing.com)

InventiveParent.com (www.inventiveparent.com); 603-926-9272

Inventors Assistance League (www.inventions.org); 877-IDEA-BIN

Inventors Insider (www.inventorsinsider.com): Internet TV show hosted by a patent attorney

Juvenile Products Manufacturing Association (www.jpma.org)

ParentWise (www.parentwise.com): Invented-by-mom incubator

Patent It Yourself, 8th Edition by David Pressman (Nolo Press, 2000)

Thomas Register of American Manufacturers (www.thomasregister.com)

United Inventors Association of the USA (www.uiausa.org); 716-359-9310

Wal-Mart Innovation Network (www.walmartstores.com/win): Invention assessment

Wisconsin Innovation Service Center (http://academics.uww.edu/business/innovate): New Product and Invention Assessment; 262-472-1365

JOB RESOURCES

General Job Boards

CareerBuilder.com (www.careerbuilder.com)

Headhunter (www.headhunter.net)

HotJobs.com (www.hotjobs.com)

Monster.com (www.monster.com)

New Mobility Jobline for Disabled Workers (www.newmobility.com/classifieds)

Flexible Work Options for Moms

Dot Com Mommies (www.dotcommommies.com)

Flexible Resources, Inc. (www.flexibleresources.com)

FlexTime Solutions (www.flextimesolutions.com)

GET A MOM (www.getamom.com)

Jobs and Moms Resource Center (www.jobsandmoms.com)

MoneyMakin' Mommy (www.moneymakingmommy.com)

WAHMfest (www.wahmfest.org); 877-271-5218

Womans-Work (www.womans-work.com)

Working Mother Best 100 Companies for Working Mothers (www.working-woman.com)

Work Options.com (www.workoptions.com)

Independent Contractors/Freelancers

Ants.com (www.ants.com)

eLance (www.elance.com)

eWork Exchange (www.ework.com)

FreeAgent.com (www.freeagent.com)

Free Agent Nation (www.freeagentnation.com)

Guru.com (www.guru.com)

icPlanet (www.icplanet.com)

Monster Talent Market (http://talentmarket.com)

Information Technology (IT) and Computer Professionals

Brainpower (www.brainpower.com)

Computer Jobs.com (www.computerjobs.com)

Dice.com (www.dice.com)

Techies.com (www.techies.com)

Part-Time/Temporary Positions

Net-Temps (www.net-temps.com)

LEGAL RESOURCES

Find Law (www.findlaw.com)

Internet Law Firm (www.internet-law-firm.com)

Law Office.com (www.lawoffice.com)

LawVantage.com Legal Documents Library (www.lawvantage.com)

Nolo (www.nolo.com): Self-Help Law Center

Marketing

Adventa.com (www.adventa.com): Opt-in e-mail lists, direct-marketing tech solutions, and database management

Banner Explode 2 (www.bannerexplode.com): Generates Web traffic through placement of banner ads

Biz Web 2000 (www.bizweb2000.com): Online marketing resource center

ClicksLink (www.clickslink.com): Affiliate resources

Direct Marketing Association (www.the-dma.org); 212-391-9683

Get Submitted (www.getsubmitted.com): Submit to search engines

Gorilla Marketing (www.gorillamarketing.com): Low-cost marketing techniques

Guerrilla Marketing Online (www.gmarketing.com): The official site of the original guerrilla marketers

How to Market a Product for Under $500: A Handbook of Multiple Exposure Marketing by Jeffrey Dobkin (Danielle Adams Publishing, 2000)

iBoost (www.iboost.com): Marketing network

Idea Marketers (www.ideamarketers.com)

Linkleads.com (www.linkleads.com): Exchange links and banner ads

Linkshare (www.linkshare.com): Affiliate resources

Mastering Guerrilla Marketing: 100 Profit Producing Insights That You Can Take to the Bank by Jay Conrad Levinson (Houghton-Miflin, 1999)

1to1 Marketing (www.1to1.com): Customer relationship marketing and personalization ideas courtesy of the pioneering Peppers & Rogers Group

Search Engine Watch (www.searchenginewatch.com): Guide to how search engines work and their ranking systems

SelfPromotion.com (www.selfpromotion.com): Search engine placement tips

Submit It! (www.submit-it.com): Offers up your site to search engines and Web directories

Targeting.com (www.targeting.com)

Toastmasters International (www.toastmasters.org): Listing of local Toastmasters chapters for learning public speaking and presentation skills

VirtualPromote.com (www.virtualpromote.com)

Wilson Internet Services (www.wilsonweb.com): Web marketing and e-commerce

Zoomerang (www.zoomerang.com): Subscription-based service to help create and send market research surveys via the Web

NETWORKING

American Businesswomen's Association (www.abwa.org)

Association for Internet Professionals (www.association.org); 800-JOINAIP

Business Network International (www.bninet.com): The word-of-mouth business referral organization

Chamber of Commerce (www.chamberofcommerce.com)

Cybergrrl.com (www.cybergrrl.com)

Cyber Sisters in Success (www.herwebbiz.com/cyber_sisters_in_success.htm): Site for African-American entrepreneurs

Digital Divas (www.digitaldivas.com): A network of digitally gifted women

FEMALE (www.femalehome.org): Formerly Employed Mothers at the Leading Edge, also known as Mothers + More—the Network for Sequencing Women

GirlGeeks.com (www.girlgeeks.com): Advice and mentoring for women in tech careers

HerPlanet (www.herplanet.com)

iVillage Work Channel (www.ivillage.com/work): Home of the Mompreneurs® message boards and chats as well as other work-from-home and entrepreneurial forums

National Association for Women in Education and Development (www.nawe.org): Advancing women's rights in the workplace

National Association of Female Executives (www.nafe.com); 800-634-NAFE

National Association of Women Business Owners (www.nawbo.org); 800-55-NAWBO

Netpreneur Exchange (www.netpreneur.org)

Networking Moms (www.networkingmoms.com): Support site for women in the workforce and those transitioning to entrepreneurship

Oxygen Media (www.oxygen.com): Multichannel network for women that includes business advice

Silicon Salley (www.siliconsalley.com): Information and support source for women building the World Wide Web

Sistah Space (www.sistahspace.com): Networking for black women; includes entrepreneurial section

Webgrrls (www.webgrrls.com): Young women working in high-tech fields

Women.com (www.women.com): Network and community for women that offers professional guidance, among other areas of expertise

Women Inc. (www.womeninc.com): Resources and connections for business-women

Women's Forum (www.womensforum.com)

OFFICE SUPPLIES/SERVICES

At Your Office.com (www.atyouroffice.com)

Buyer Zone.com (www.buyerzone.com)

Federal Express (www.fedex.com)

Office By Design (www.officebydesign.com)

Office Depot (www.officedepot.com)

Office Max (www.officemax.com)

OfficeMe.com (www.officeme.com)

Simply Postage (www.simplypostage.com)

SmartShip (www.smartship.com)

Stamps.com (www.stamps.com)

Staples Office Supply (www.staples.com)

Your Office Business Centers (www.youroffice.com)

PUBLICITY

Internet News Bureau (www.newsbureau.com): Distribution of press releases on the Web

Internet Wire (www.internetwire.com): Online press release distribution

Media Mentor (www.mediamentor.com): Online media training and coaching

NETrageous Publicity Resource Center (www.netrageousresults.com/pr)

Press Kits (www.presskits.com): Custom printing of kits

Press Releases (www.press-release-writing.com)

Promote Yourself (www.promoteyourself.com): Articles and advice for publicizing a business

The Publicity Hound (www.publicityhound.com): Tips, tricks, and tools for low-or no-cost publicity

Web Marketing Today (www.webmarketingtoday.com): Source of online publicity services

Women's News Bureau (www.womensnewsbureau.com): Daily business news, tools, articles, and PR for businesswomen

SCAM AND SPAM PROTECTION

Better Business Bureau (www.bbb.org): 703-276-0100

Internet Scambusters (www.scambusters.com)

National Fraud Information Center (www.fraud.org); 800-876-7060

Network Abuse Clearinghouse (www.abuse.net)

The Federal Trade Commission's Consumer Response Center (www.ftc.gov/ftc/consumer.htm); 877-FTC-HELP

The Internet Fraud Complaint Center (www.ifccfbi.gov)

Scamwatch (www.scamwatch.com): Part of InterGov—the worldwide Internet watchdog

Trader List (www.traderlist.com): Source for good and bad collectible traders

United States Postal Inspection Service (www.usps.gov/websites/depart/inspect/emplmenu.htm)

WebAssured Watch List (www.webassured.com)

TAX HELP

Digital Daily (www.IRS.gov): IRS guide to income tax regulations, forms, and publications

Internet Connect (www.icaccounting.com): For finding accountants

Minding Her Own Business, 3rd Edition: The Self-Employed Woman's Guide to Taxes and Recordkeeping by Jan Zobel (Adams Media Corporation, 2000)

The Tax Prophet (www.taxprophet.com)

1040.com (www.1040.com)

TECH TOOLS

ClickMarks (www.clickmarks.com): Personal wireless portals

CNET (www.cnet.com): Latest hardware and Web tools

Lsoft (www.lsoft.com): Lists management software and hosting

PalmGear H.Q. (www.palmgear.com)

Same-Page eStudio (www.same-page.com): Online creative project management system

SasEz! Palm Pilot Files (www.palmpilotfiles.com)

Tech Web (www.techweb.com)

Ureach.com (www.ureach.com): All-in-one phone, e-mail, and fax message management service

WebEx.com (www.webex.com): Web-based meetings, videoconferencing, and online training

Wireless News Factor (www.wirelessnewsfactor.com): e-Zine covering latest in wireless technology

ZDNet.com (www.zdnet.com)

TELECOMMUTING

About.com's Telecommuting Center (http://telecommuting.about.com)

Gil Gordon's Telecommuting, Telework and Alternative Officing (www.gilgordon.com)

International Telework Association & Council (www.telecommute.org); 202-547-6157

June Langhoff's Telecommuting Resource Center (www.langhoff.com)

101 Tips for Telecommuters: Successfully Manage Your Work, Team, Technology and Family by Debra A. Dinnocenzo and Ronald C. Fetzer (Berrett-Koehler Publishers, 1999)

Telecommute Magazine: e-Zine for Today's Flexible Workplace (www.telecommutemagazine.com)

Telecommuting Jobs (www.tjobs.com)

Telework Connection (www.telework-connection.com): Telecommuting job opportunites, products, and other resources

Work Center Plus (www.workcenterplus.com)

Workaholics4Hire.com (www.workaholics4hire.com): Jobs for telecommuters

TRADEMARKS (*See Copyrights/Trademarks*)

VIRUS PROTECTION

AntiViral Toolkit Pro (www.avpve.com)

McAfee Virus Scan Software (www.mcafee.com)

Symantec AntiVirus Research Center (www.sarc.com)

WAREHOUSES/SHIPPING/FULFILLMENT

Fulfillforyou.com (www.fulfillforyou.com)

Ifulfill.com (www.ifulfill.com)

Kohl Packing (www.kohlpacking.com); 877-381-2300

Shipsmo.com (www.shipsmo.com)

ShipXact.com (www.shipxact)

WEB DESIGN

About.com (www.webdesign.about.com)

Art Today (www.arttoday.com): Clip art and graphics

Builder.com (www.builder.com): How-tos for building a website

Cool Home Pages (www.coolhomepages.com)

Digital Art Shop (ww.digitalartshop.com): Clip art and graphics

Clip Art Warehouse (www.coolclipart.com)

Web Diner (www.webdiner.com)

Website Tips (www.websitetips.com)

WEBHOSTING

Host Index (www.hostindex.com)

TopHosts.com (www.tophosts.com): Changing list of best ISPs

Webhosters (www.webhosters.com)

Webhosting.com (www.webhosting.com): Complete webhosting resource

WEBSITE DEVELOPMENT

Bigstep.com (www.bigstep.com): Turnkey site allows hands-on learning as you set up your site

CNET Web Services (http://webservices.cnet.com)

HTML: A Beginner's Guide by Wendy Willard (Osborne/McGraw-Hill, 2000; www.willardesigns.com)

HTML Writers Guild (www.hwg.org)

HTML Is Not Rocket Science: You Can Create & Update Your Own Website by Linda Caroll (available at www.lindacaroll.com)

Jim World (www.jimworld.com)

Webmonkey (www.webmonkey.com)

Web Site Garage (www.websitegarage.com)

ZD Net.com (www.zdnet.com/ecommerce)

WHOLESALE SUPPLIES

Surplus.Net (www.surplus.net)

Wholesale Central (www.wholesalecentral.com): Wholesale industry resource

Here's the basic terminology you'll need to do business on the Internet.

Bandwidth: The transmission capacity of your Internet connection; the higher the bandwidth, the faster your connection and the more features you can include. Multimedia features like streaming video require a high bandwidth.

Banner: A graphic image on a Web page that advertises another e-Business; clicking on the graphic can take you directly to that website.

Browser: A program such as *Internet Explorer* or *Netscape* that allows you to navigate the World Wide Web and access information.

Cable Modem: A modem connected to a cable TV line to provide access to the Internet; it's usually faster than a dial-up telephone line modem.

Chat: "Real-time" discussions held in designated online areas or "chat rooms" constructed on websites.

Dial-Up Modem: A modem connected to your Internet Service Provider's (ISP's) server via a telephone line; provides access to the Internet.

Directory: A human-compiled Web guide that lists websites by categories; can be used as a search engine. Examples are www.dmoz.org, LookSmart, and Yahoo!.

Domain Name: The unique name that identifies your website on the Internet. The most common domain names end with a dot.com, as in mompreneursonline.com. Other suffixes in use now or in the near future include .gov, .org., .net, .edu, .biz, and .tv.

Download: The transfer of files or data from the Internet or an e-mail attachment to your computer's hard drive.

DSL: The abbreviation for Digital Subscriber Line, it's the technology for bringing high-speed Internet access to homes and small businesses.

E-Commerce: Short form of electronic commerce; it refers to all the business transactions, buying, and selling that's conducted on the Web.

E-Zine: An electronic publication written, produced, distributed, and read online.

Flame: Angry e-mail or nasty online comments in response to unsolicited e-mails or discussion threads in message boards, newsgroups, or chats.

Frame: A design tool that divides the browser window and enables viewers to see two or more Web pages on a site at the same time.

GIF: Short for Graphics Interchange Format; a file format used to display simple digital images, such as clip art.

Home Page: The opening or main page of a website.

Host: The server on which your website is stored.

HTML: Abbreviation for Hypertext Markup Language; the coding language used to create text for websites, e-zines, and other Web documents.

Hyperlink: A highlighted word or graphic image on a Web page. Hyperlinks are "live," so when you click on them, you're taken to another part of the website or another website entirely.

Instant Messaging: A system used to conduct online conversations in "real time" with people you select and keep in a database.

ISP: The term used for Internet Service Provider—the company that provides you with Internet access. ISPs range from tiny local providers to industry giants like AOL.

Java: Programming language used by Web designers to create animation, sound effects, and other special features on websites.

Javascript: Scripting language embedded into HTML documents on the Web.

JPEG: Short for Joint Photographic Experts Group; a file used to compress, transfer, and display full-color photos on the Web.

Keyword: A word written in HTML code so it can be picked up easily by the search engines. The keywords you choose on your website should relate to your business.

Listserv: An Internet discussion group that takes place through e-mail; subscribers join in the discussion by posting comments/responses that are then e-mailed to everyone on the list.

Meta Tag: Pieces of HTML code (see above) that help search engines find and index your website.

Newsgroup: A discussion group among people with similar interests; operated on the Internet through UseNet.

Personal Digital Assistant (PDA): A wireless handheld electronic device that can be used to record appointments, create and send e-mail, access the Internet and voice mail, download information from a desktop or laptop computer, and carry out a multitude of other tasks.

Portal: A website that attracts a large number of visitors by offering free information, chats, message boards, an online community, and the ability to explore the Web. Two popular portals are Yahoo! and Excite.

Search Engine: An Internet database that enables viewers to locate websites and find the information they need online. Google and GoTo.com are two examples of search engines.

Secure Server: An ISP or Web host that provides an SSL (Secure Sockets Layer), which protects your credit card information by encrypting or scrambling it before it's sent over the Internet.

Server: The computer or virtual "home" on which your website is stored.

Sig File: Short for "signature file"; a small block of text that automatically attaches to your e-mail notes and provides additional information about you (phone number, URL, etc.).

Spam: Unsolicited or inappropriate promos, ads, and other information sent to your e-mail address or posted on message boards and in discussion groups.

T1: A telephone line that provides faster Internet access than a dial-up modem.

T3: A high-bandwidth telephone line that can deliver very high-speed Internet access—the equivalent of 28 T1 lines.

URL: Abbreviation for Uniform Resource Locater; your website's home page address on the Internet. URLs usually start with "www" and end with a suffix such as .com, .org, or .net. In the middle of your URL is the domain name you've chosen (see above).

Venture Capitalist: An individual or firm that invests sizable amounts of money in start-ups and small businesses with the hopes of growing them into successful enterprises and reaping a share of the profits.

Webmaster: The person in charge of maintaining a website.

Patricia Cobe and **Ellen H. Parlapiano** are recognized as leading authorities on working from home and have offered entrepreneurial advice on *Oprah, NBC Nightly News*, CNN, CNBC, *Good Morning America*, Fox News Network, *Good Day New York*, Lifetime's *New Attitudes*, NPR, and others. Devoted moms with over twenty-five years of work-from-home experience between them, they are experts on juggling a home business and family. Their weekly "Mompreneurs®" advice column, message board, and chats appear on iVillage.com, which is visited by seven million women each month.

You can e-mail the Mompreneurs® and learn more about their upcoming speaking engagements through their website at www.mompreneurs-online.com.